GHETTO BROTHER

WARRIOR TO PEACEMAKER

Julian Voloj
and
Claudia Ahlering

NBM ComicsLit

Based on true events.
ISBN 9781561639489
© 2015 Julian Voloj and Claudia Ahlering
Rights arranged through Nicolas Grivel Agency

Library of Congress control number: 2015931382
Printed in China
First printing May 2015
Second printing November 2015

This book is also available digitally wherever e-books are sold.

NBMPUB.COM

we have over 200 titles available
Catalog upon request
NBM
160 Broadway, Suite 700, East Wing
New York, NY 10038
If ordering by mail add $4 P&H 1st item, $1 each addt'l

Comicslit is an imprint
and trademark of

NANTIER • BEALL • MINOUSTCHINE
Publishing inc.
new york

Introduction
Jeff Chang

Benjamin "Yellow Benjy" Melendez's story is one that everyone should know. Told here with grit and empathy by Julian Voloj and Claudia Ahlering, his story intersects with New York City's late 20th century rebirth and the emergence of a global hip-hop movement from the pastimes of youth of the forsaken Bronx. For these reasons alone, it should be passed on from generation to generation. But his is also a personal story of identity, hope, and redemption. In other words, it's a classic American narrative.

Benjy was born August 3, 1952 in San Juan, Puerto Rico. Shortly after his birth, his family moved to the Greenwich Village area. Displaced by Robert Moses' plans to transform Manhattan's working-class neighborhoods into exclusive enclaves for the white and wealthy, the Melendezes moved to the Bronx as part of an exodus of African Americans and Puerto Ricans.

By the time Melendez had reached his teens, the borough had been ripped apart by deindustrialization, white desertion, and finally, governmental disinvestment. Between 1960 and 1970, four in ten manufacturing jobs disappeared. Three in five youths were unemployed. Half of the white population fled the borough, many for new whites-only suburbs in New Jersey, Queens, or Westchester County. Even a liberal city government had turned its back on the Bronx.

Young people like Benjy came of age amidst malign neglect, resegregation, and the politics of abandonment. They sought solidarity, security, and kicks in gangs. Benjy was slightly older than those who would become the pioneers of hip-hop, including his counterpart and friend in the Black Spades gang, Afrika Bambaataa. But he shared their desire to find The One—both in the musical sense and the social sense.

Benjy's story runs on three parallel tracks—in the GBs, he finds voice, structure, and violence; with his first wife Mei Lin, he finds support and companionship; and among elders like his father, Rita Fecher, and Evelina Antonetty, he is pushed toward growth and responsibility. At an early age, Benjy was forced into extraordinary circumstances. Here, amidst the intense creativity, fervent activism, and shocking violence of his youth, is where his story intersected with

History. Benjy was an agent of his own change, and the work that he did in this period has had lasting impact. If it were not for the events of 1971 and the actions he and his peers took, we would not be talking about hip-hop today.

I was privileged to meet Benjy through Henry Chalfant and his creative partner, the artist Rita Fecher. Rita and her then-husband Manny Dominguez had both been teachers at John Dwyer Junior High in the South Bronx, and were involved in helping their students secure gang peace. From the late 1960s through the early 1970s, she also shot video of the youth, keeping a rare visual record of a lost era.

Rita was a generous soul. Through her untimely passing in 2003, she not only kept a copious archive of the gang era, she maintained strong ties to many of the former gang members. She hosted regular get-togethers with them at her home in the Chelsea Hotel. She never gave up believing in them.

Perhaps best known for his landmark work with Martha Cooper documenting the New York subway art era, the influential Henry Chalfant had been interested in making a movie about the Bronx youth gangs ever since he had first immersed himself in the graffiti scene and hip-hop movement. During the late 1980s, he met Benjy at a reception—Benjy was flying GB colors—and they struck up a conversation. Benjy introduced Henry to Rita, and the two went on to make the powerful documentary "Flying Cut Sleeves."

As a document of the gang era, Rita and Henry's film only has two precedents—Tony Batten's 1972 film of the Ghetto Brothers and the truce meeting (when it screened on New York public television, it was followed by a townhall meeting with many of the gangs); and Gary Weis's movie "Eighty Blocks From Tiffany's", which captures the aging members of the Savage Nomads and Savage Skulls in the mid-1970s. Of the three, "Flying Cut Sleeves", which contrasts Rita's early movies with late 80s interviews she and Henry had with many of the same gang members, is the least sensational or romanticized.

The Ghetto Brothers' only album, the amazing "Power/Fuerza!" has now been re-released by Truth and Soul Records. Its sound could only have come together in the Bronx. In its explosive energy, rich Afrodiasporicisms, and feverish breaks, the album is a perfect snapshot of the moment right before hip-hop.

And now we have Julian's faithful account of Benjy's story, matched by Claudia's liquid graphics. At the center of all these is Benjy, a man whose wisdom and compassion came early, even before he had fully grown into himself. The beauty of this book is that it truly captures the plainspoken rhythms of his singular voice, even as it reveals the large-hearted way that Benjy sees an often ugly world.

Benjy remains a respected voice for peace and overstanding, a man committed to his family and community. May his story continue to be heard and retold.

Jeff Chang
January 2015

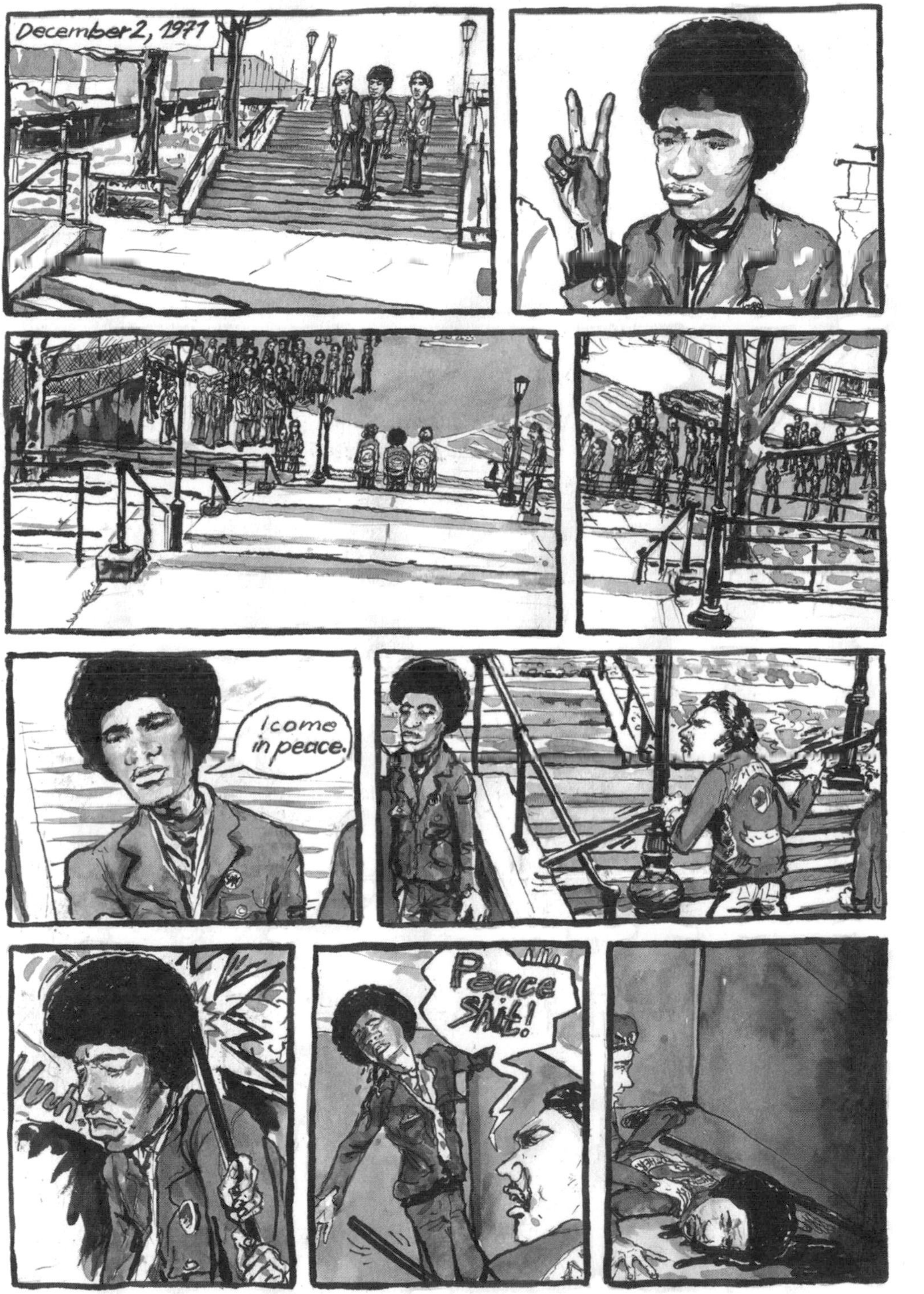
December 2, 1971
I come in peace.
Uuuh
Peace Shit!

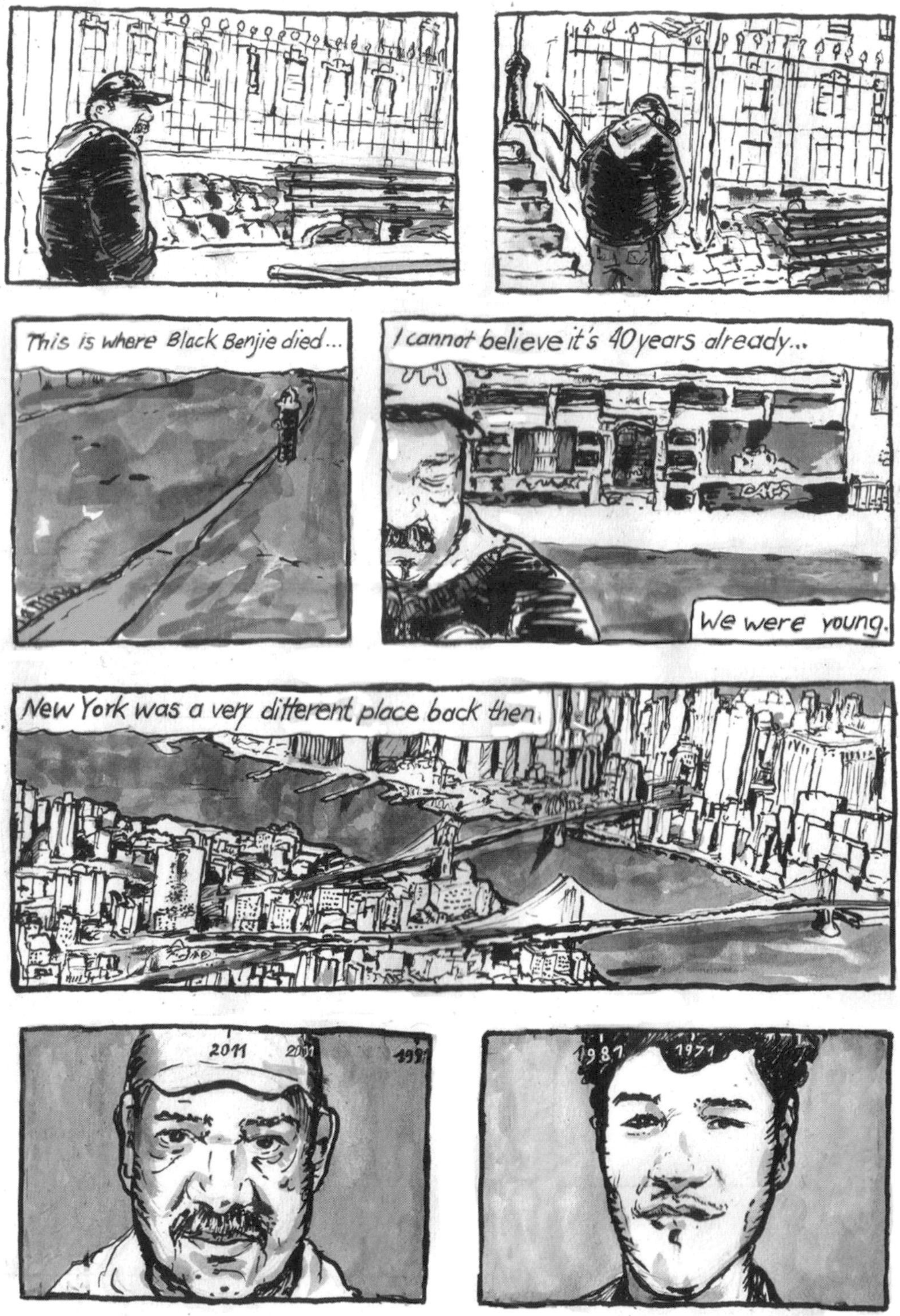
This is where Black Benjie died...
I cannot believe it's 40 years already...
We were young.
New York was a very different place back then.
2011
2001
1981
1971

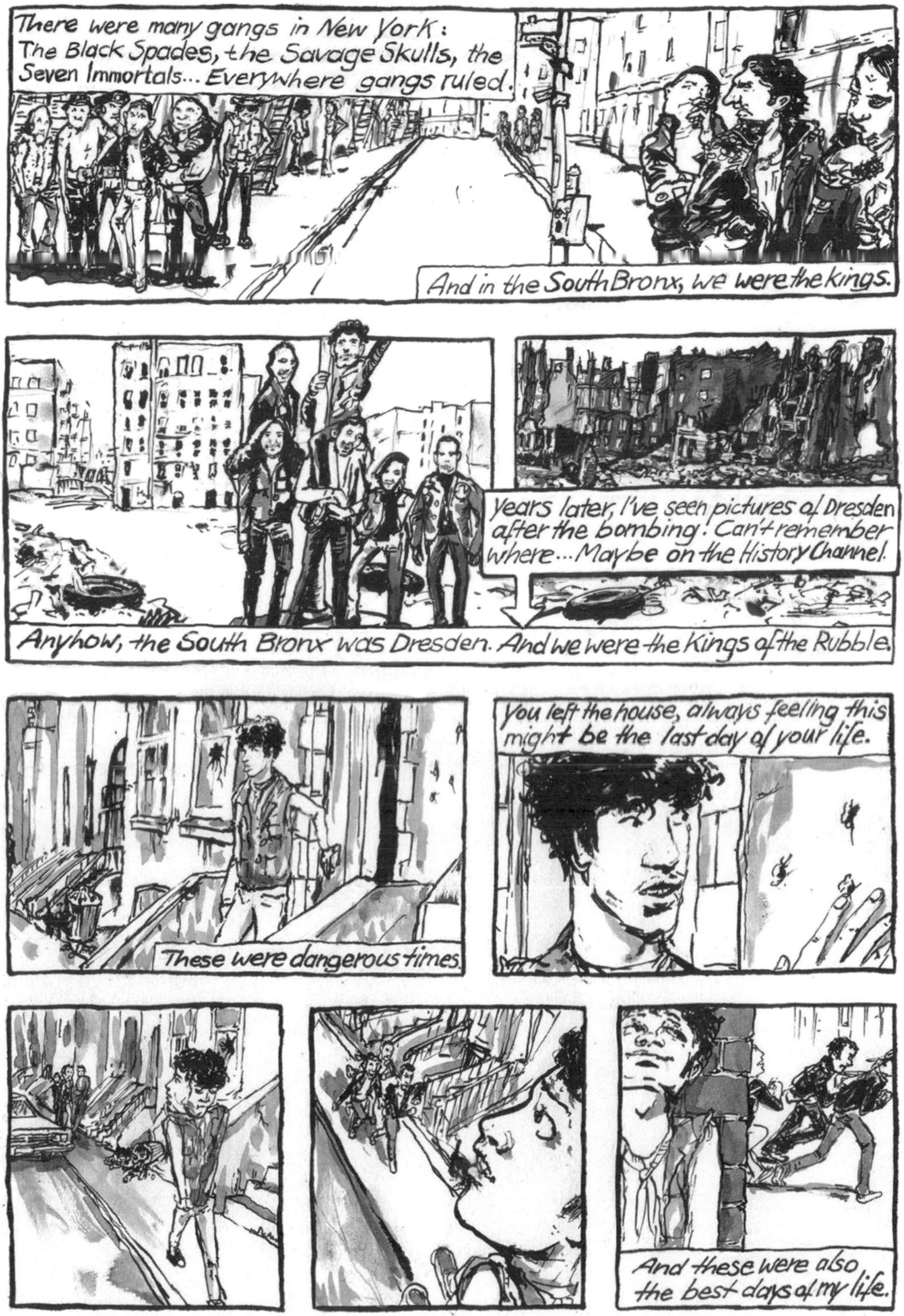
There were many gangs in New York: The Black Spades, the Savage Skulls, the Seven Immortals... Everywhere gangs ruled.
And in the South Bronx, we were the kings.
Years later, I've seen pictures of Dresden after the bombing. Can't remember where... Maybe on the History Channel.
Anyhow, the South Bronx was Dresden. And we were the Kings of the Rubble.
These were dangerous times.
You left the house, always feeling this might be the last day of your life.
And these were also the best days of my life.

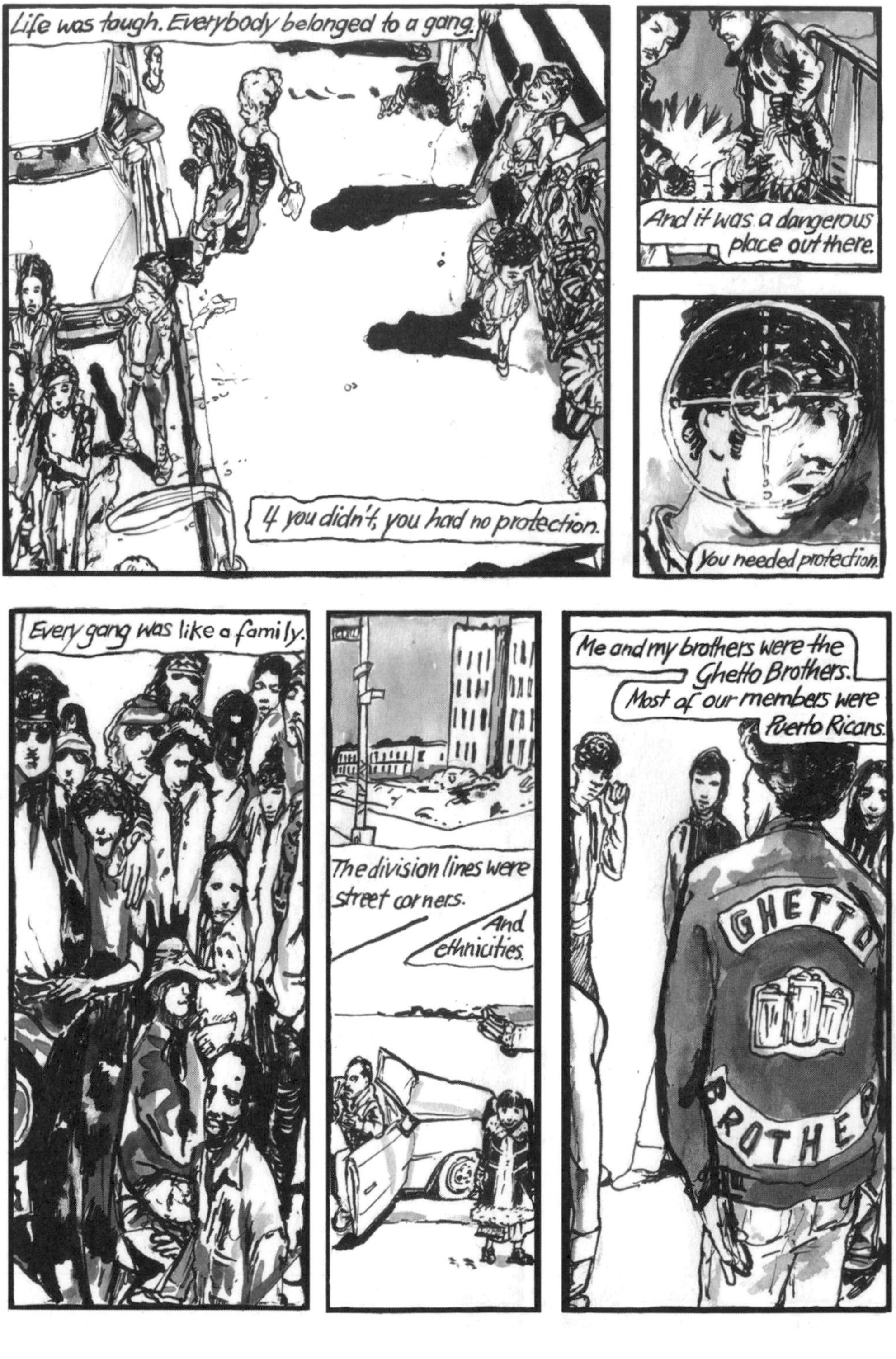
Life was tough. Everybody belonged to a gang.
If you didn't, you had no protection.
And it was a dangerous place out there.
You needed protection.
Every gang was like a family.
The division lines were street corners.
And ethnicities.
Me and my brothers were the Ghetto Brothers.
Most of our members were Puerto Ricans.
GHETTO
BROTHER

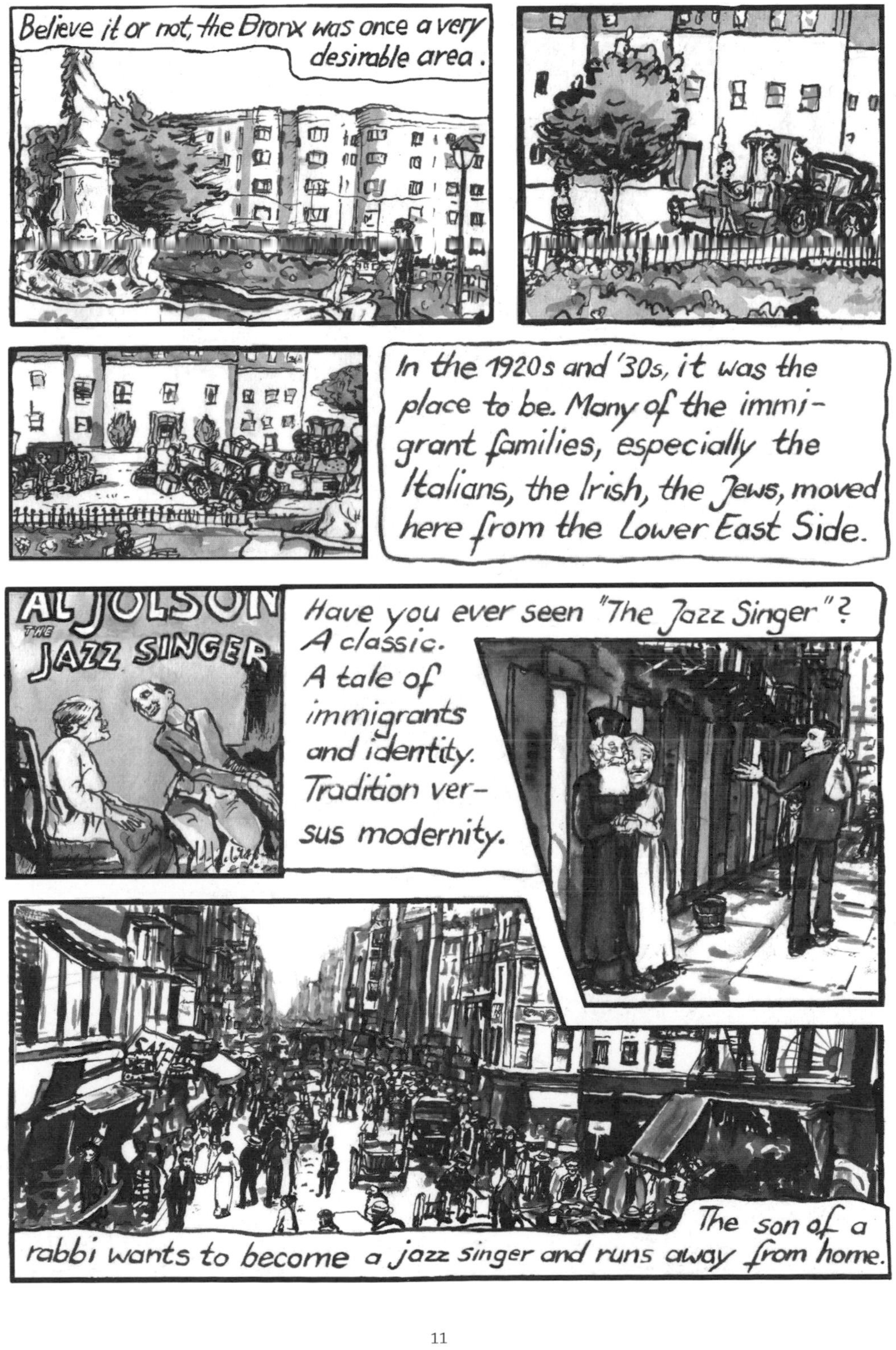

Believe it or not, the Bronx was once a very desirable area.
In the 1920s and '30s, it was the place to be. Many of the immigrant families, especially the Italians, the Irish, the Jews, moved here from the Lower East Side.
AL JOLSON
THE JAZZ SINGER
Have you ever seen "The Jazz Singer"?
A classic.
A tale of immigrants and identity.
Tradition versus modernity.
SALE
The son of a rabbi wants to become a jazz singer and runs away from home.

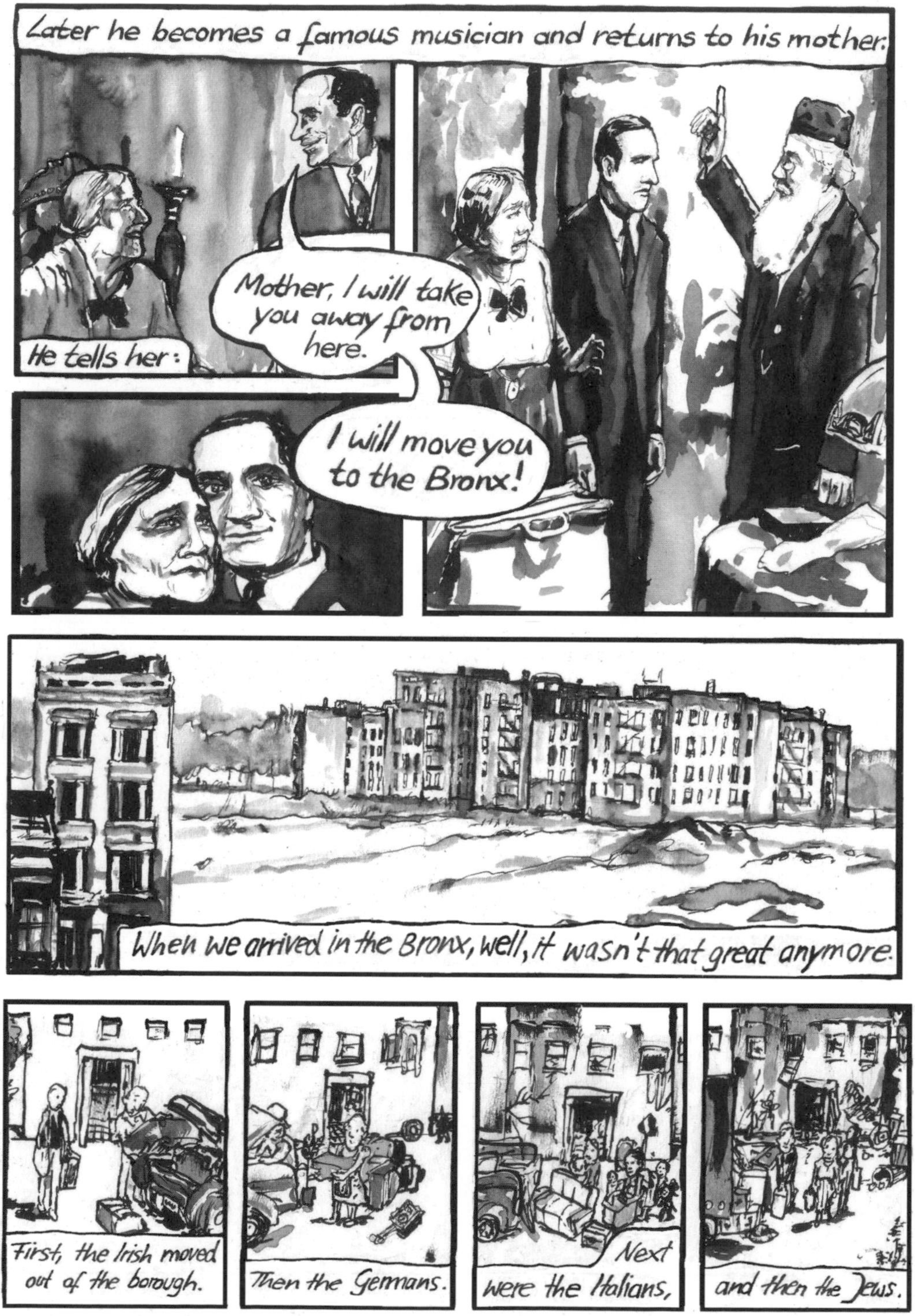
Later he becomes a famous musician and returns to his mother.
He tells her:
Mother, I will take you away from here.
I will move you to the Bronx!
When we arrived in the Bronx, well, it wasn't that great anymore.
First, the Irish moved out of the borough.
Then the Germans.
Next were the Italians,
and then the Jews.

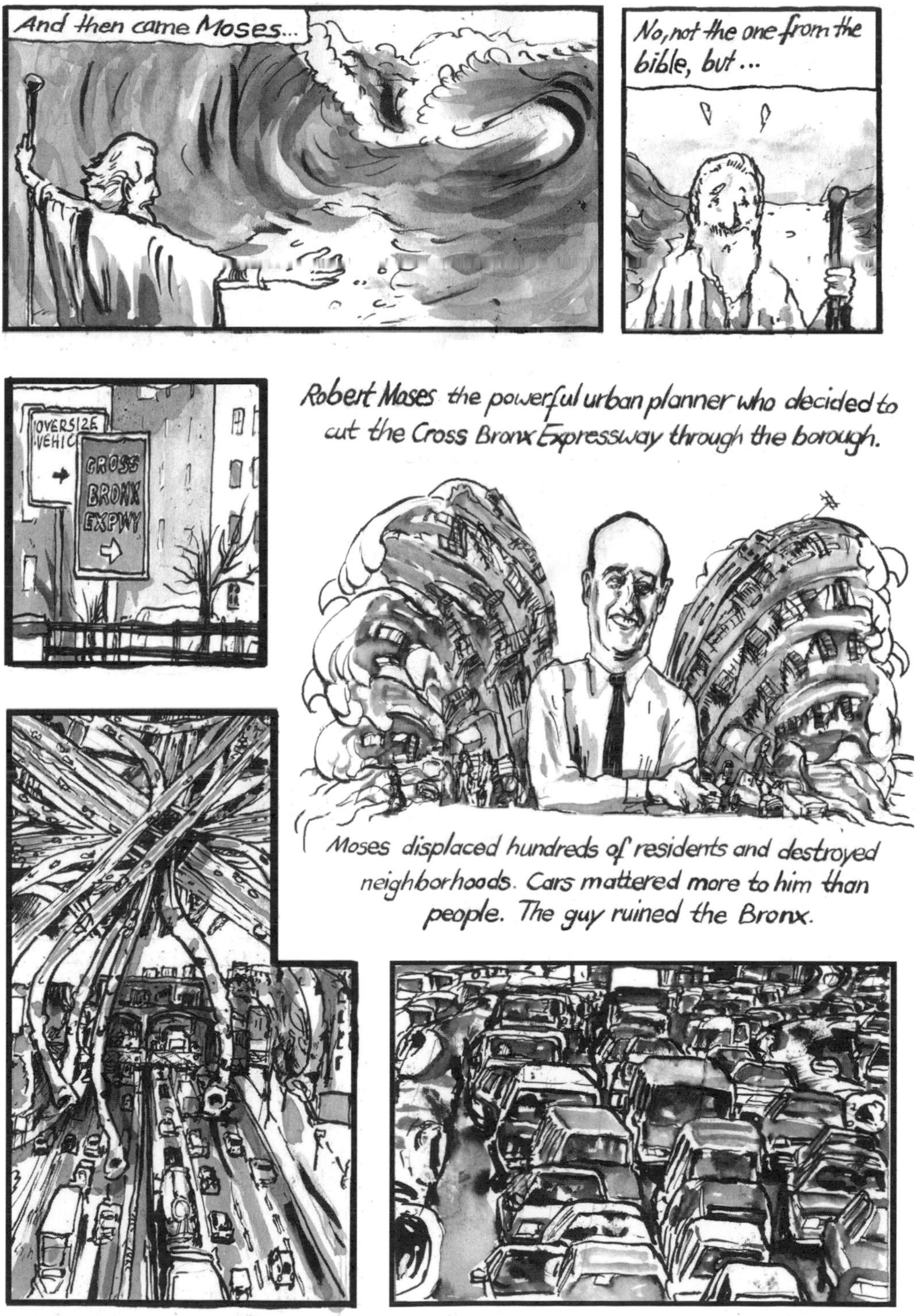
And then came Moses...
No, not the one from the bible, but...
OVERSIZE VEHIC
CROSS BRONX EXPWY
Robert Moses the powerful urban planner who decided to cut the Cross Bronx Expressway through the borough.
Moses displaced hundreds of residents and destroyed neighborhoods. Cars mattered more to him than people. The guy ruined the Bronx.

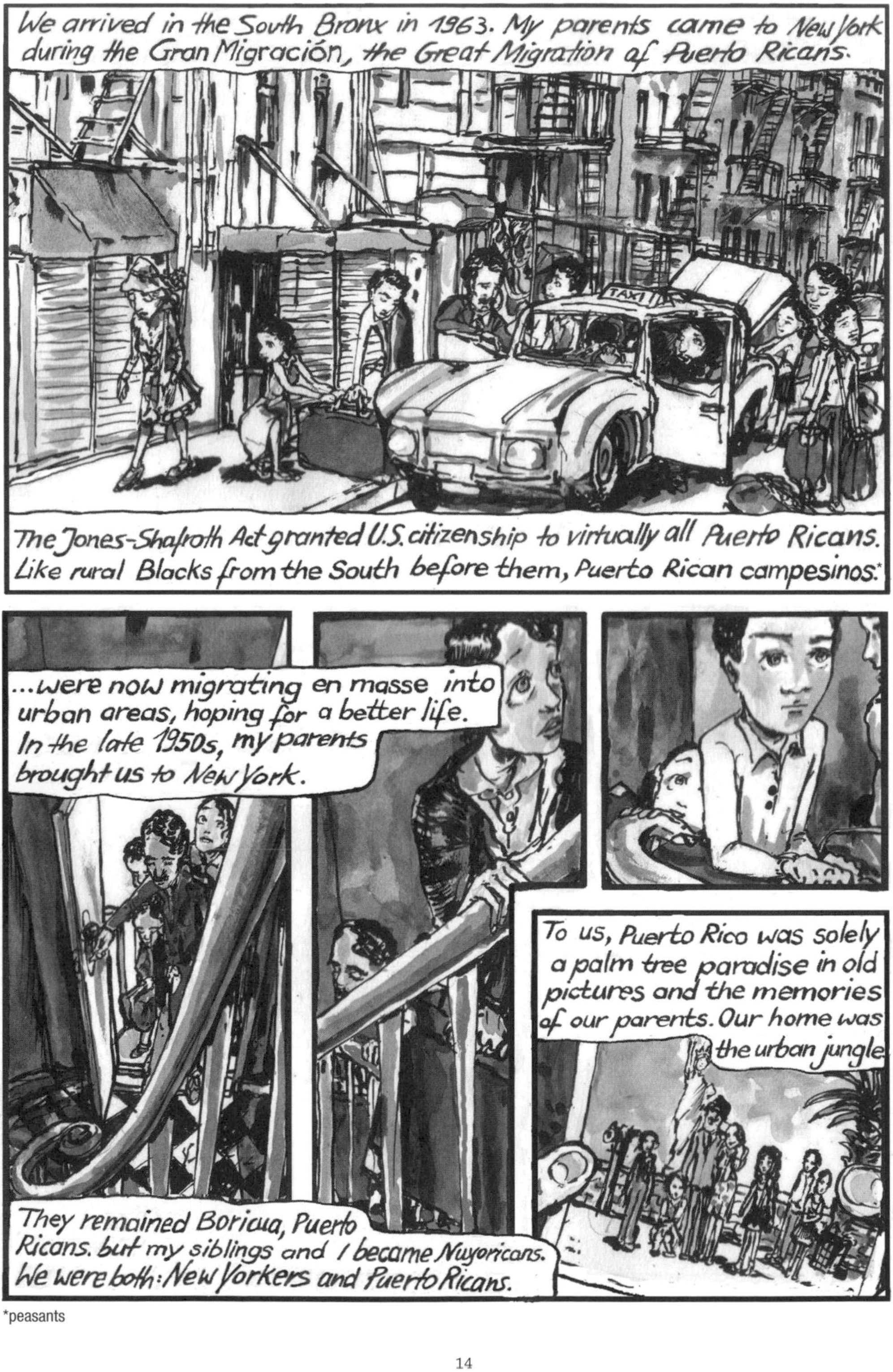
We arrived in the South Bronx in 1963. My parents came to New York during the Gran Migración, the Great Migration of Puerto Ricans.
TAXI
The Jones-Shafroth Act granted U.S. citizenship to virtually all Puerto Ricans. Like rural Blacks from the South before them, Puerto Rican campesinos.*
...were now migrating en masse into urban areas, hoping for a better life. In the late 1950s, my parents brought us to New York.
They remained Boricua, Puerto Ricans. but my siblings and I became Nuyoricans. We were both: New Yorkers and Puerto Ricans.
To us, Puerto Rico was solely a palm tree paradise in old pictures and the memories of our parents. Our home was the urban jungle

*peasants

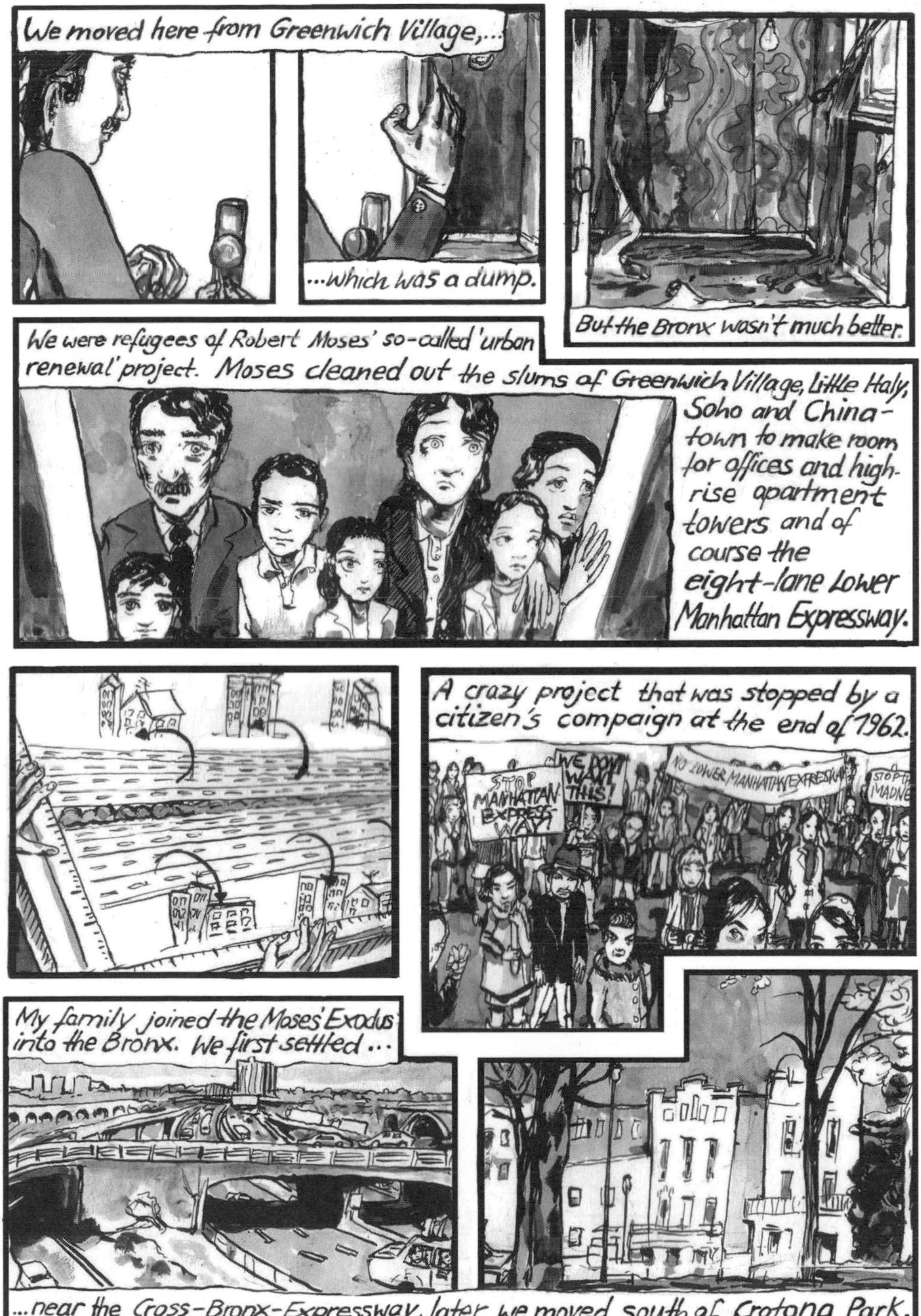

We moved here from Greenwich Village,...
...which was a dump.
But the Bronx wasn't much better.
We were refugees of Robert Moses' so-called 'urban renewal' project. Moses cleaned out the slums of Greenwich Village, Little Italy, Soho and Chinatown to make room for offices and high-rise apartment towers and of course the eight-lane Lower Manhattan Expressway.
A crazy project that was stopped by a citizen's compaign at the end of 1962.
STOP MANHATTAN EXPRESS-WAY!
WE DON'T WANT THIS!
NO LOWER MANHATTAN EXPRESSWAY
My family joined the Moses' Exodus into the Bronx. We first settled...
...near the Cross-Bronx-Expressway, later we moved south of Crotona Park.

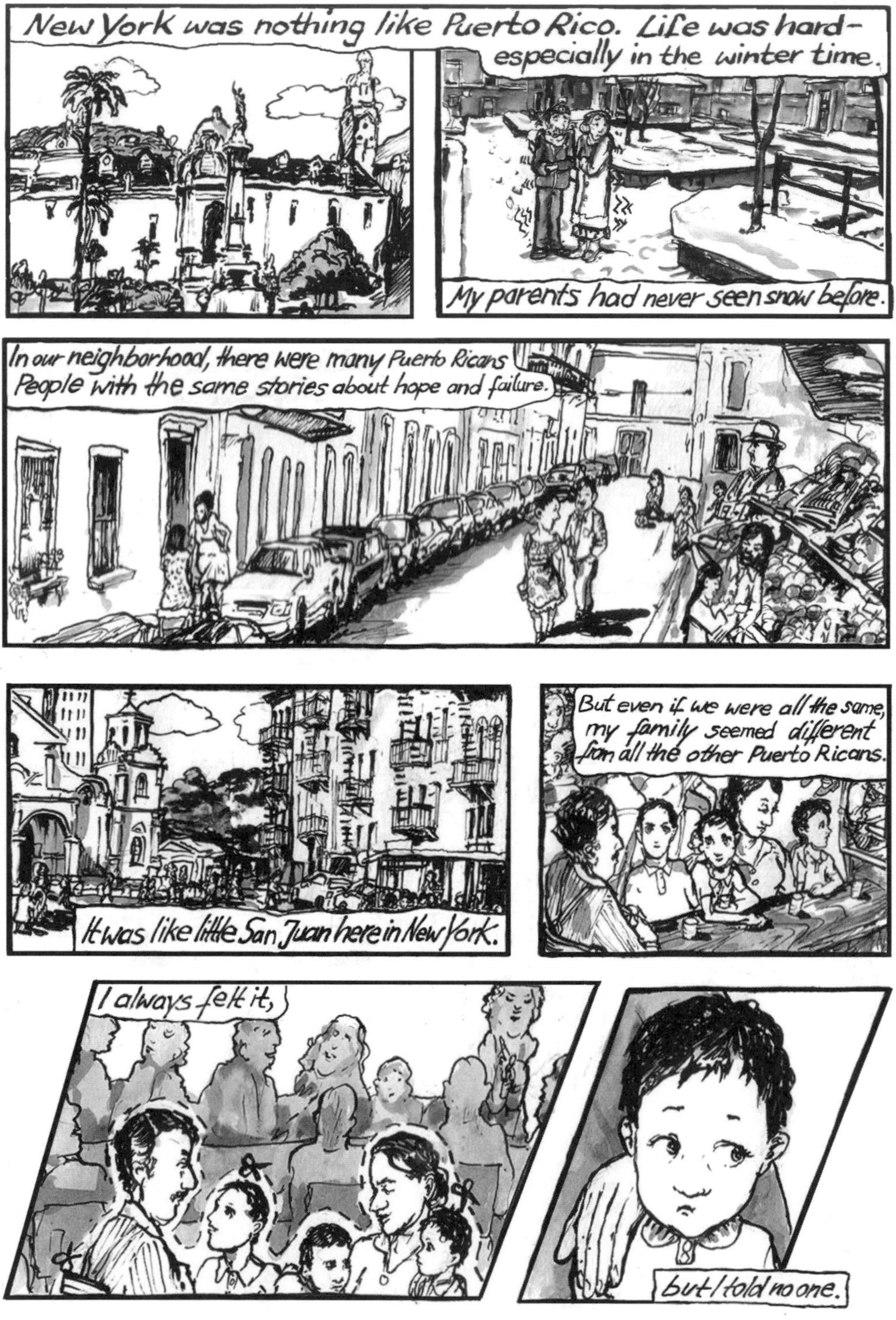
New York was nothing like Puerto Rico. Life was hard-
especially in the winter time.
My parents had never seen snow before.
In our neighborhood, there were many Puerto Ricans
People with the same stories about hope and failure.
It was like little San Juan here in New York.
But even if we were all the same,
my family seemed different
from all the other Puerto Ricans.
I always felt it,
but I told no one.

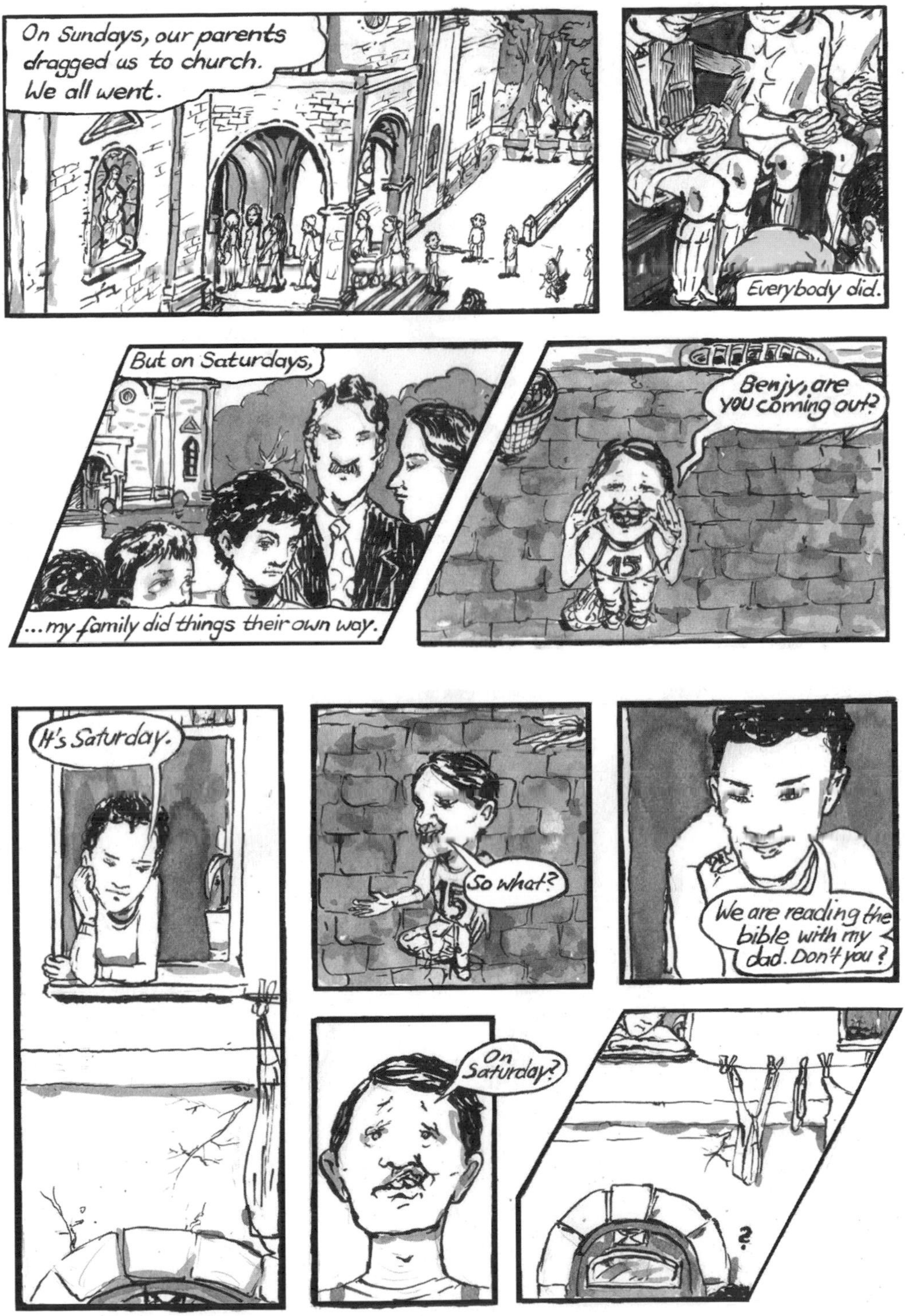
On Sundays, our parents dragged us to church. We all went.
Everybody did.
But on Saturdays,
...my family did things their own way.
Benjy, are you coming out?
It's Saturday.
So what?
We are reading the bible with my dad. Don't you?
On Saturday?
?

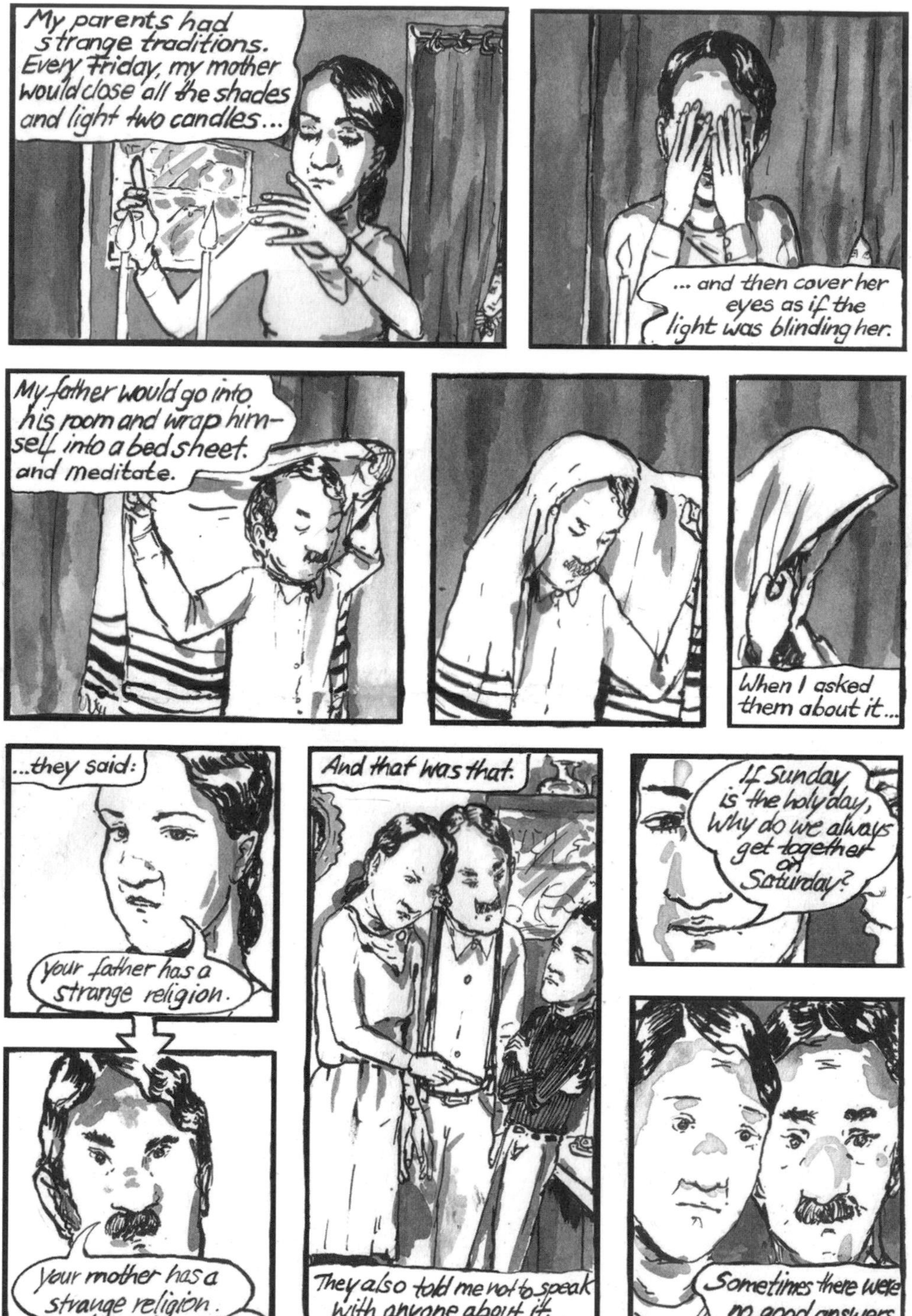
My parents had strange traditions. Every Friday, my mother would close all the shades and light two candles...
... and then cover her eyes as if the light was blinding her.
My father would go into his room and wrap him-self into a bed sheet. and meditate.
When I asked them about it...
...they said:
your father has a strange religion.
your mother has a strange religion.
And that was that.
They also told me not to speak with anyone about it.
If Sunday is the holy day, Why do we always get together on Saturday?
Sometimes there were no good answers.

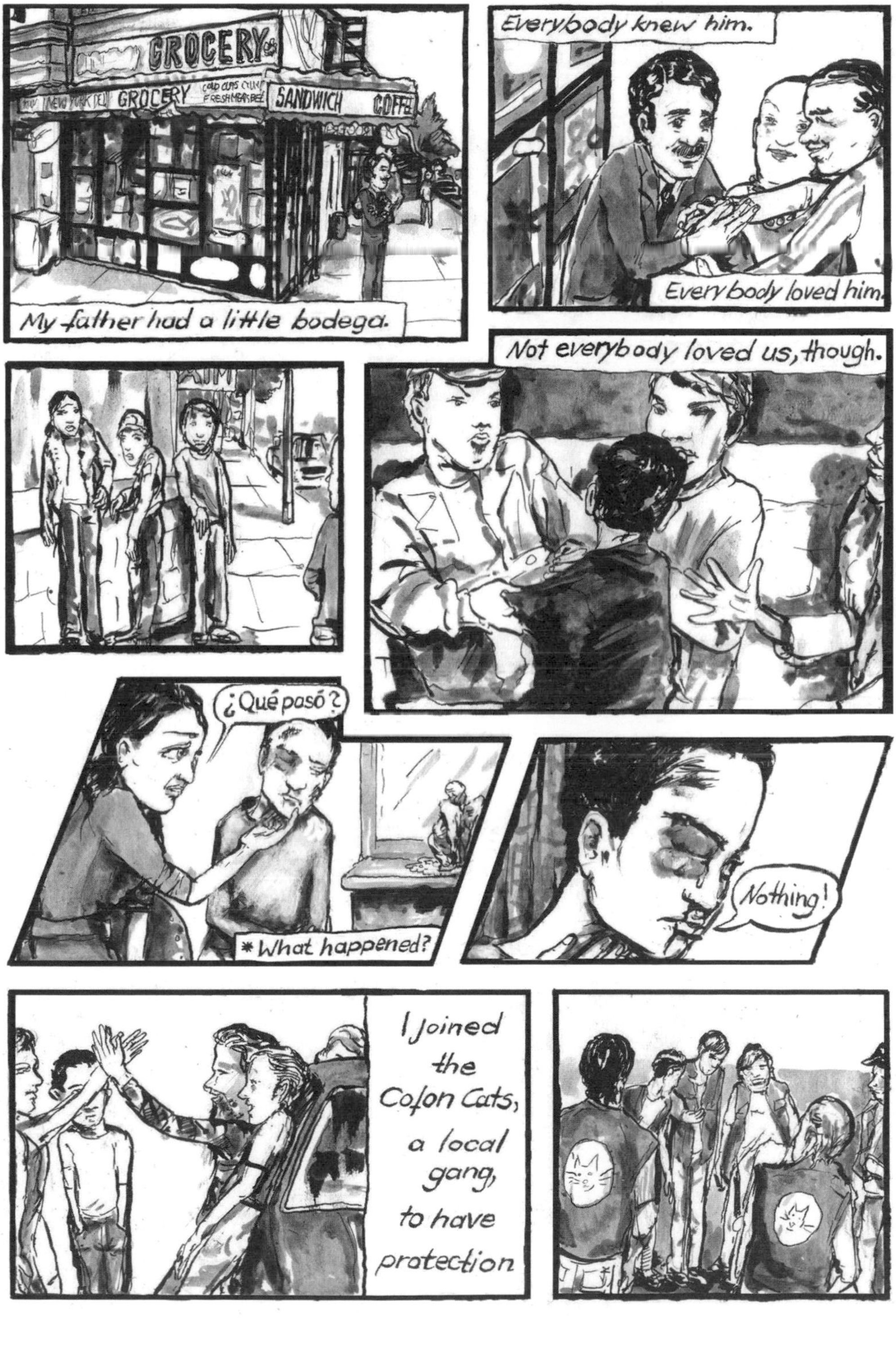
GROCERY
NEW YORK DELI
GROCERY
SANDWICH
COFFE
My father had a little bodega.
Everybody knew him.
Everybody loved him.
Not everybody loved us, though.
¿Qué pasó?
*What happened?
Nothing!
I joined the Colon Cats, a local gang, to have protection

To join a gang you have to go through the so-called Apache Line.

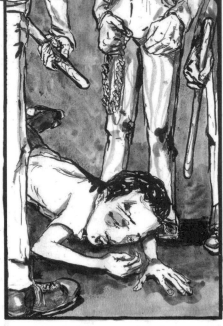

If you do not make it all the way to the end,...

you have to start over again.

My parents were not happy when they saw me.

But I was happy.

I was now part of a gang.

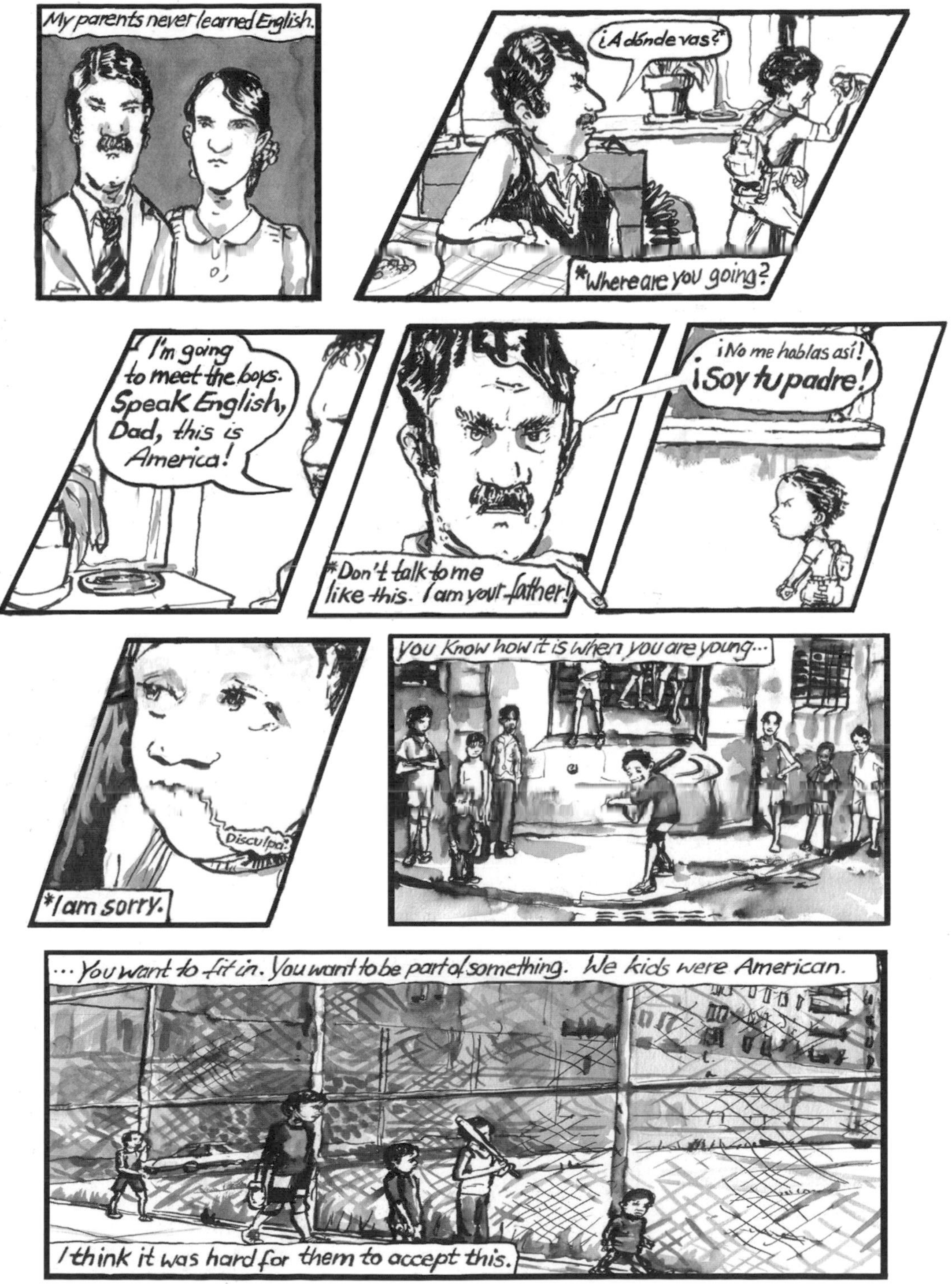
My parents never learned English.
¿A dónde vas?*
*Where are you going?
I'm going to meet the boys. Speak English, Dad, this is America!
¡No me hablas así! ¡Soy tu padre!
*Don't talk to me like this. I am your father!
Disculpa*
*I am sorry.
You know how it is when you are young...
...You want to fit in. You want to be part of something. We kids were American.
I think it was hard for them to accept this.

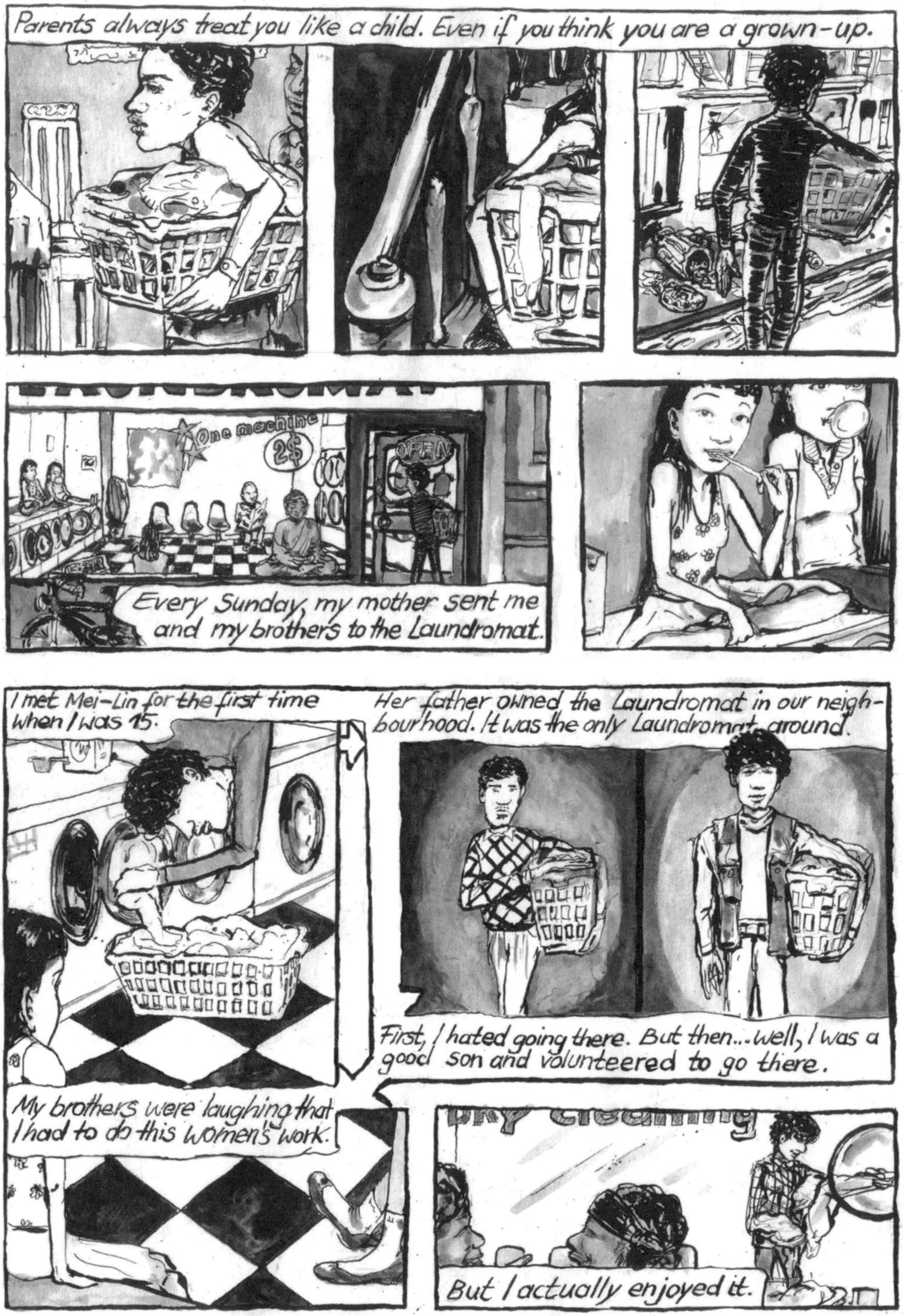
Parents always treat you like a child. Even if you think you are a grown-up.
One machine
2$
OPEN
Every Sunday, my mother sent me and my brothers to the Laundromat.
I met Mei-Lin for the first time when I was 15.
Her father owned the Laundromat in our neighbourhood. It was the only Laundromat around.
First, I hated going there. But then... well, I was a good son and volunteered to go there.
My brothers were laughing that I had to do this women's work.
But I actually enjoyed it.

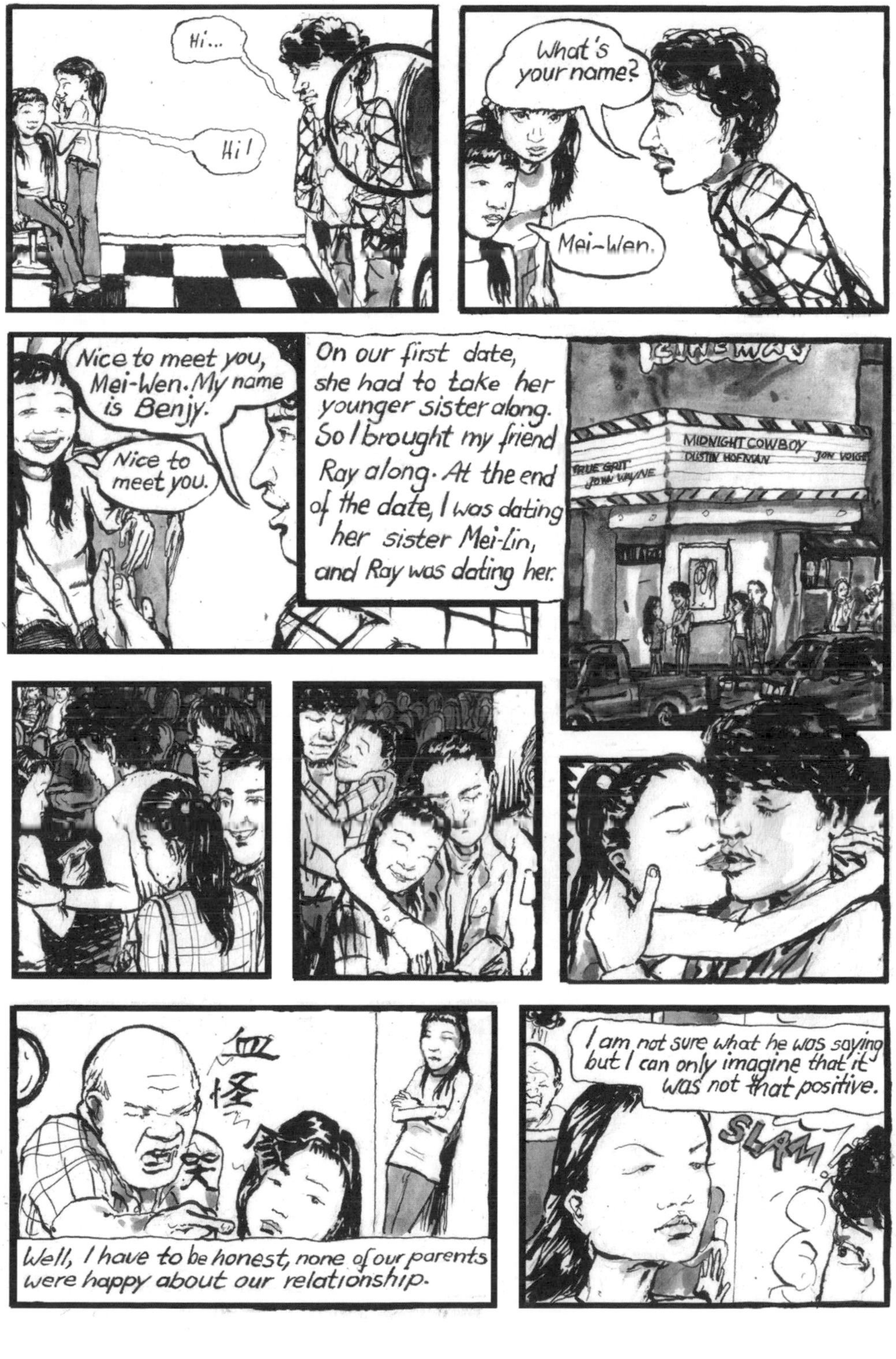
Hi...
Hi!
What's your name?
Mei-Wen.
Nice to meet you, Mei-Wen. My name is Benjy.
Nice to meet you.
On our first date, she had to take her younger sister along. So I brought my friend Ray along. At the end of the date, I was dating her sister Mei-Lin, and Ray was dating her.
MIDNIGHT COWBOY
DUSTIN HOFMAN
JON VOIGHT
TRUE GRIT
JOHN WAYNE
血
怪
Well, I have to be honest, none of our parents were happy about our relationship.
I am not sure what he was saying but I can only imagine that it was not that positive.
SLAM!

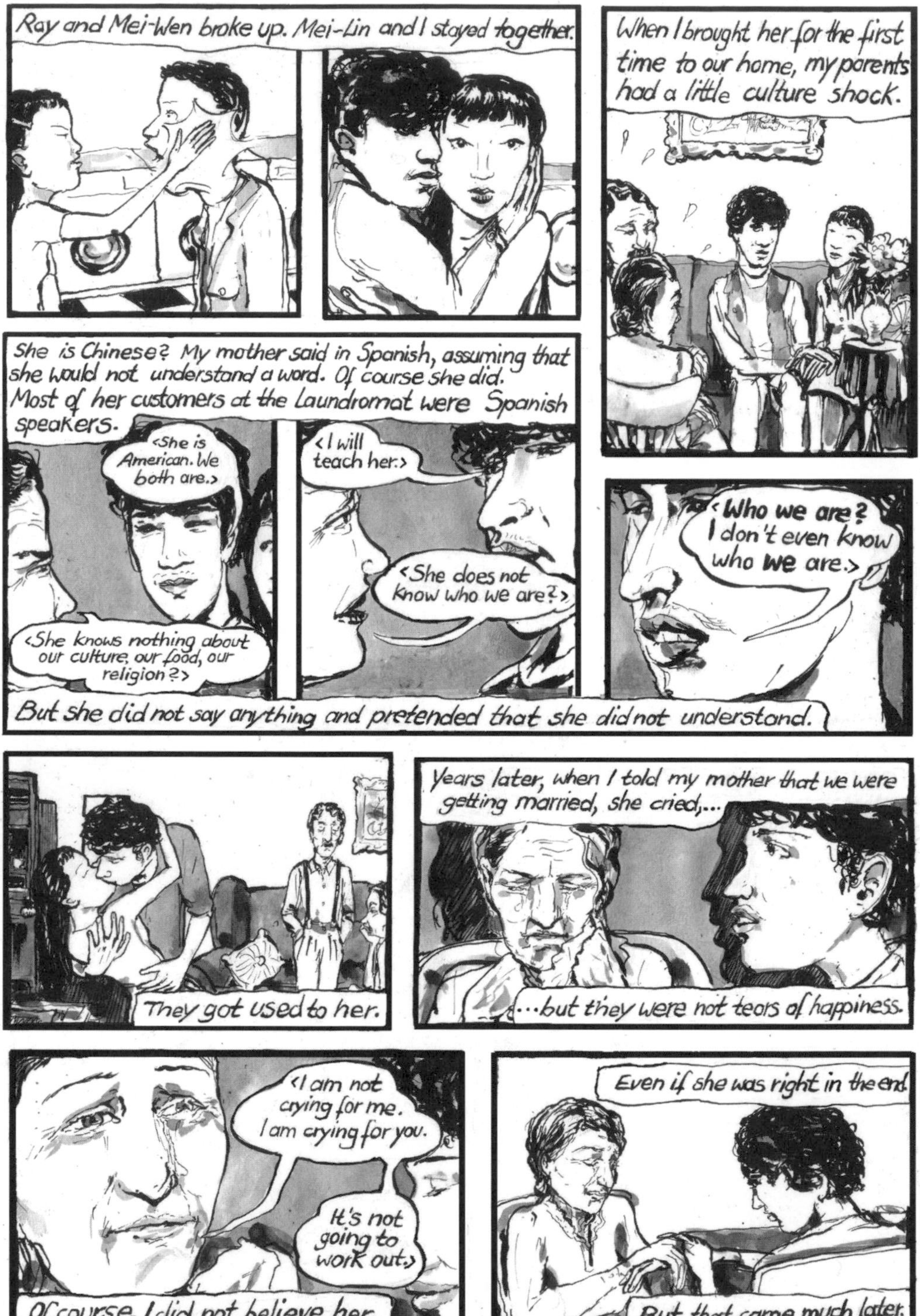
Ray and Mei-Wen broke up. Mei-Lin and I stayed together.
When I brought her for the first time to our home, my parents had a little culture shock.
She is Chinese? My mother said in Spanish, assuming that she would not understand a word. Of course she did. Most of her customers at the Laundromat were Spanish speakers.
<She is American. We both are.>
<She knows nothing about our culture, our food, our religion?>
<I will teach her.>
<She does not know who we are?>
<Who we are? I don't even know who we are.>
But she did not say anything and pretended that she did not understand.
They got used to her.
Years later, when I told my mother that we were getting married, she cried,...
...but they were not tears of happiness.
<I am not crying for me. I am crying for you.
It's not going to work out.>
Of course, I did not believe her.
Even if she was right in the end.
But that came much later.

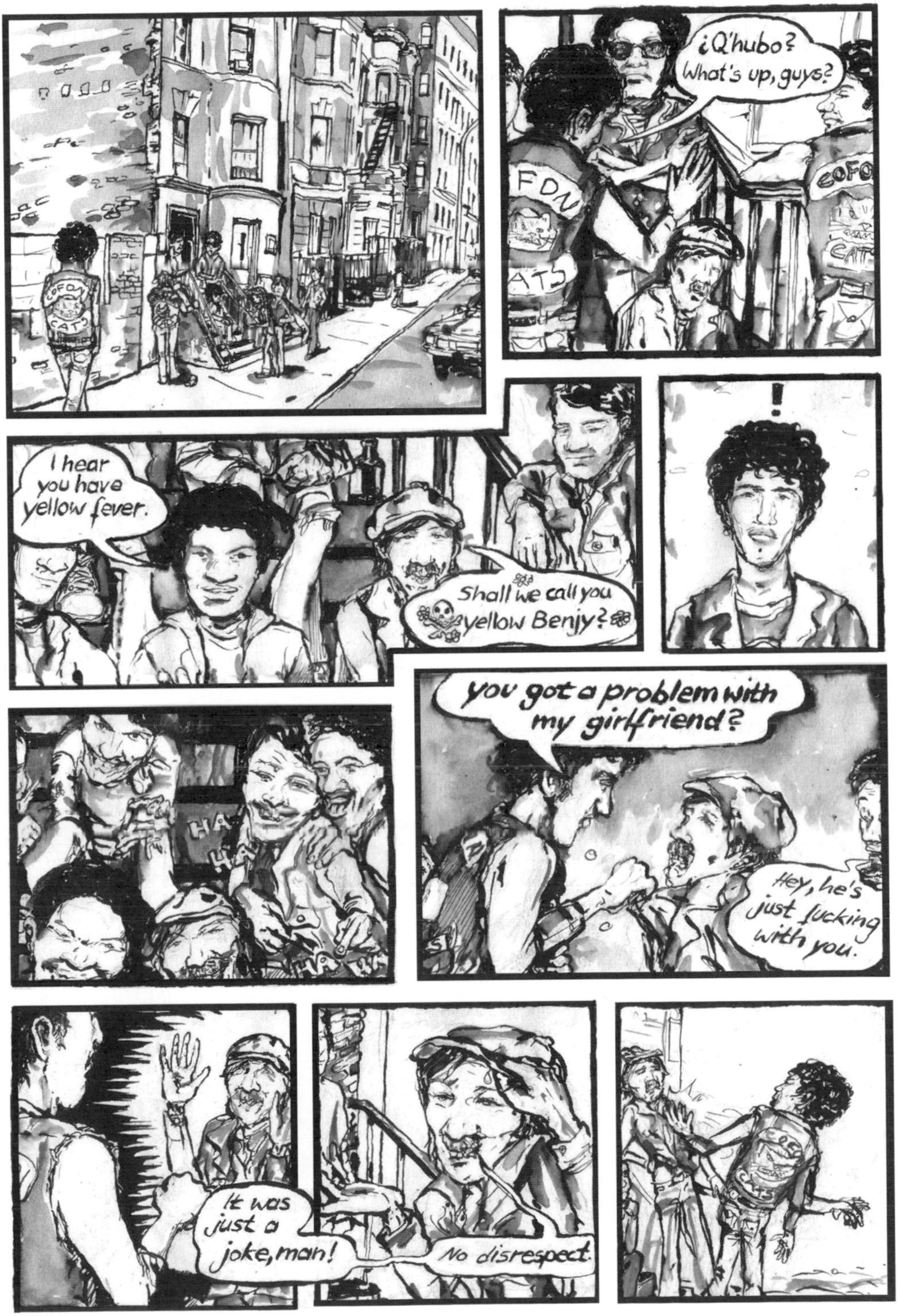
¿Q'hubo? What's up, guys?
I hear you have yellow fever.
Shall we call you yellow Benjy?
!
you got a problem with my girlfriend?
Hey, he's just fucking with you.
It was just a joke, man!
No disrespect.

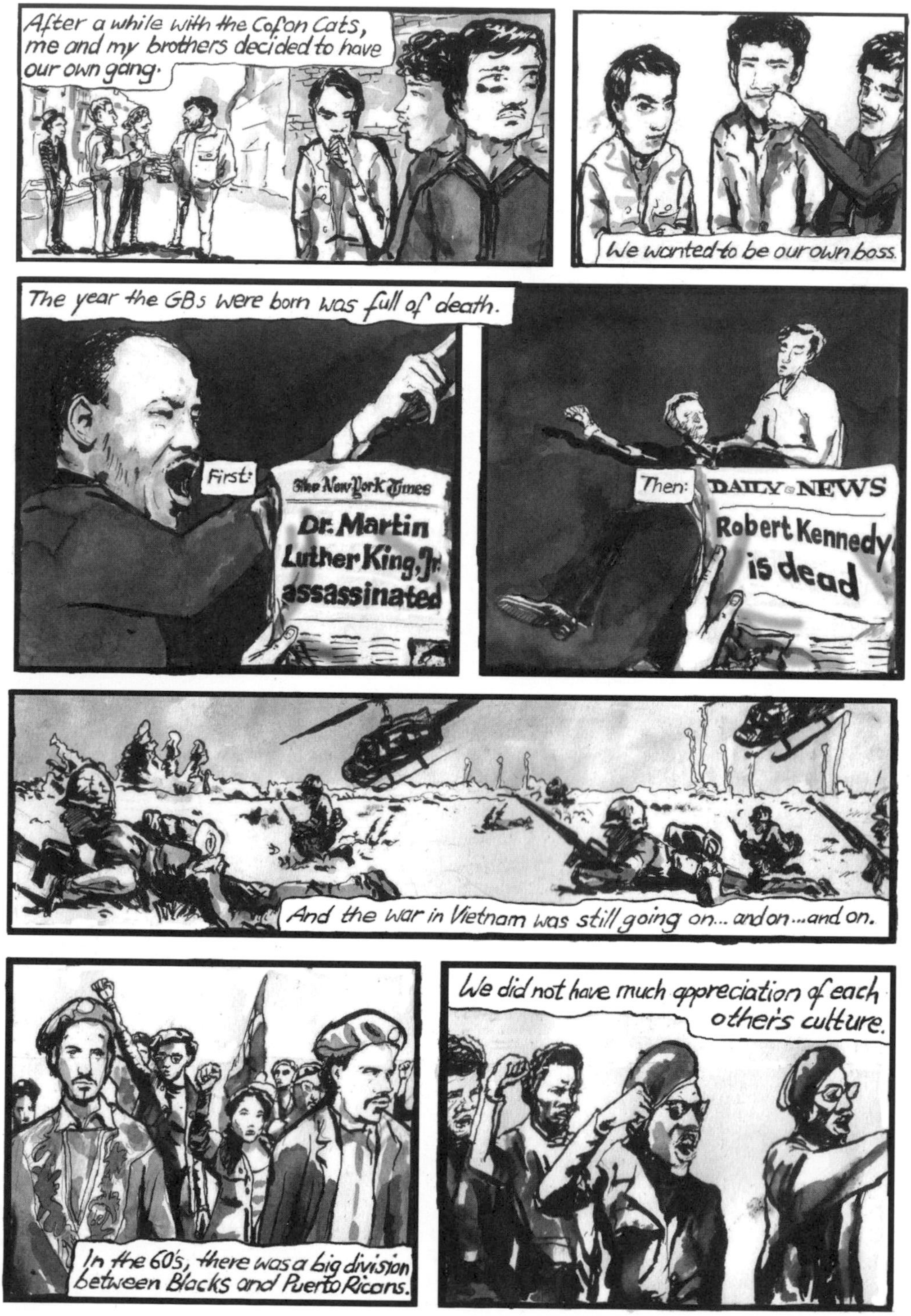
After a while with the Cofon Cats, me and my brothers decided to have our own gang.
We wanted to be our own boss.
The year the GBs were born was full of death.
First:
The New York Times
Dr. Martin Luther King, Jr. assassinated
Then:
DAILY NEWS
Robert Kennedy is dead
And the war in Vietnam was still going on... and on... and on.
In the 60's, there was a big division between Blacks and Puerto Ricans.
We did not have much appreciation of each other's culture.

It's ironic, because of poverty we all wound up in the same neighborhoods.

But instead of fighting the man, we saw each other as the enemy.

However, very few gangs were totally segregated.

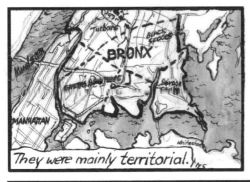

They were mainly territorial.

Some people later called the area "the inner city", but we simply called it the Ghetto.

So me and my brothers, we called ourselves the Ghetto Brothers.

27

We defended our turf.

You crossed our path without permission...

...You were in big trouble.

AAAAAGH

Oh man! We had a lot of fun.

Back in England, knights had their Coat of Arms.

Here in the ghetto, every gang had its own Coat of Arms, the colors.

Originally, back in the days, gangs used to paint their colors in the back of their jackets.

But then came the Hells Angels.

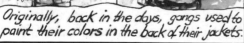

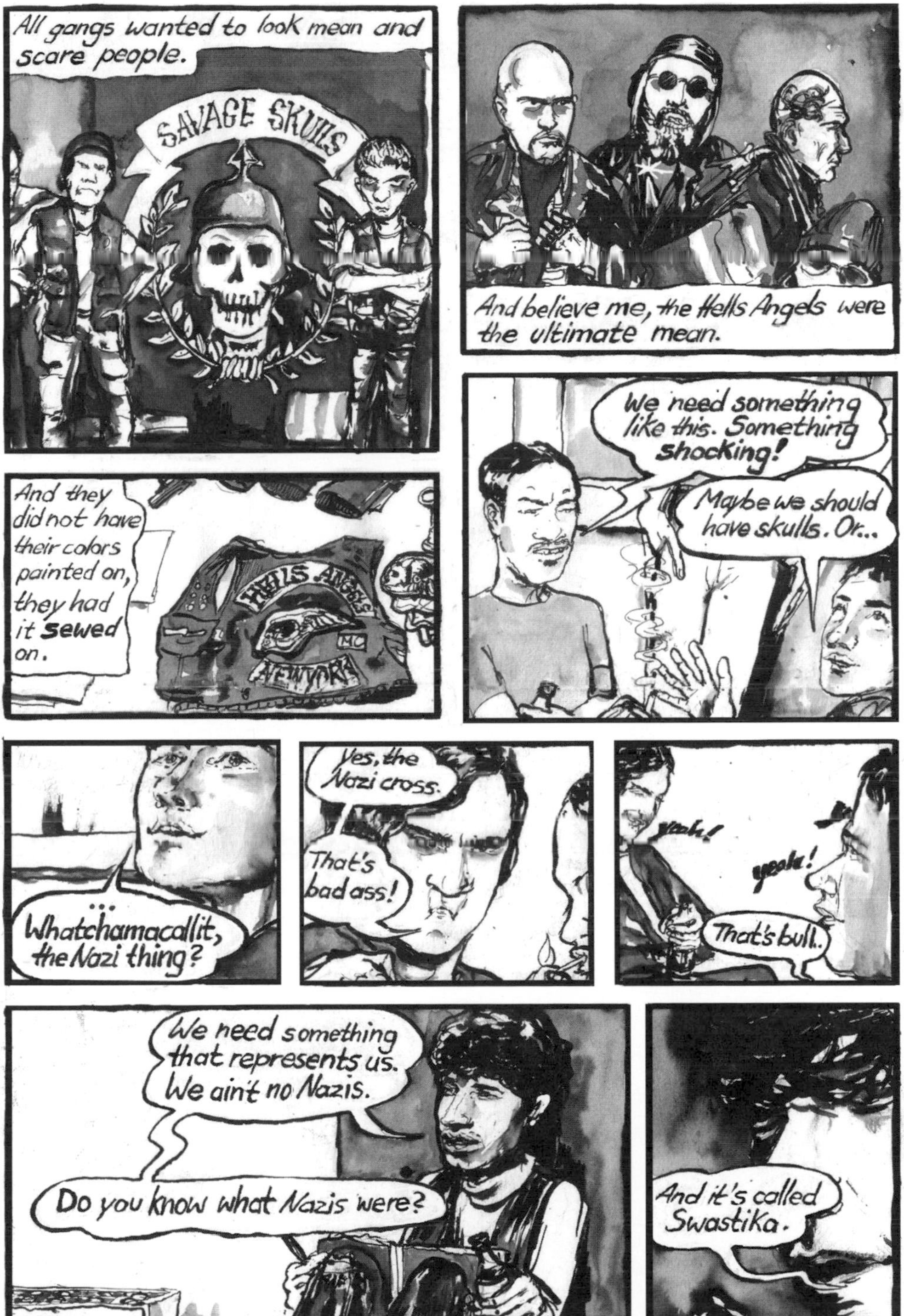
All gangs wanted to look mean and scare people.
SAVAGE SKULLS
And believe me, the Hells Angels were the ultimate mean.
And they did not have their colors painted on, they had it **sewed** on.
HELLS ANGELS
MC
NEW YORK
We need something like this. Something **shocking!**
Maybe we should have skulls. Or...
... Whatchamacallit, the Nazi thing?
Yes, the Nazi cross.
That's bad ass!
yeah!
yeah!
That's bull..
We need something that represents us. We ain't no Nazis.
Do you know what Nazis were?
And it's called Swastika.

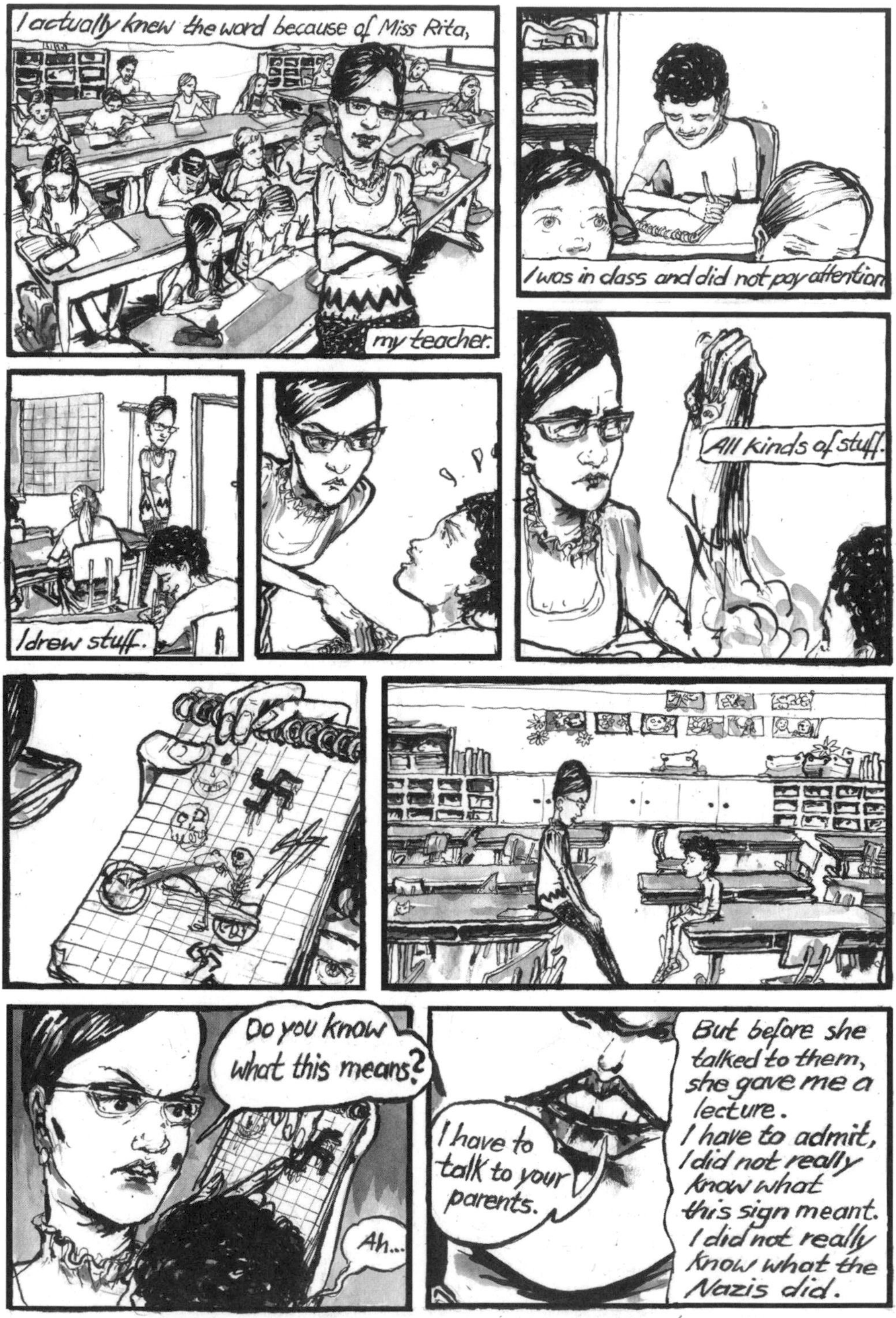
I actually knew the word because of Miss Rita,
my teacher.
I was in class and did not pay attention
I drew stuff.
All kinds of stuff.
Do you know what this means?
Ah...
I have to talk to your parents.
But before she talked to them, she gave me a lecture.
I have to admit, I did not really know what this sign meant.
I did not really know what the Nazis did.

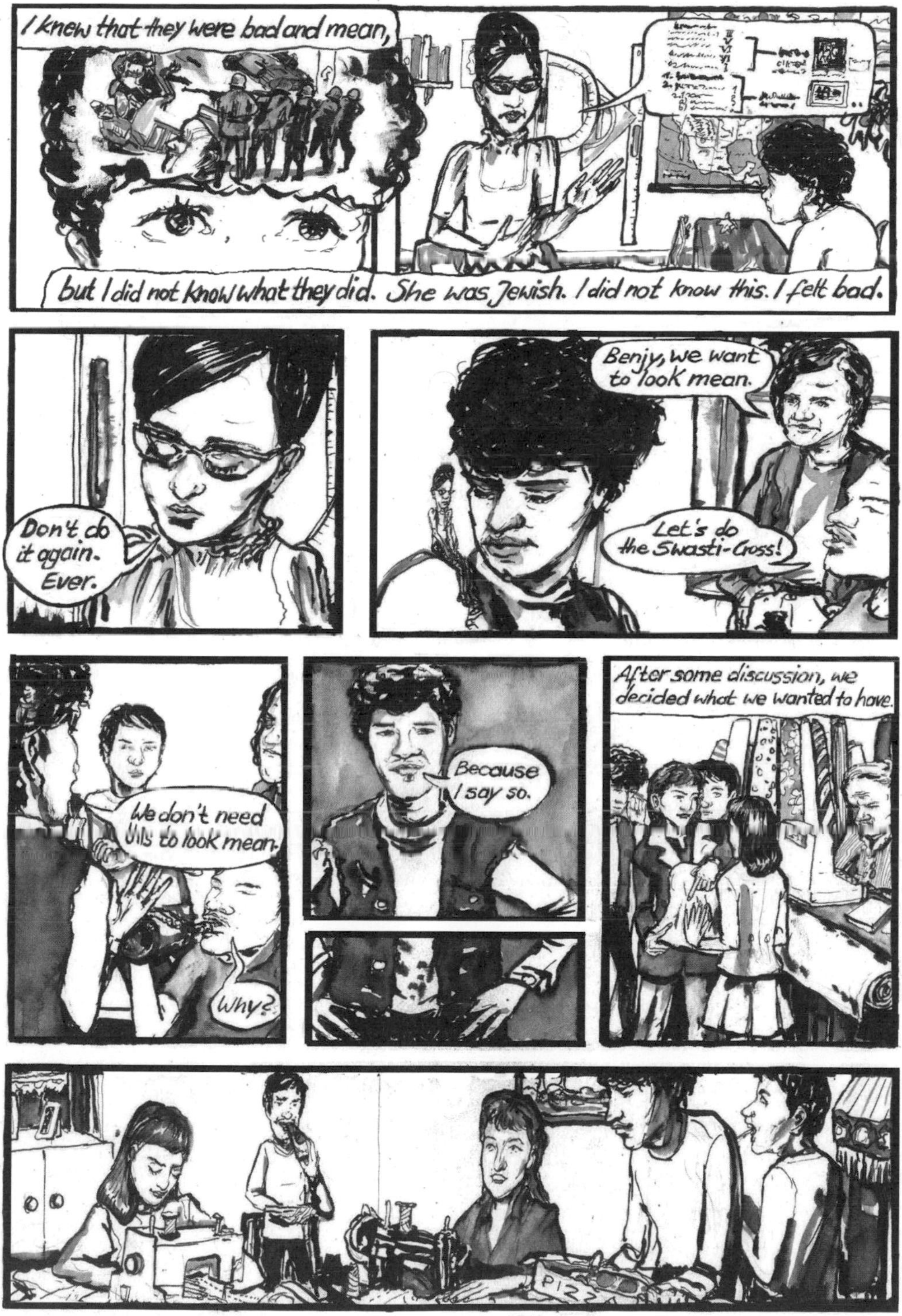
I knew that they were bad and mean,
but I did not know what they did. She was Jewish. I did not know this. I felt bad.
Don't do it again. Ever.
Benjy, we want to look mean.
Let's do the Swasti-Cross!
We don't need Ulls to look mean.
Why?
Because I say so.
After some discussion, we decided what we wanted to have.
PIZZ

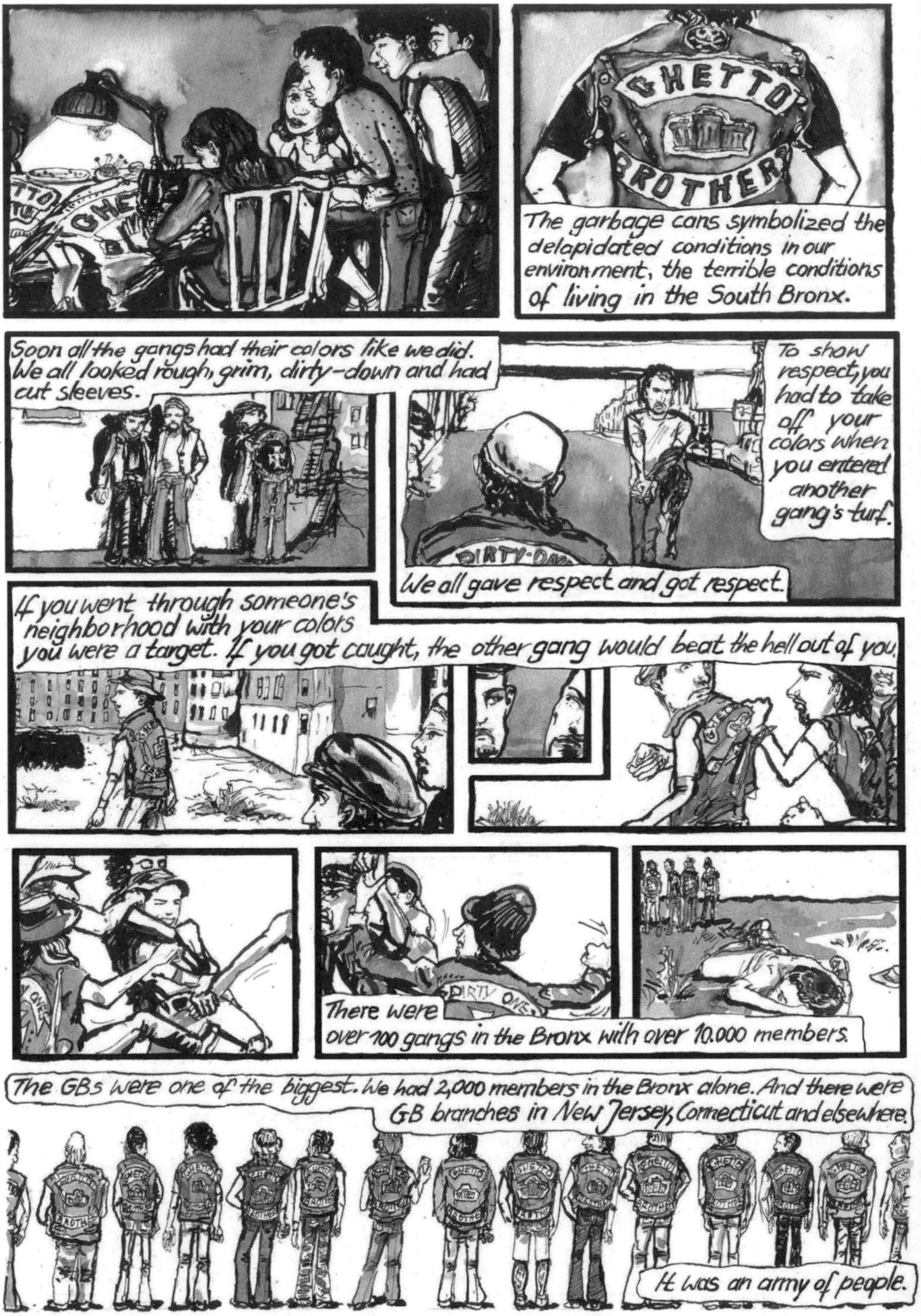
GHETTO
BROTHERS
The garbage cans symbolized the delapidated conditions in our environment, the terrible conditions of living in the South Bronx.
Soon all the gangs had their colors like we did. We all looked rough, grim, dirty—down and had cut sleeves.
To show respect, you had to take off your colors when you entered another gang's turf.
We all gave respect and got respect.
If you went through someone's neighborhood with your colors you were a target. If you got caught, the other gang would beat the hell out of you.
DIRTY ONES
There were over 100 gangs in the Bronx with over 10.000 members.
The GBs were one of the biggest. We had 2,000 members in the Bronx alone.. And there were GB branches in New Jersey, Connecticut and elsewhere.
It was an army of people.

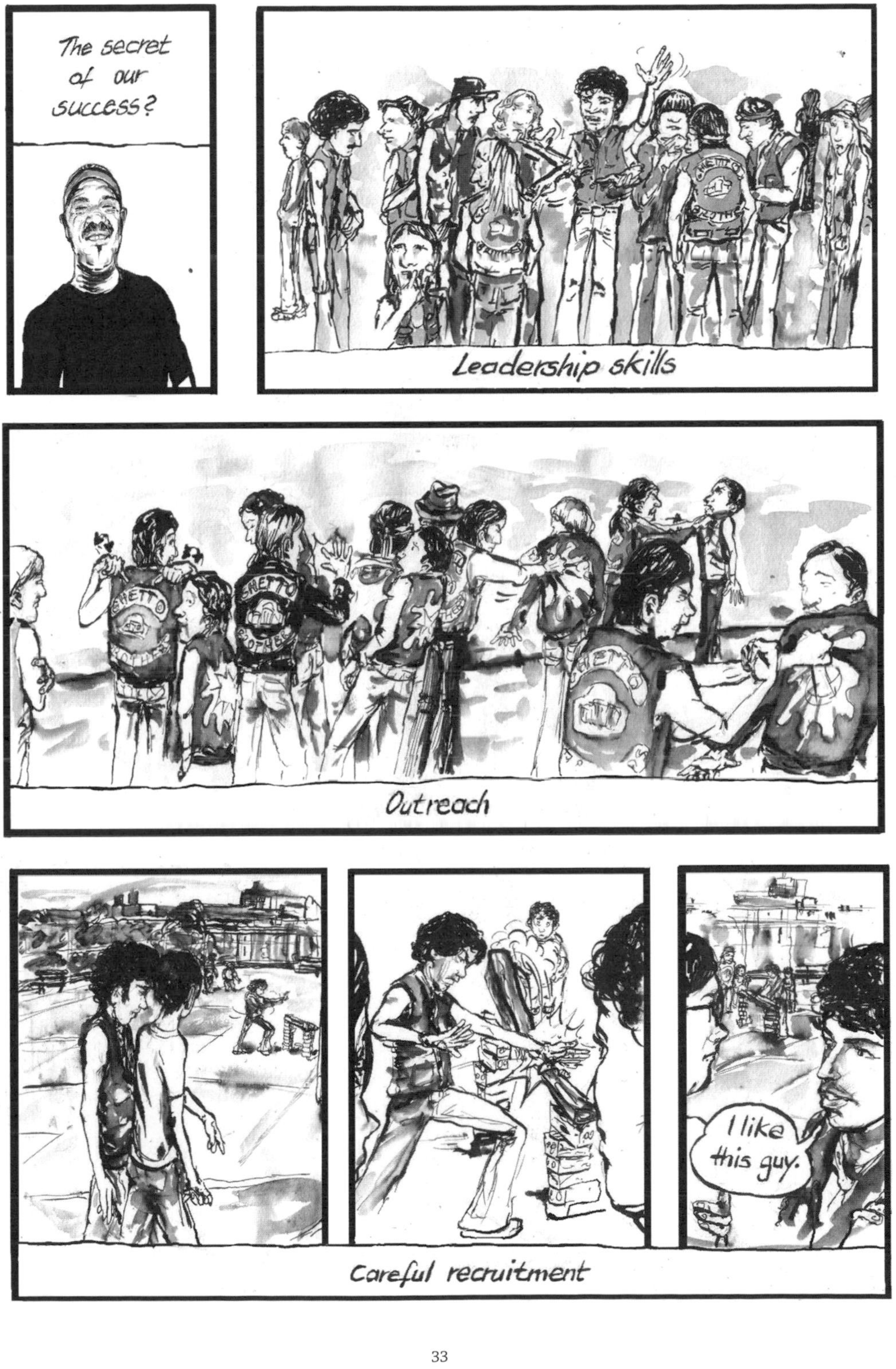
The secret of our success?
Leadership skills
Outreach
I like this guy.
Careful recruitment

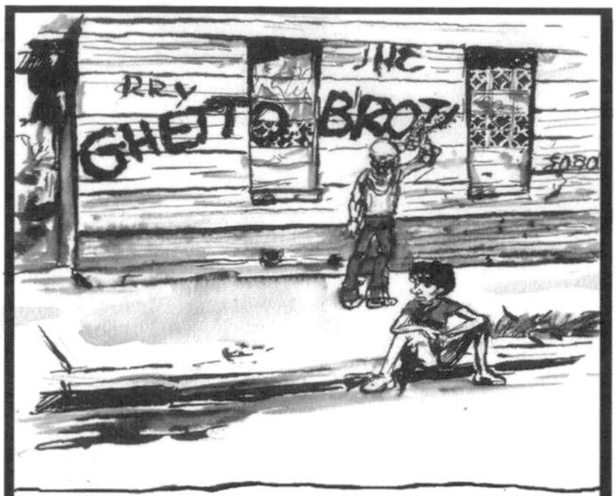
THE
GHETTO BROT

Good public relations

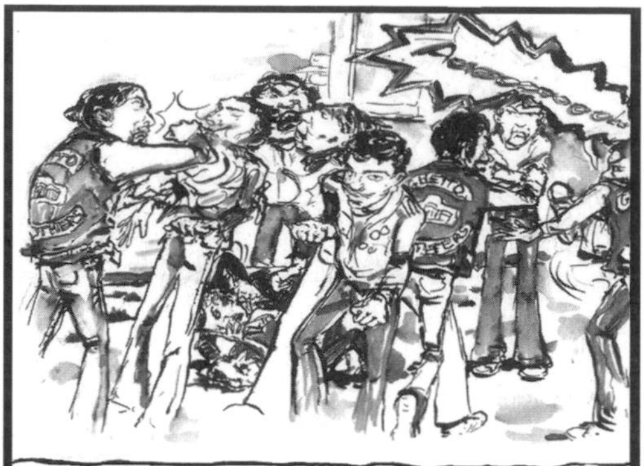

Diplomacy

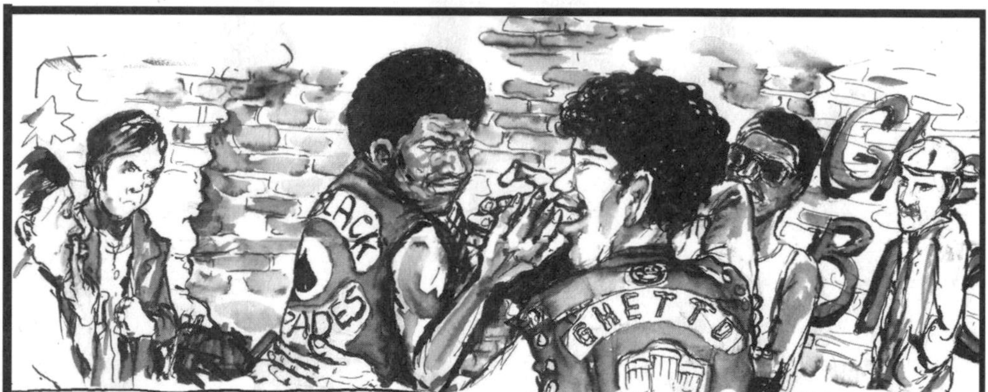
BLACK SPADES
GHETTO

Coalition building

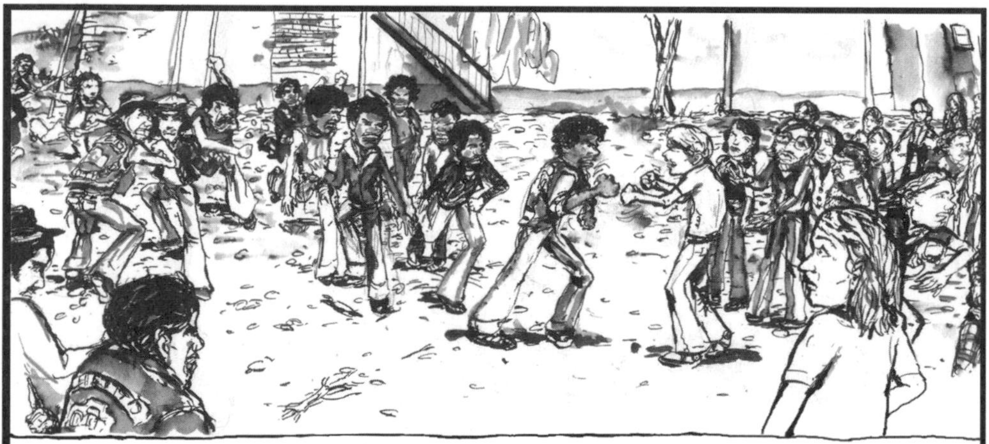

And sometimes also hostile take overs.

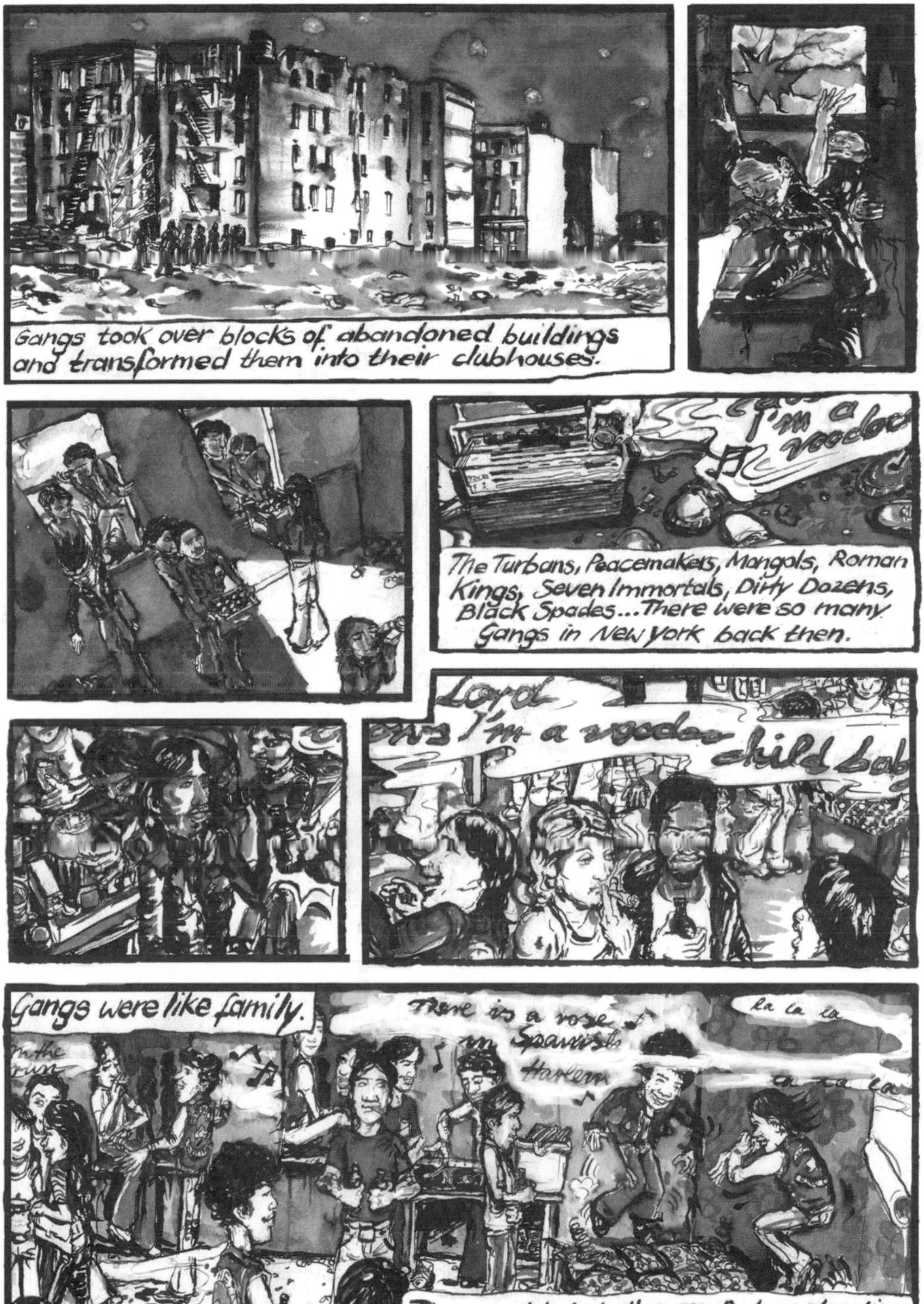
Gangs took over blocks of abandoned buildings and transformed them into their clubhouses.
I'm a
The Turbans, Peacemakers, Mongols, Roman Kings, Seven Immortals, Dirty Dozens, Black Spades... There were so many Gangs in New York back then.
Lord
I'm a voodoo child
Gangs were like family.
There is a rose in Spanish Harlem
la la la
They provided shelter, comfort, protection.

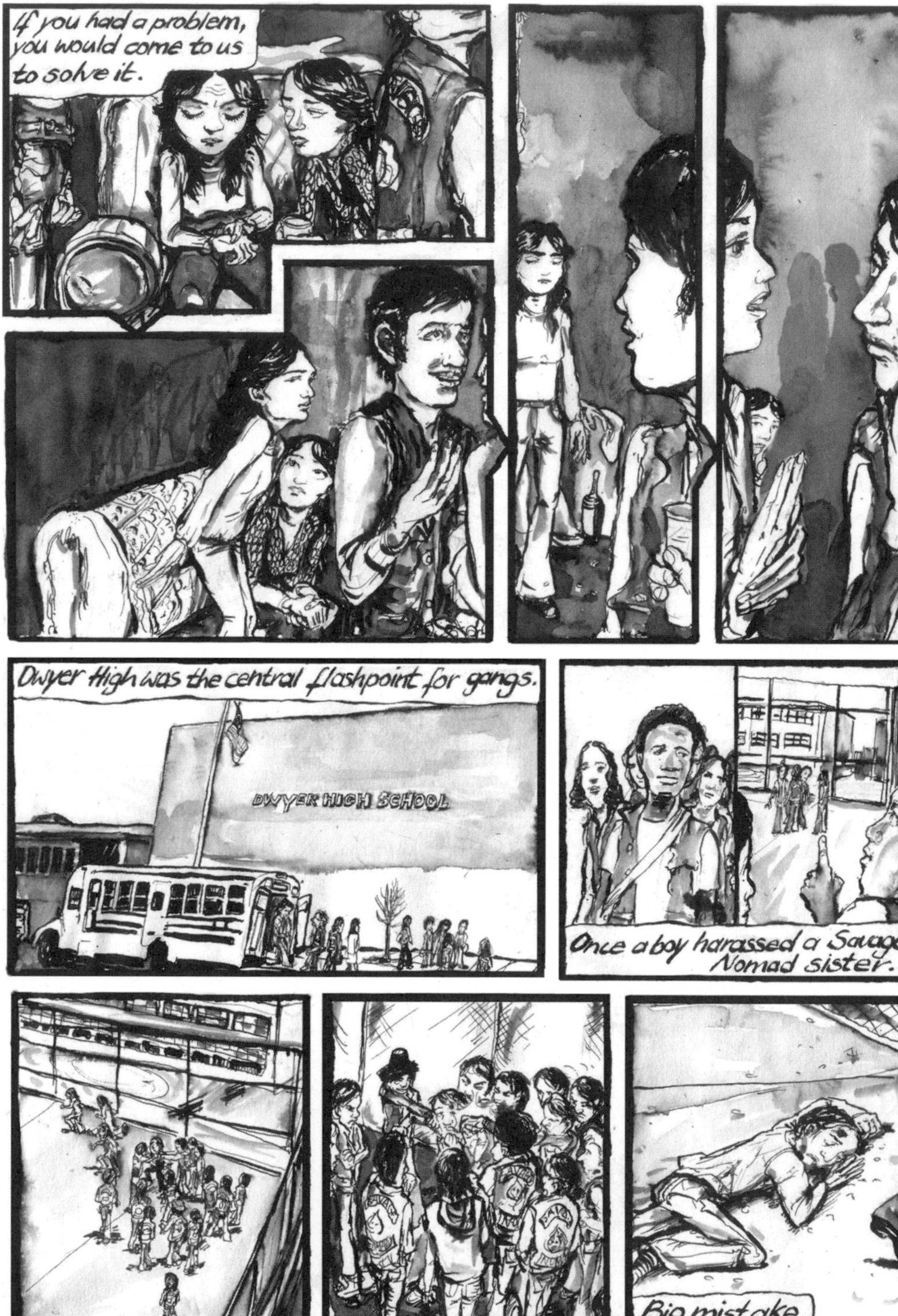
If you had a problem, you would come to us to solve it.
Dwyer High was the central flashpoint for gangs.
DWYER HIGH SCHOOL
Once a boy harassed a Savage Nomad sister.
Big mistake.

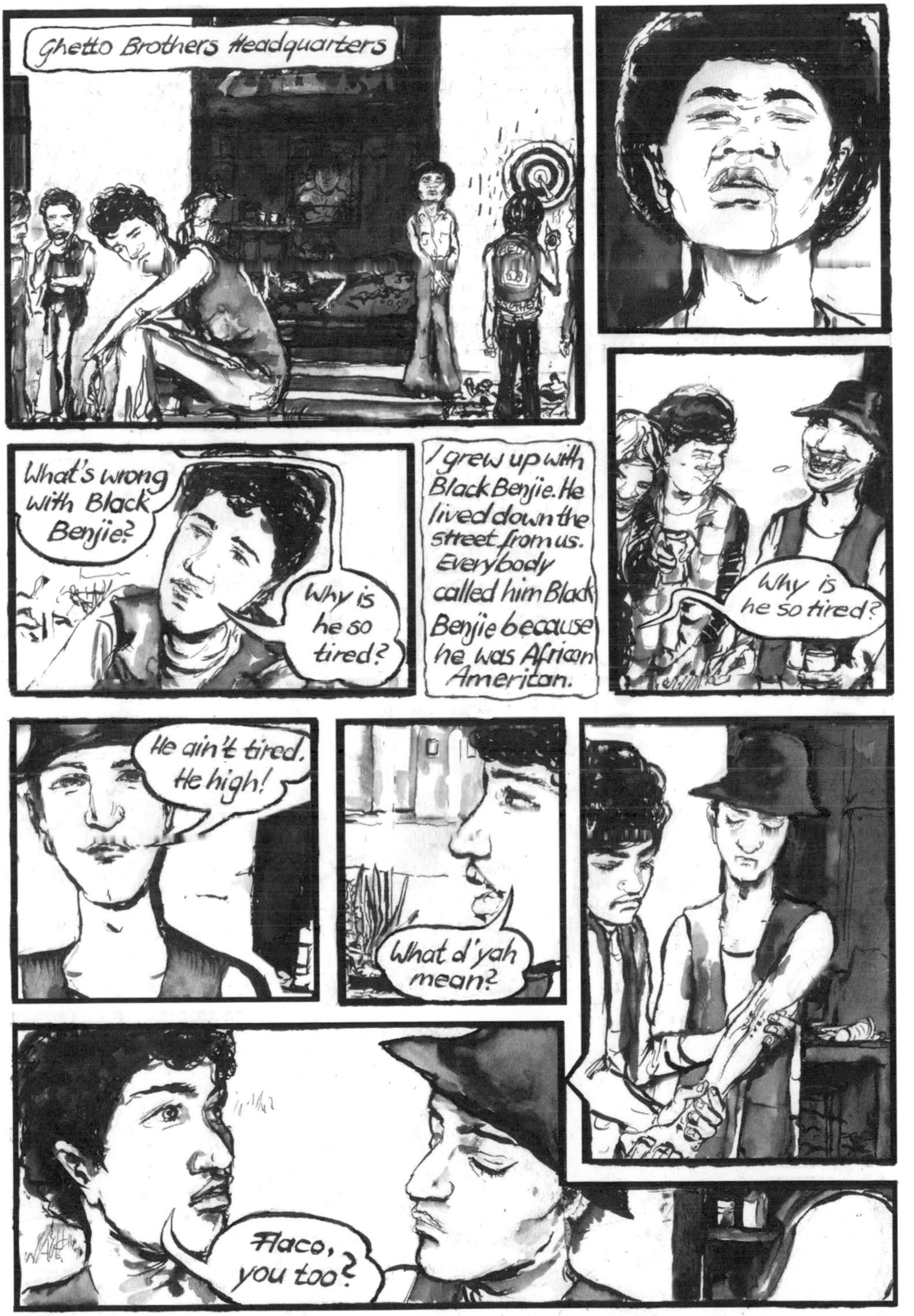
Ghetto Brothers Headquarters
What's wrong with Black Benjie?
Why is he so tired?
I grew up with Black Benjie. He lived down the street from us. Everybody called him Black Benjie because he was African American.
Why is he so tired?
He ain't tired. He high!
What d'yah mean?
Flaco, you too?

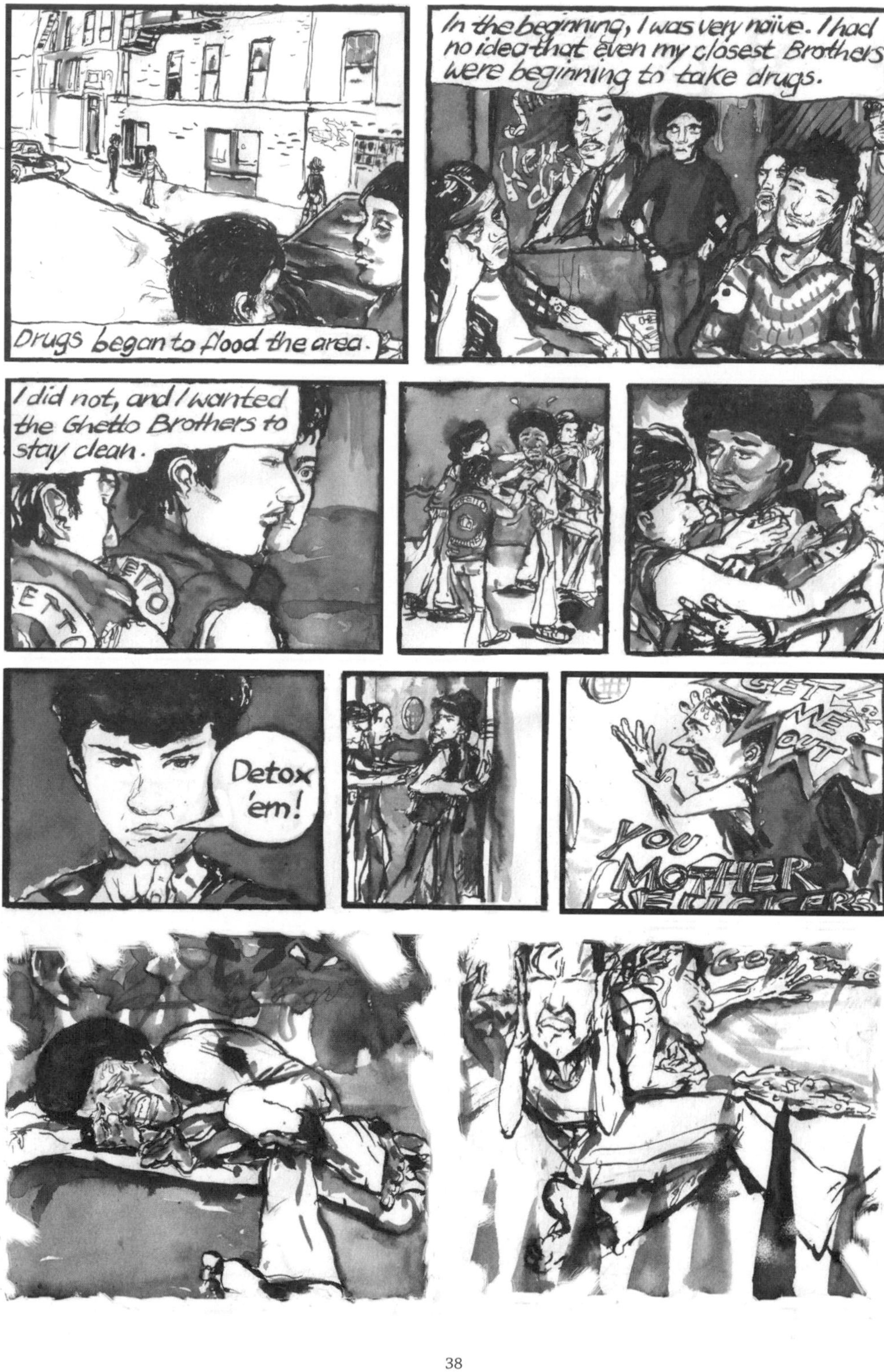
Drugs began to flood the area.
In the beginning, I was very naïve. I had no idea that even my closest Brothers were beginning to take drugs.
I did not, and I wanted the Ghetto Brothers to stay clean.
Detox 'em!
GET ME OUT
YOU MOTHER

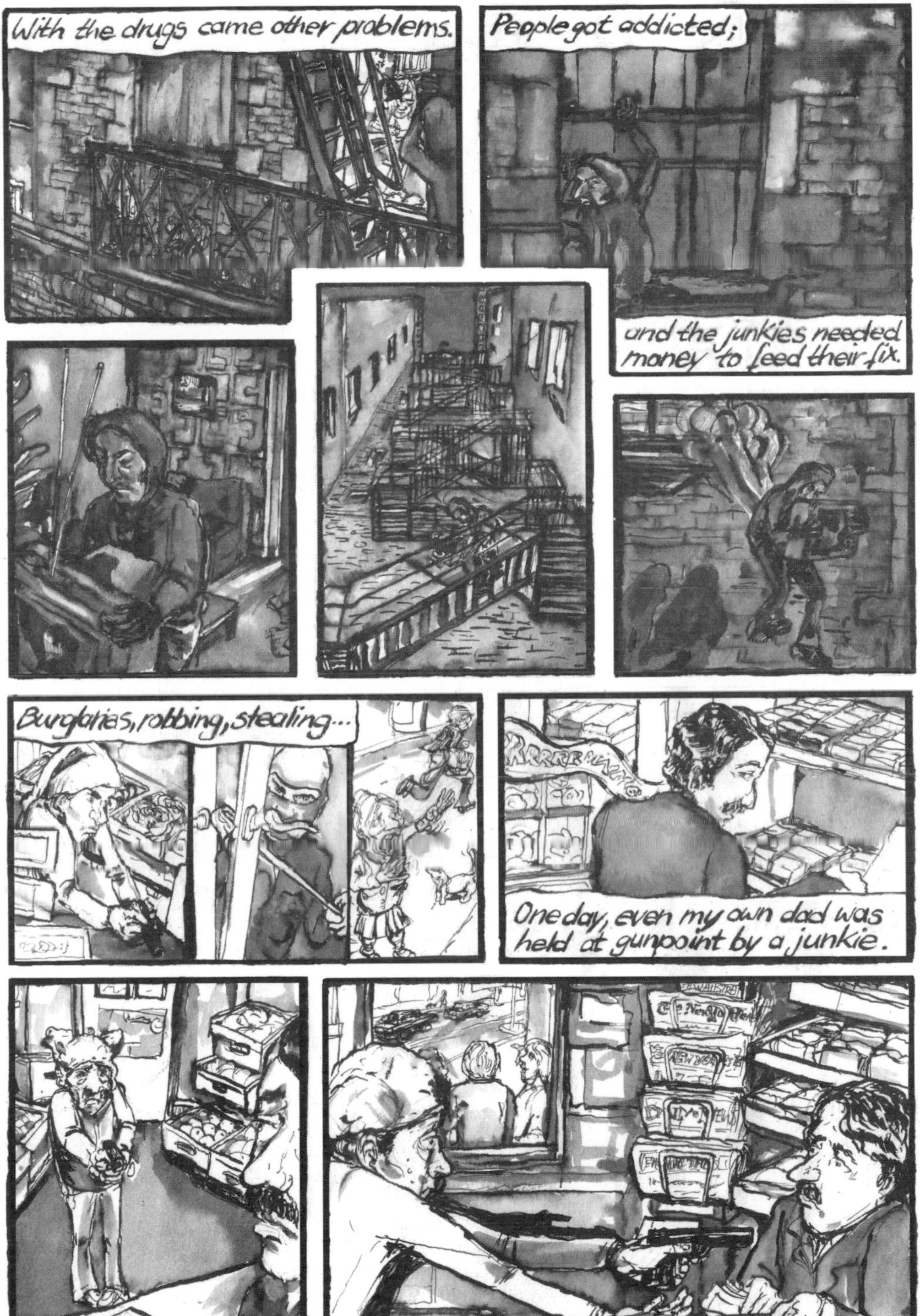
With the drugs came other problems.
People got addicted;
and the junkies needed money to feed their fix.
Burglaries, robbing, stealing...
One day, even my own dad was held at gunpoint by a junkie.

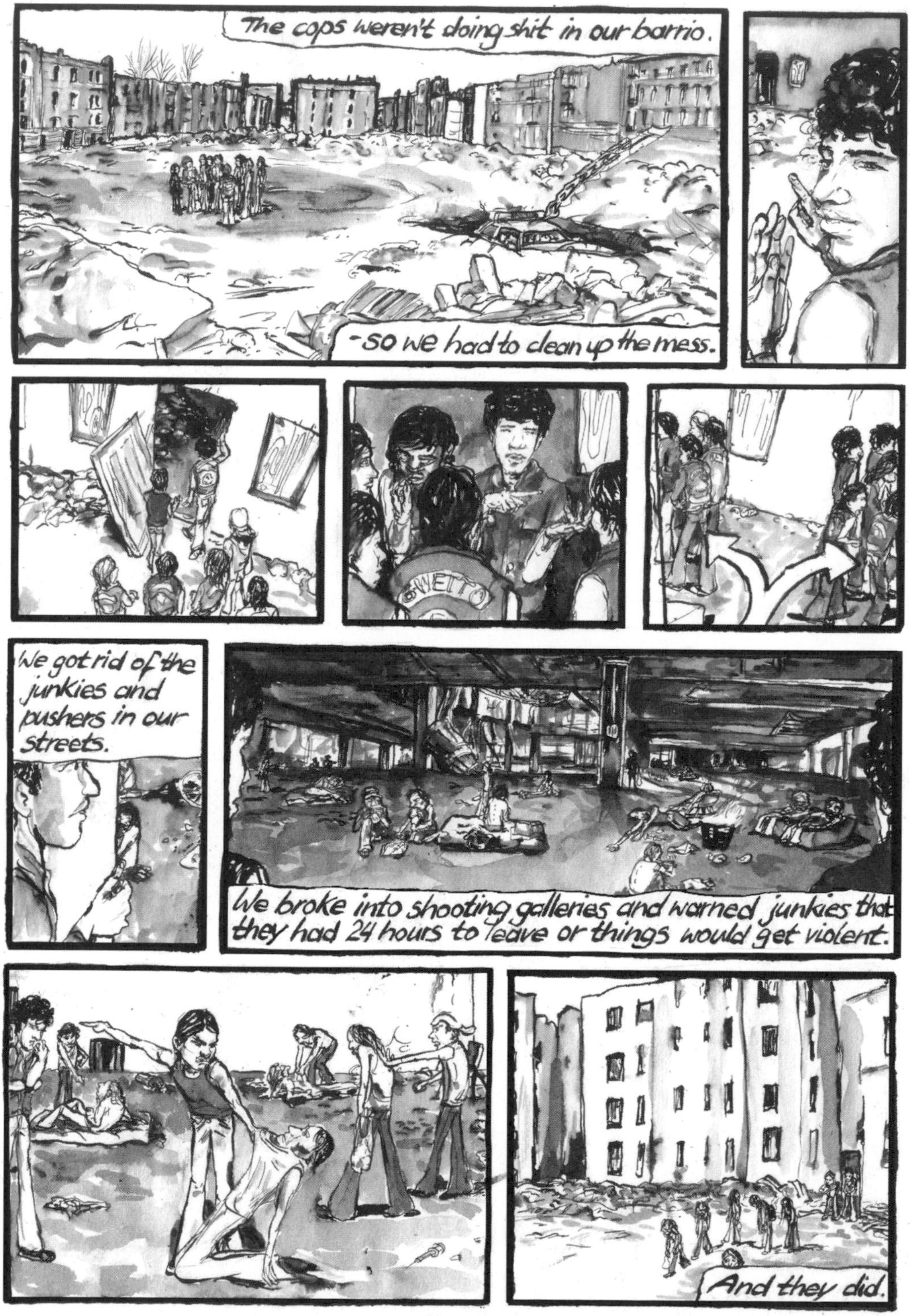
The cops weren't doing shit in our barrio.
-so we had to clean up the mess.
We got rid of the junkies and pushers in our streets.
We broke into shooting galleries and warned junkies that they had 24 hours to leave or things would get violent.
And they did.

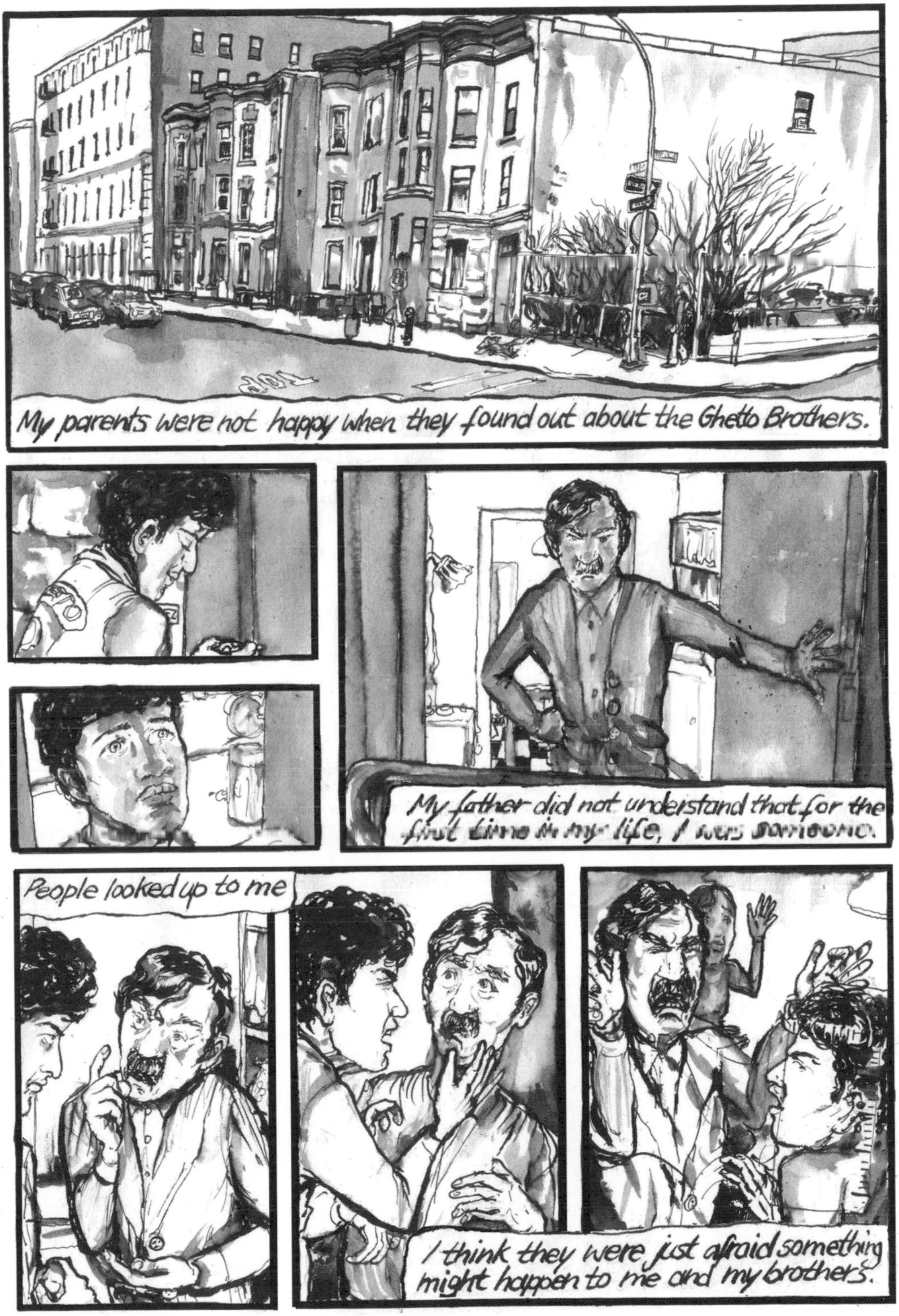

My parents were not happy when they found out about the Ghetto Brothers.
My father did not understand that for the first time in my life, I was someone.
People looked up to me
I think they were just afraid something might happen to me and my brothers.

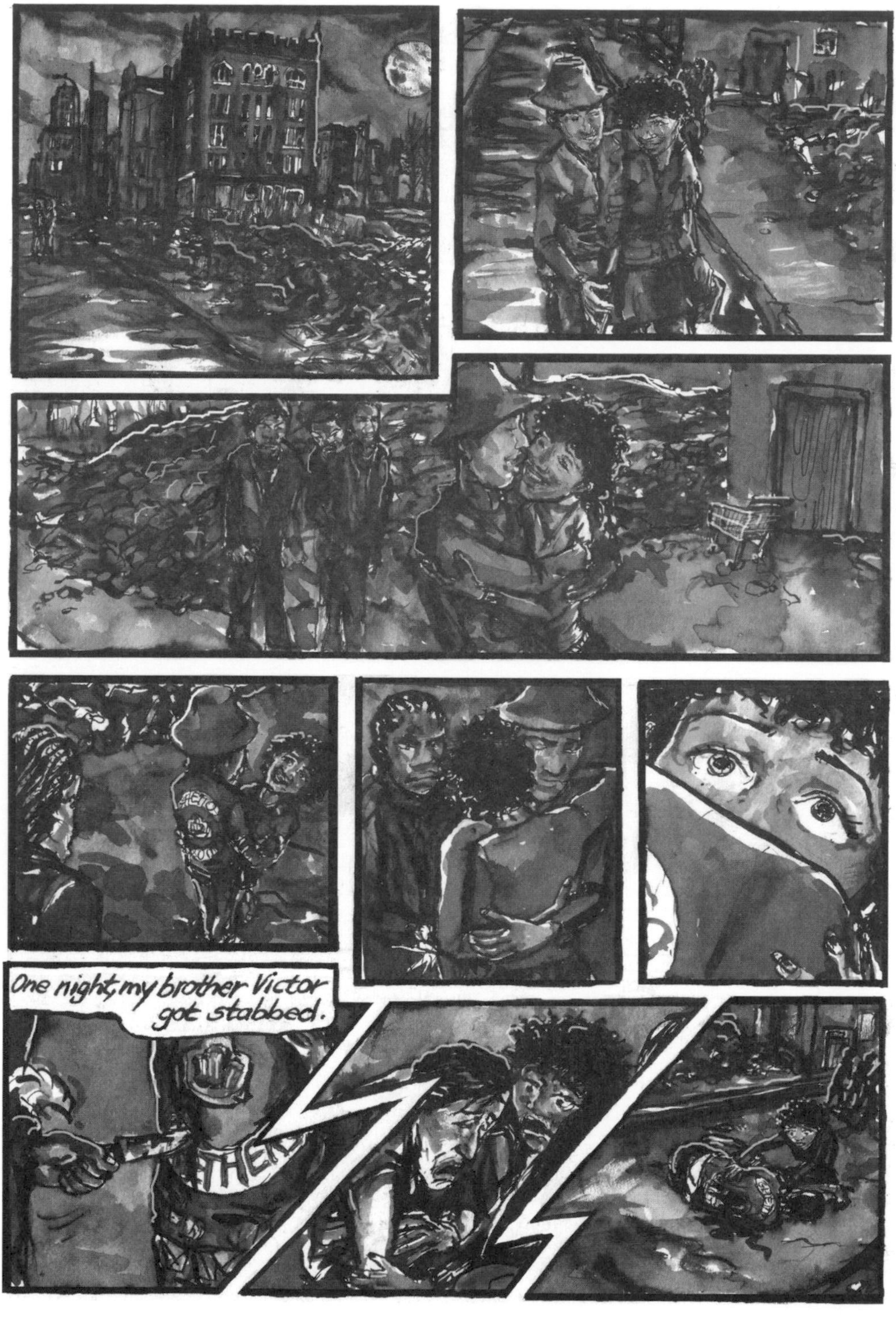
One night, my brother Victor got stabbed.

We figured that the Mongols were behind this.

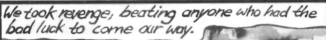

We took revenge, beating anyone who had the bad luck to come our way.

But violence begat more violence.

EEEE
EEE
E

EEEEEEEEEEE

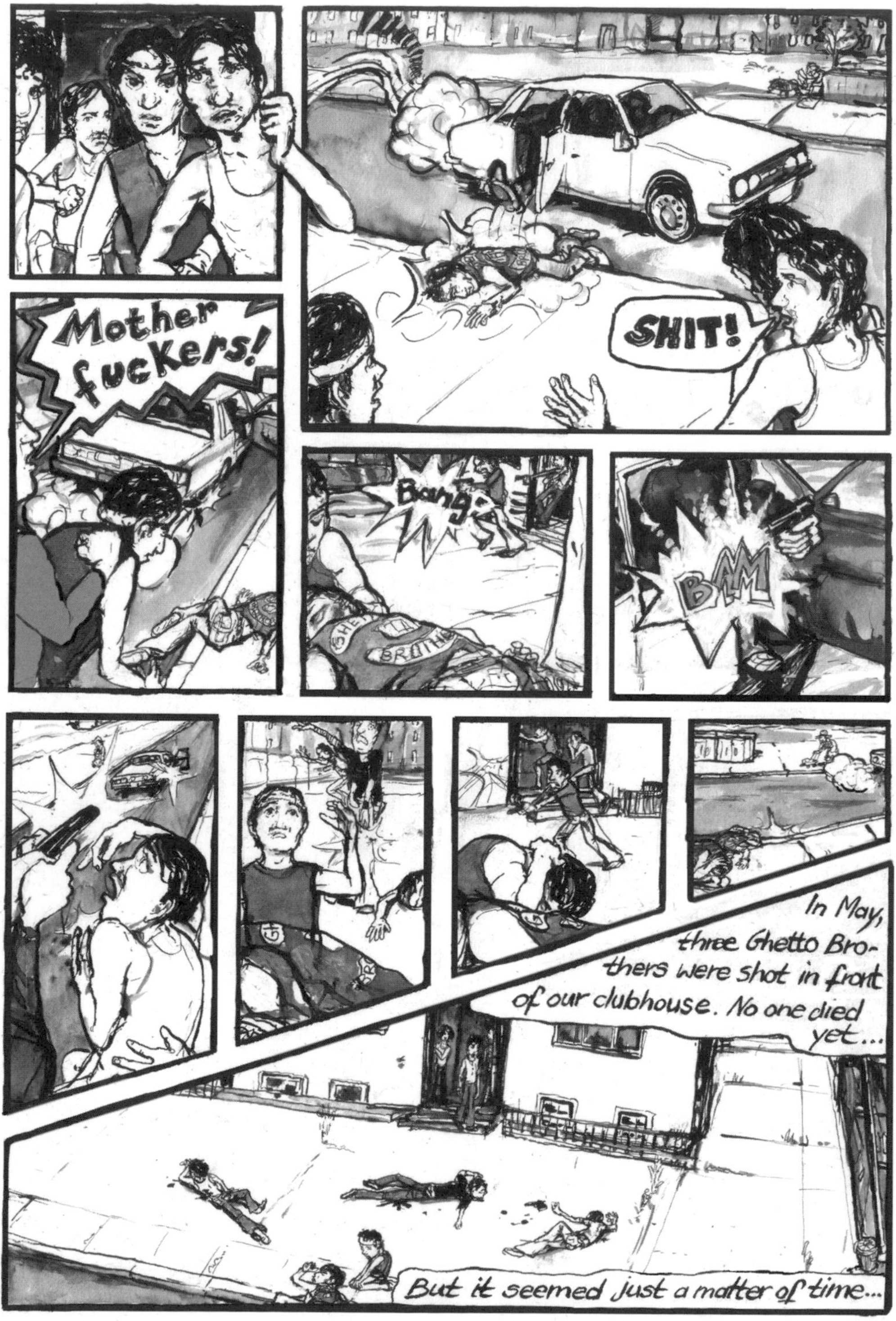
SHIT!
Mother fuckers!
Bang
BAM
In May, three Ghetto Brothers were shot in front of our clubhouse. No one died yet...
But it seemed just a matter of time...

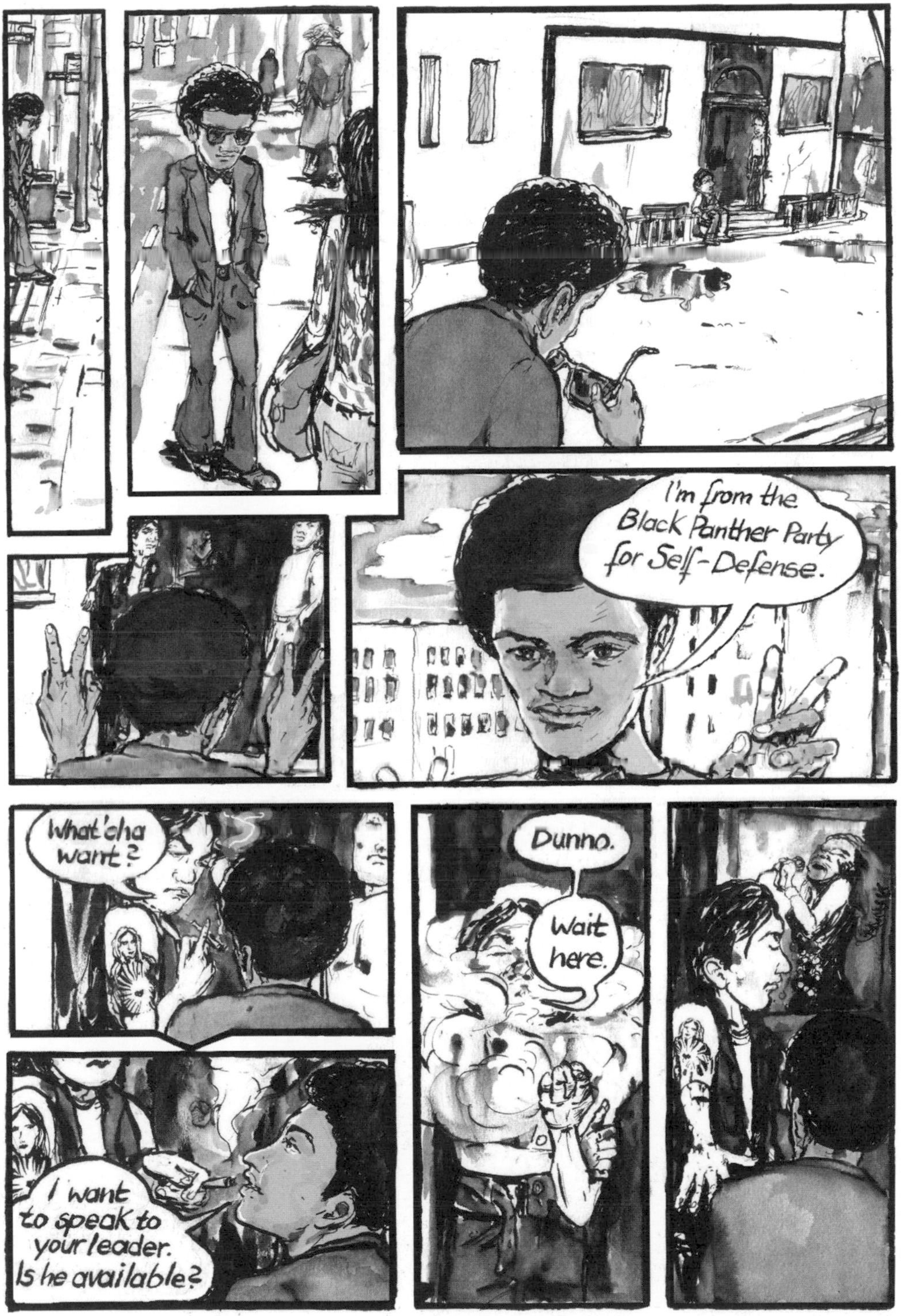
I'm from the Black Panther Party for Self-Defense.
What'cha want?
I want to speak to your leader. Is he available?
Dunno.
Wait here.

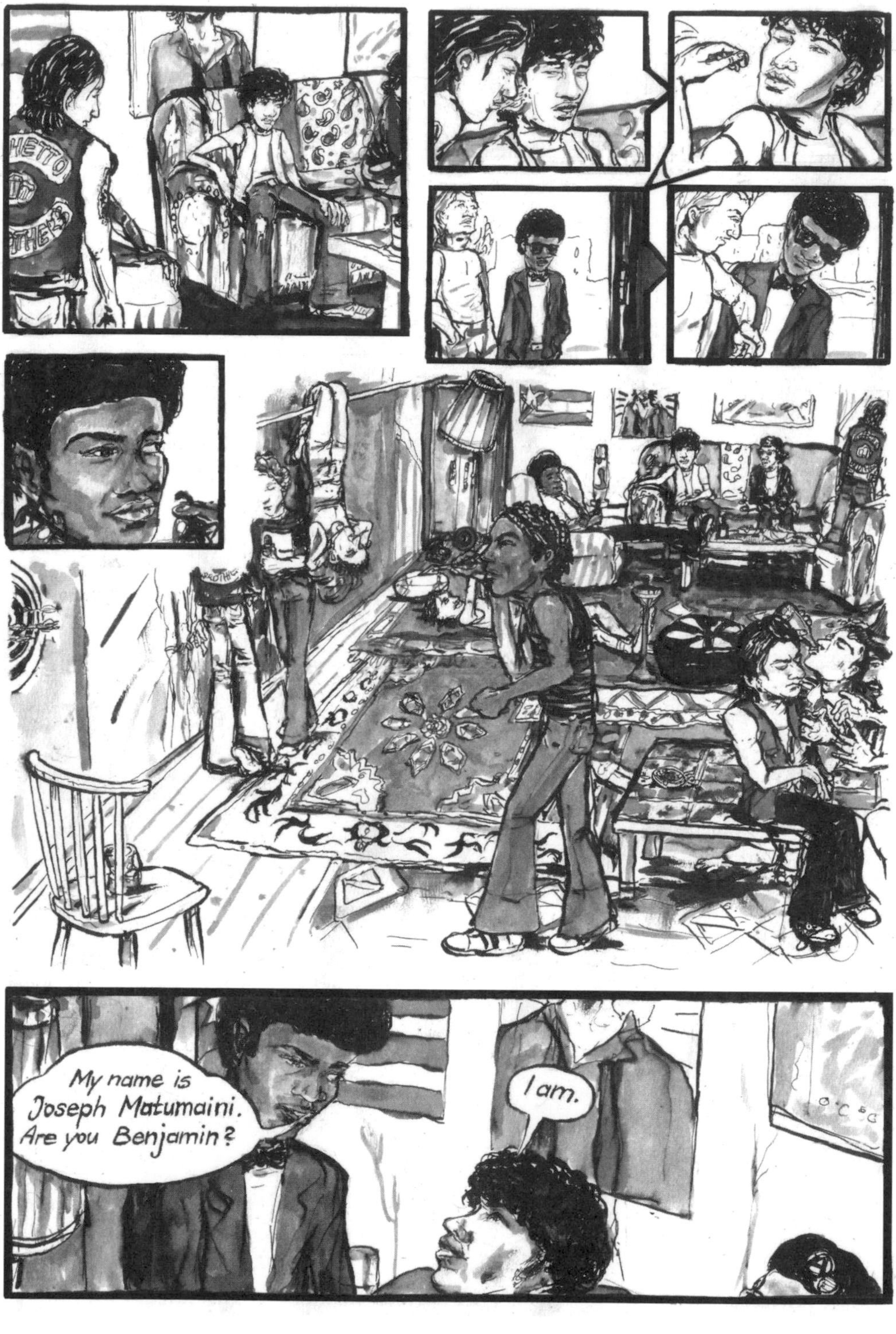

My name is Joseph Matumaini. Are you Benjamin?
I am.

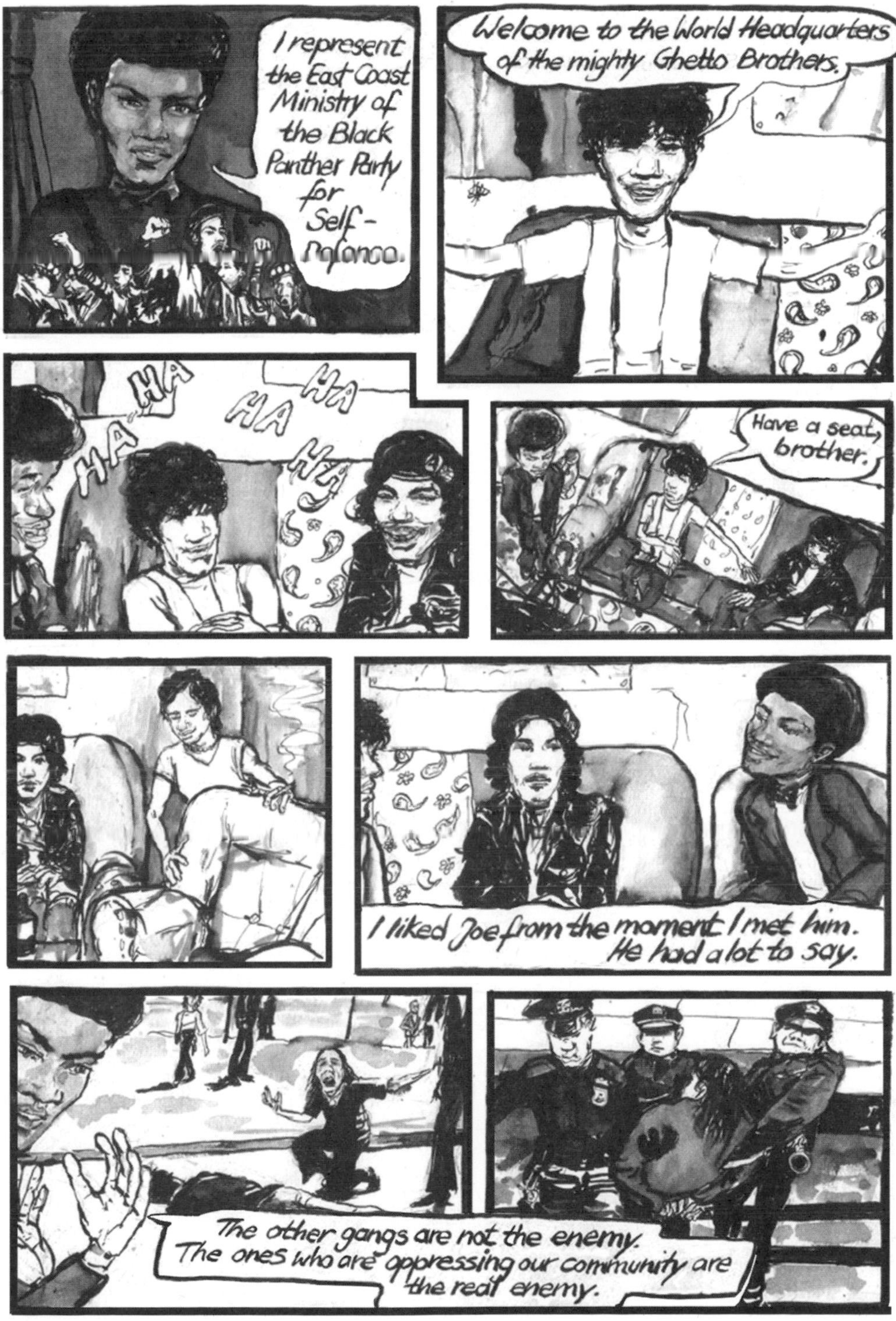
I represent the East Coast Ministry of the Black Panther Party for Self-Defense.
Welcome to the World Headquarters of the mighty Ghetto Brothers.
HA HA HA HA HA
Have a seat, brother.
I liked Joe from the moment I met him. He had a lot to say.
The other gangs are not the enemy. The ones who are oppressing our community are the real enemy.

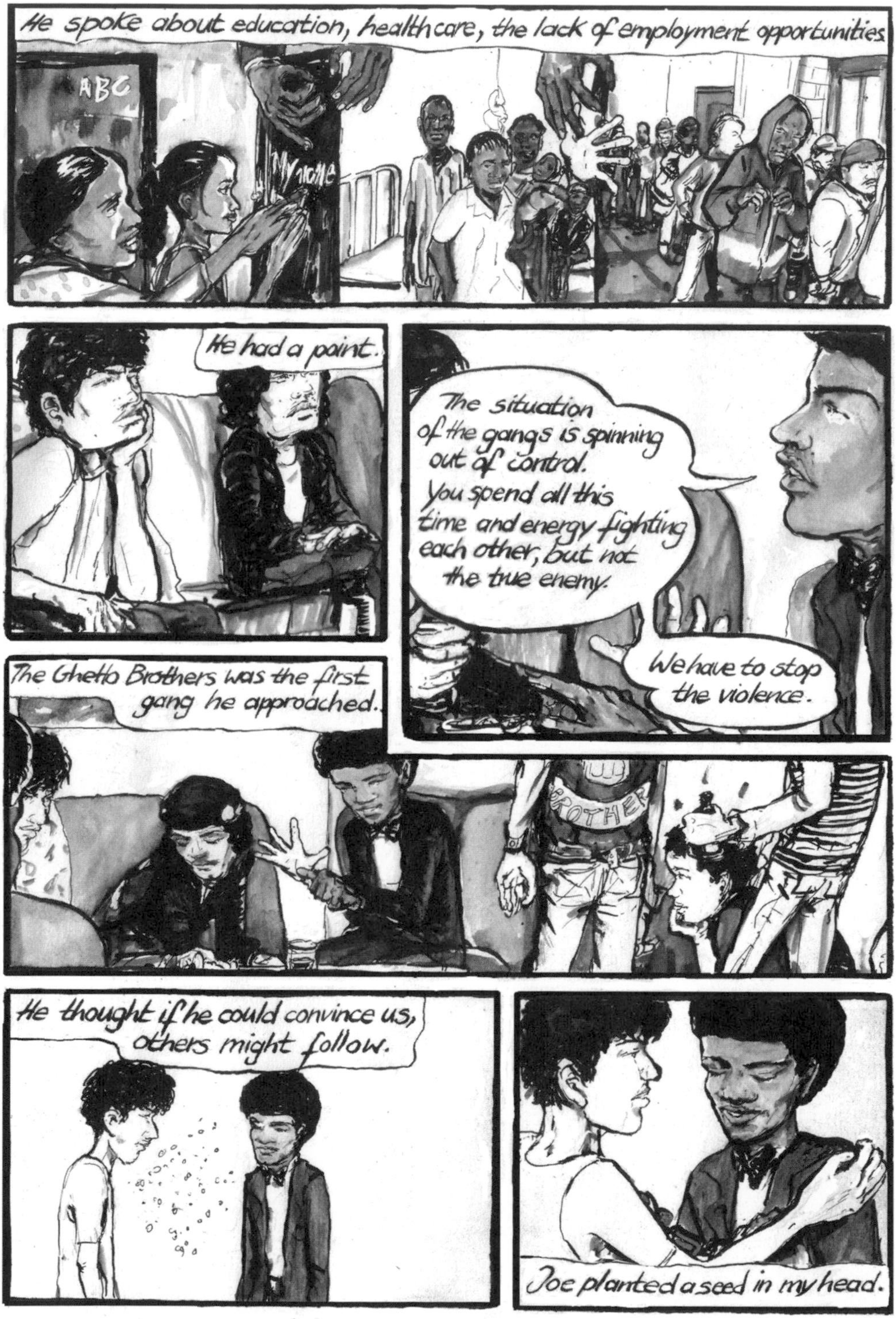
He spoke about education, healthcare, the lack of employment opportunities
ABC
He had a point.
The situation of the gangs is spinning out of control. You spend all this time and energy fighting each other, but not the true enemy.
We have to stop the violence.
The Ghetto Brothers was the first gang he approached.
BROTHER
He thought if he could convince us, others might follow.
Joe planted a seed in my head.

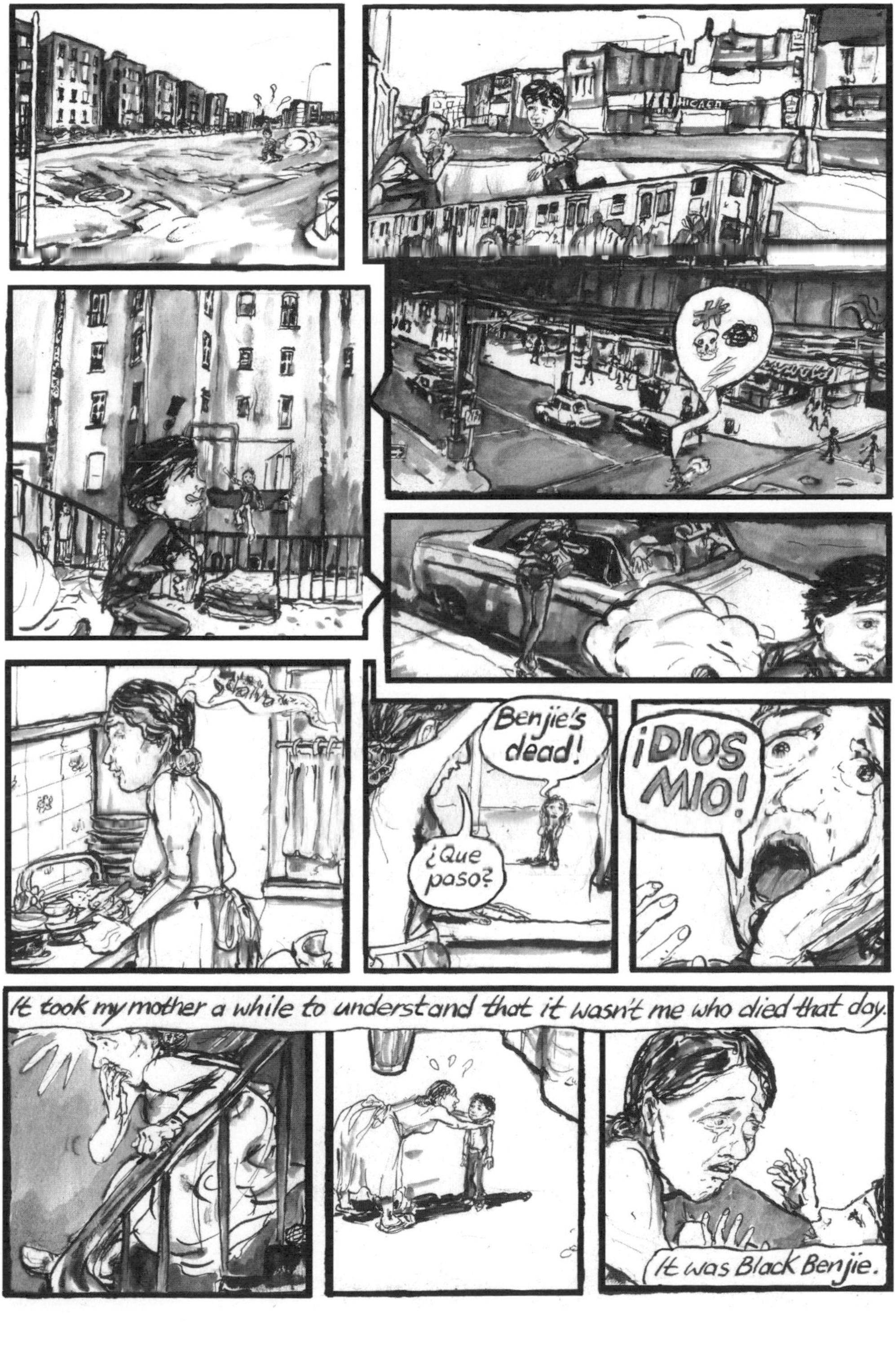
Benjie's dead!
¿Que paso?
¡DIOS MIO!
It took my mother a while to understand that it wasn't me who died that day.
It was Black Benjie.

That day, everything changed.

Violence was escalating. November had been the peak of the wars. An emergency summit was held in Central Park, but nothing concrete came of it.

News reached us that the Mangols, Seven Immortals and Black Spades were entering GB turf, attacking people.

50

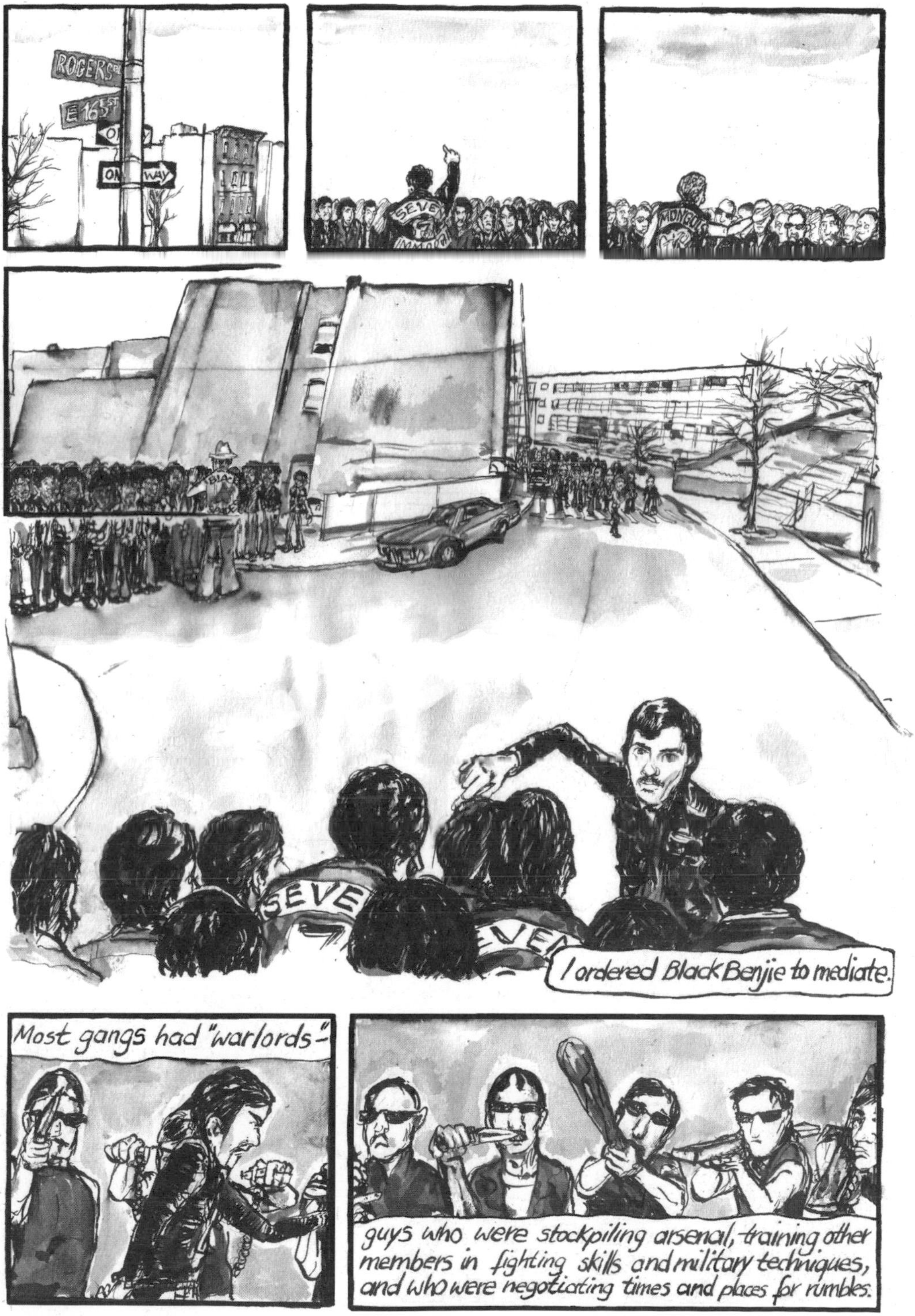
ROGERS PL
E 165 ST
ONE WAY
SEVEN
MONGUS
BLACK
SEVEN
SEVEN
I ordered Black Benjie to mediate.
Most gangs had "warlords"-
guys who were stockpiling arsenal, training other members in fighting skills and military techniques, and who were negotiating times and places for rumbles.

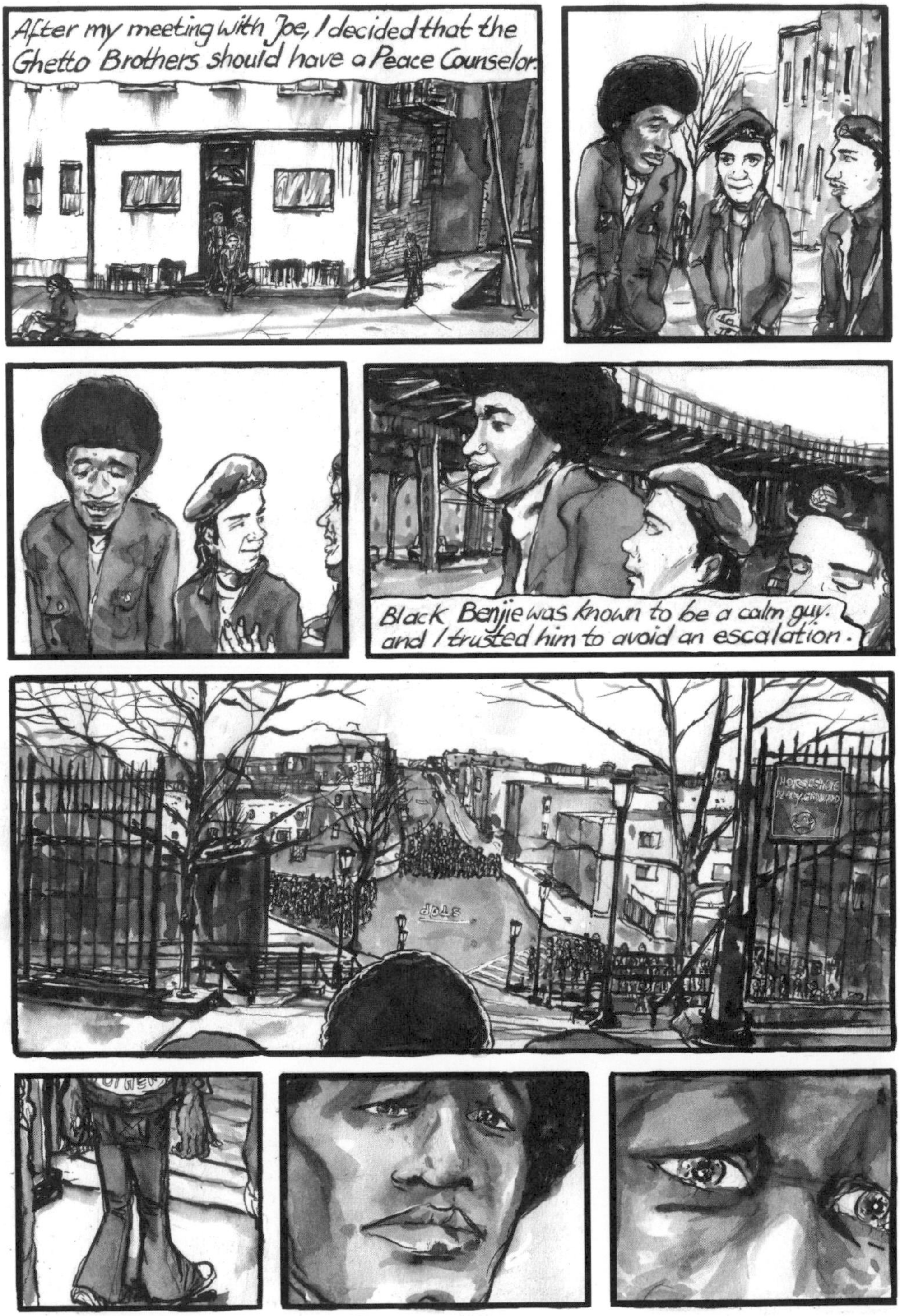
After my meeting with Joe, I decided that the Ghetto Brothers should have a Peace Counselor.
Black Benjie was known to be a calm guy. and I trusted him to avoid an escalation.

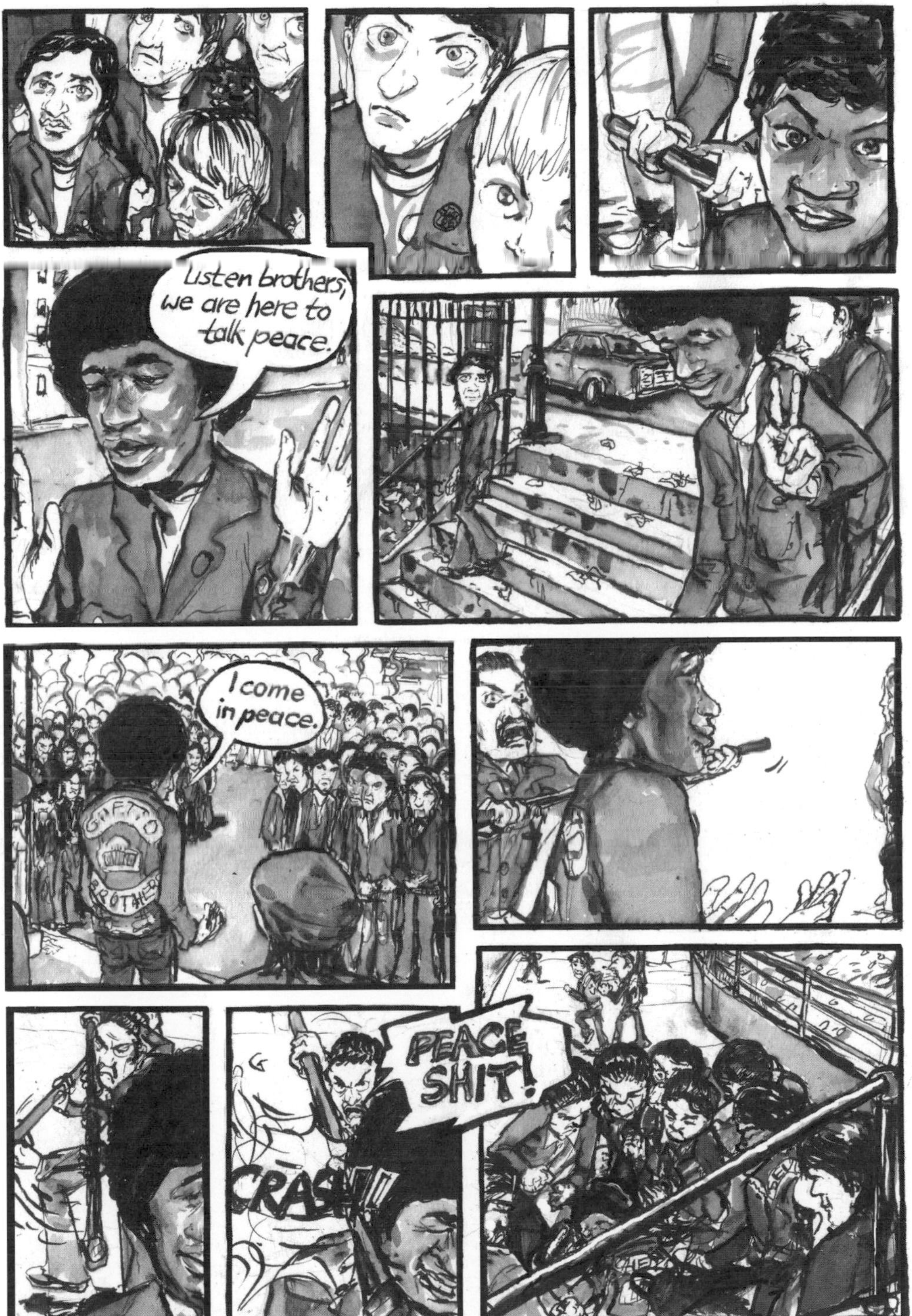

Listen brothers, we are here to talk peace.
I come in peace.
PEACE SHIT!
CRASH!

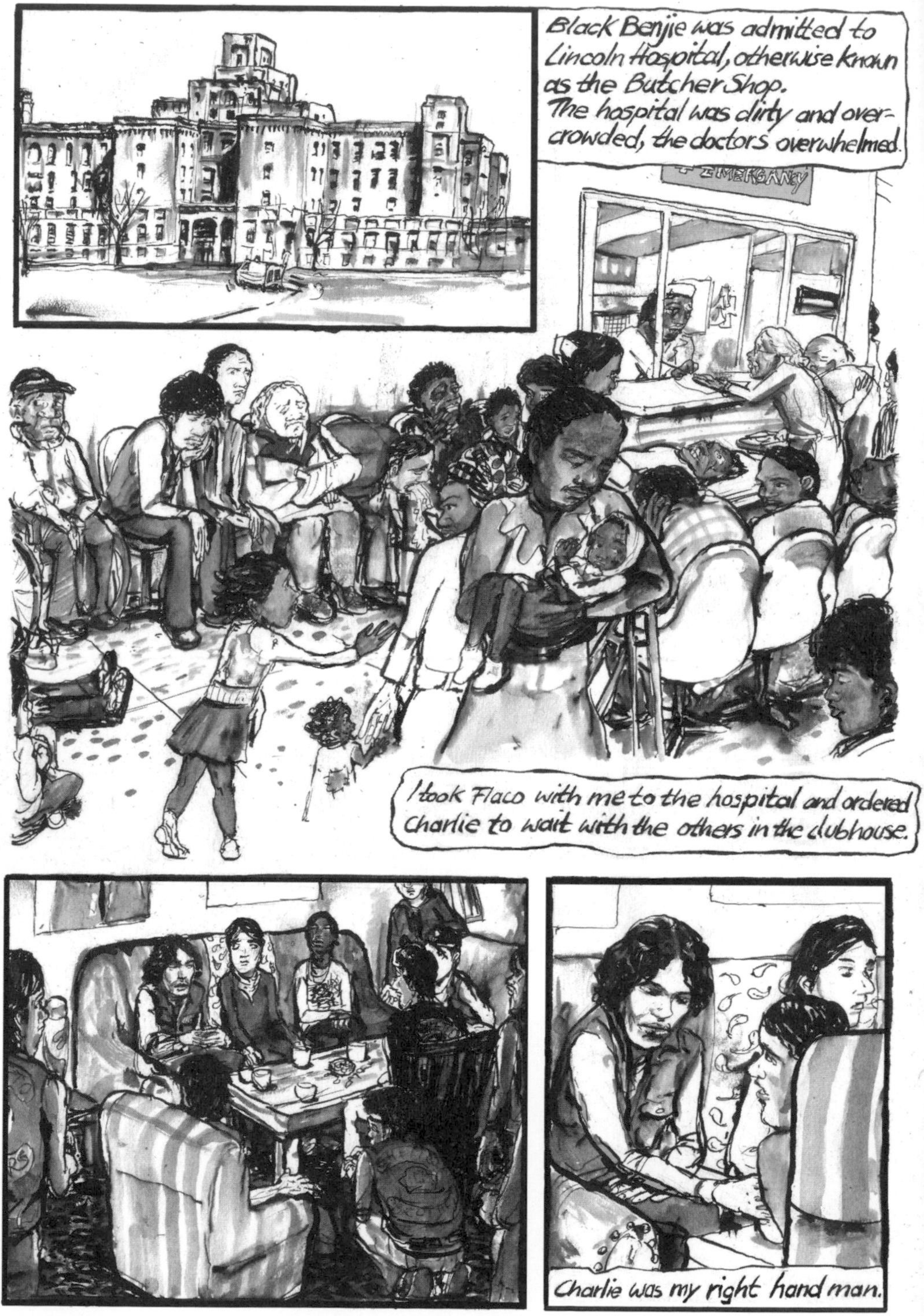
Black Benjie was admitted to Lincoln Hospital, otherwise known as the Butcher Shop. The hospital was dirty and over-crowded, the doctors overwhelmed.
I took Flaco with me to the hospital and ordered Charlie to wait with the others in the clubhouse.
Charlie was my right hand man.

He had joined the Marines, but went AWOL and joined the Ghetto Brothers.

I have no business fighting in Vietnam when we have a war in our own back-yard to fight.

He took off the uniform of the US army, and took on the uniform of the street.

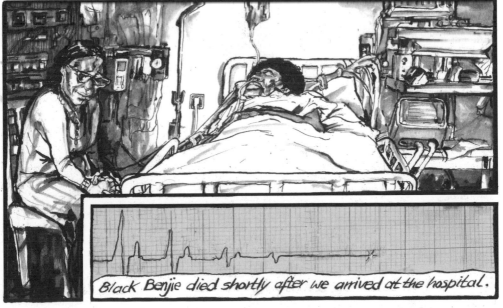

Black Benjie died shortly after we arrived at the hospital.

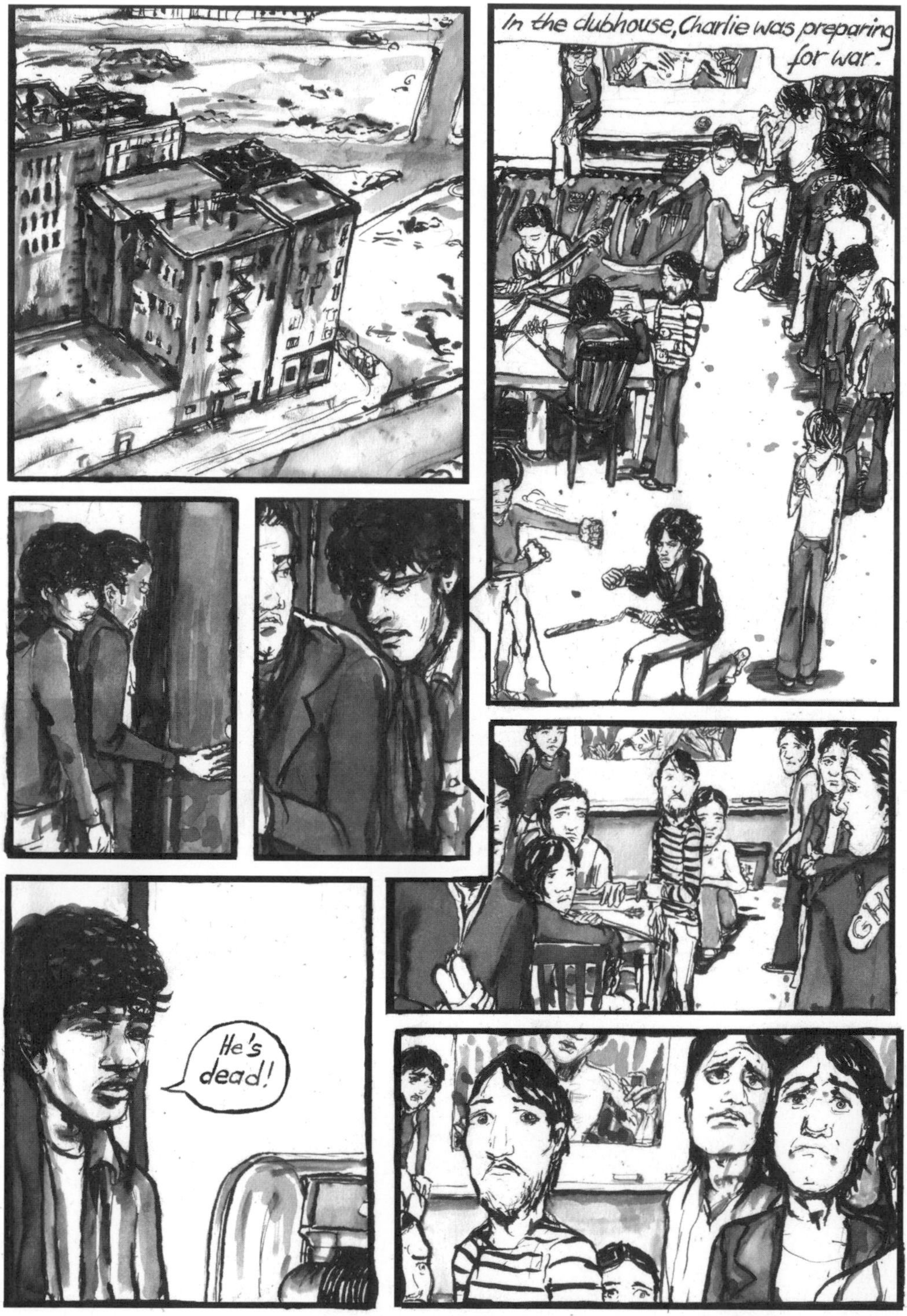
In the clubhouse, Charlie was preparing for war.
He's dead!

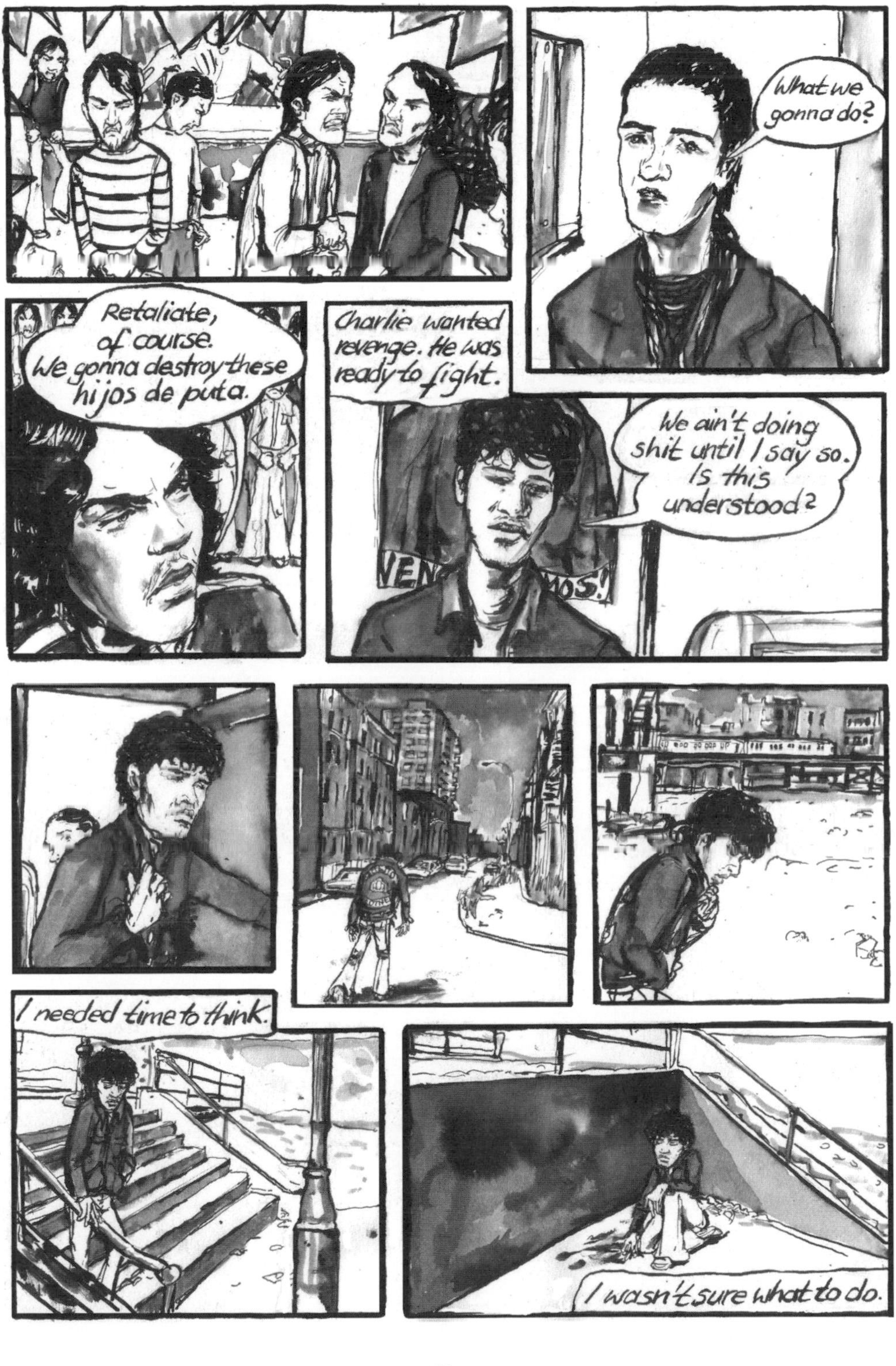
What we gonna do?
Retaliate, of course. We gonna destroy these hijos de puta.
Charlie wanted revenge. He was ready to fight.
We ain't doing shit until I say so. Is this understood?
I needed time to think.
I wasn't sure what to do.

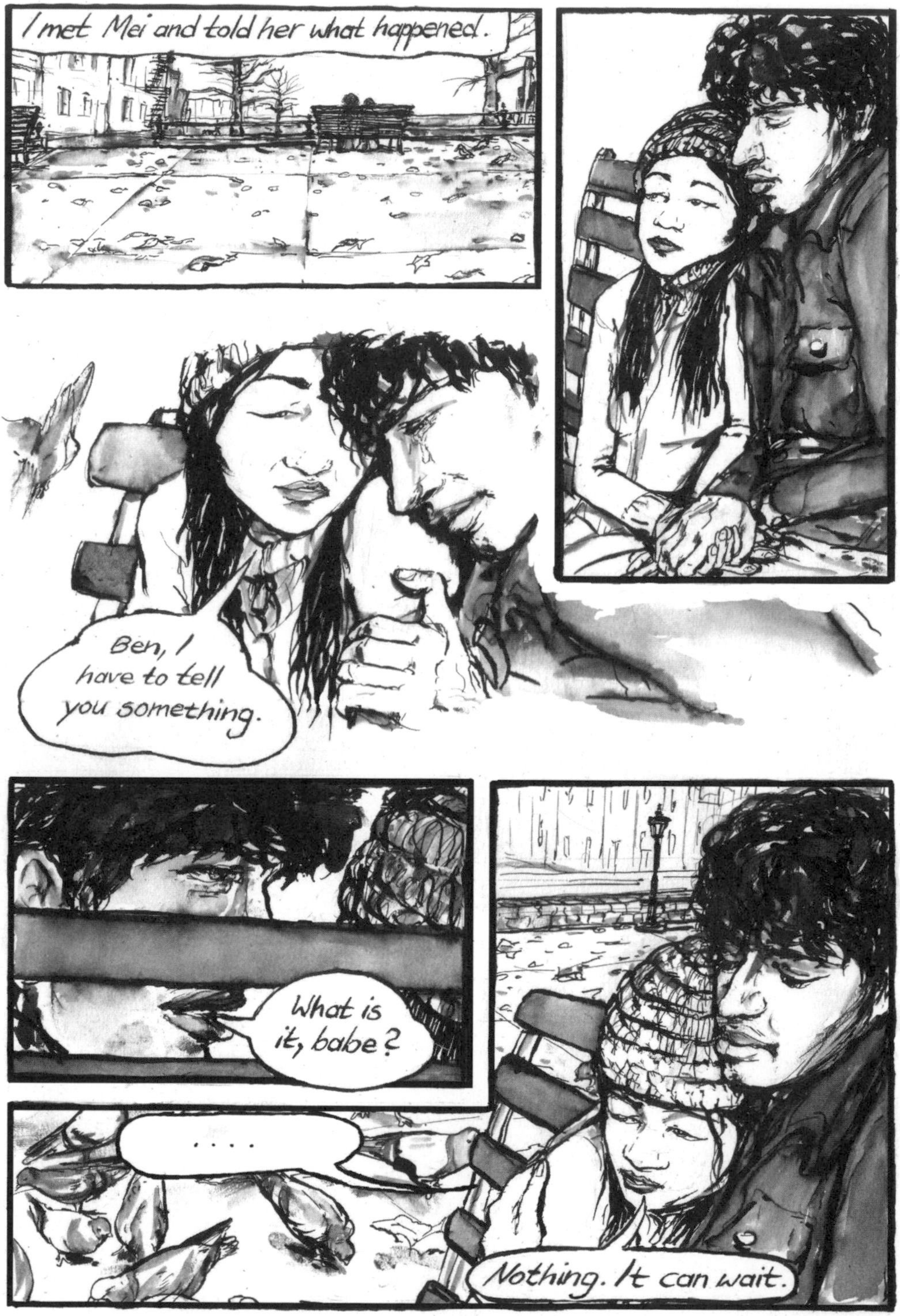
I met Mei and told her what happened.
Ben, I have to tell you something.
What is it, babe?
. . . .
Nothing. It can wait.

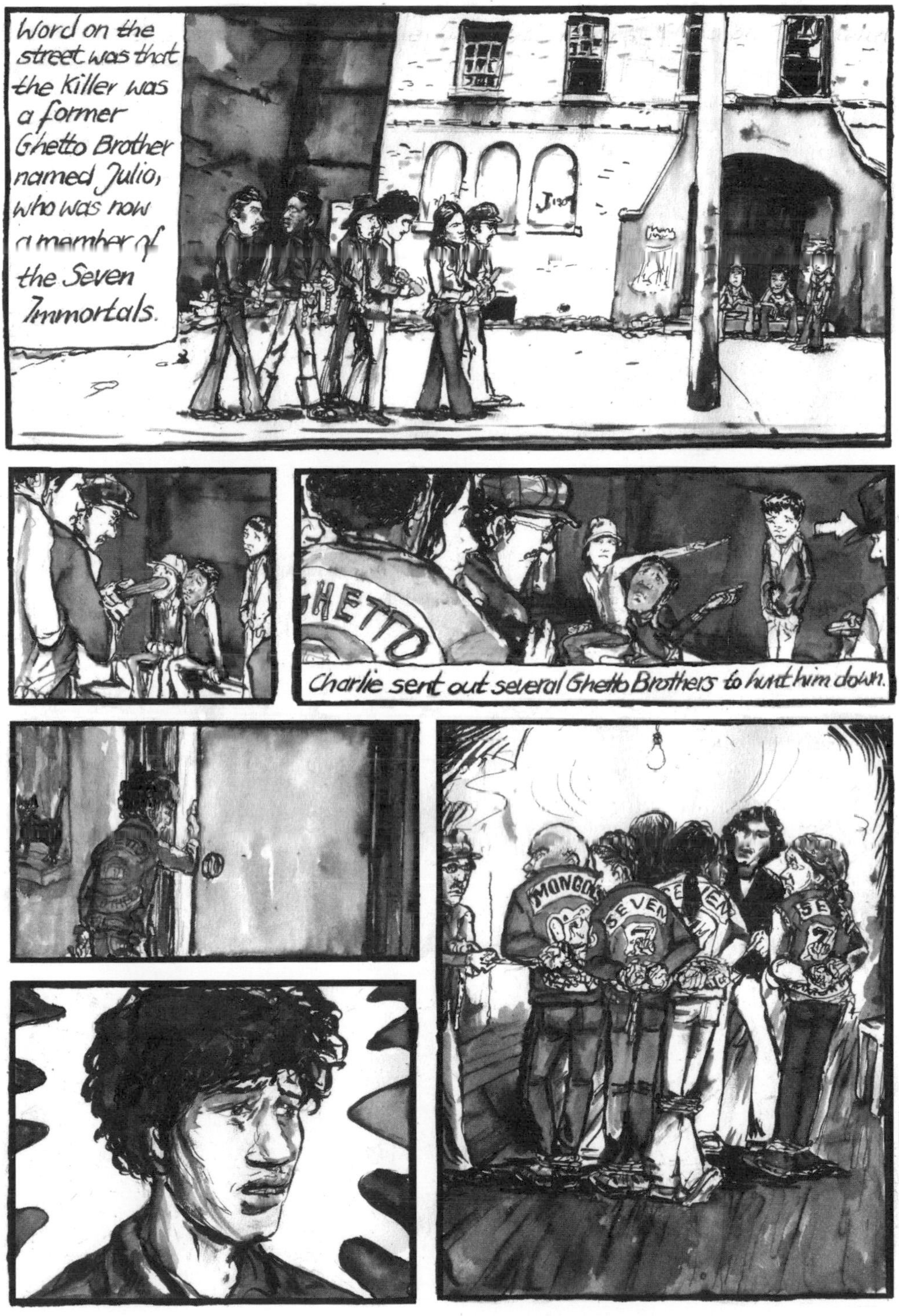
Word on the street was that the Killer was a former Ghetto Brother named Julio, who was now a member of the Seven Immortals.
GHETTO
Charlie sent out several Ghetto Brothers to hunt him down.
MONGOLS
SEVEN
SEVEN

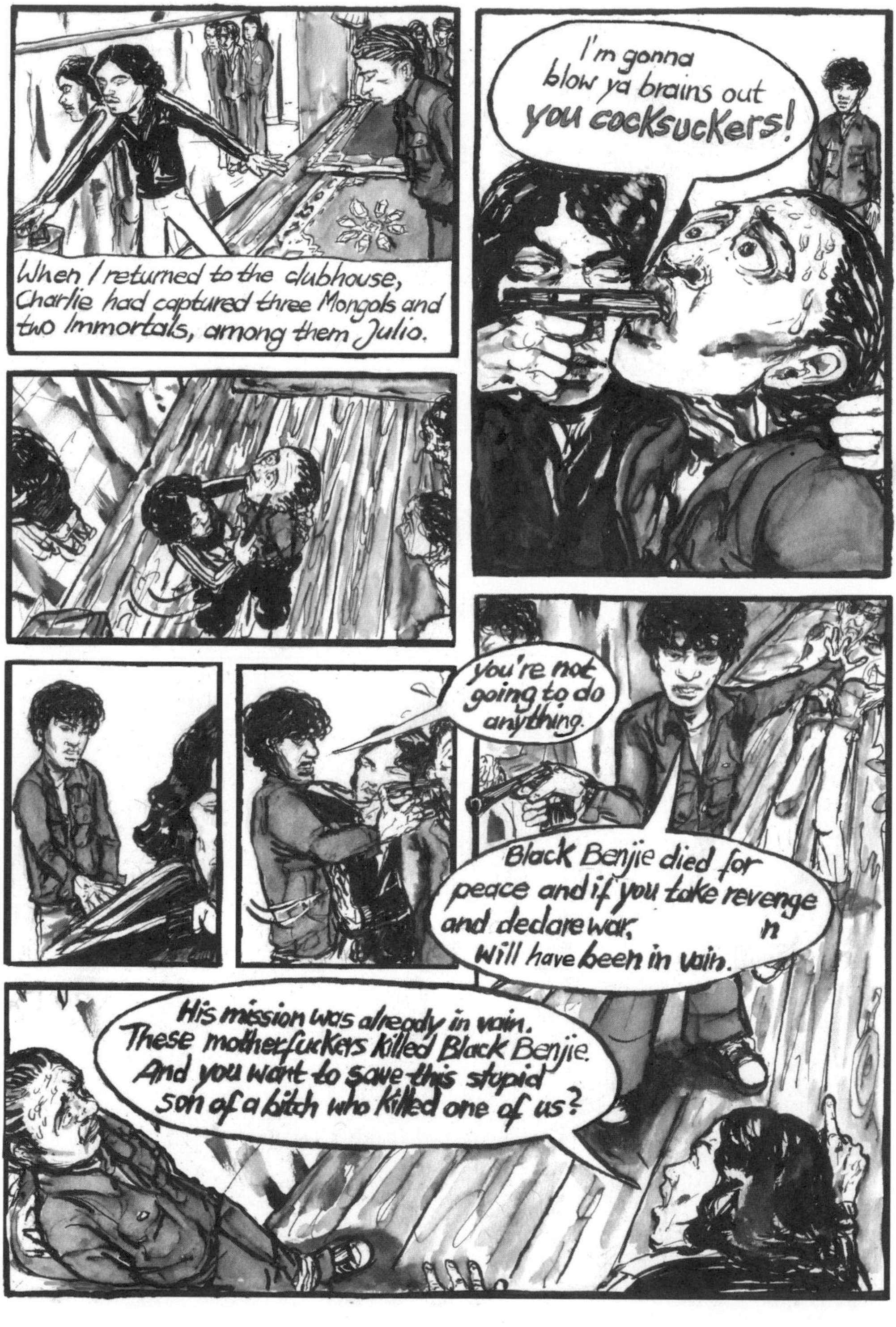
When I returned to the clubhouse, Charlie had captured three Mongols and two Immortals, among them Julio.
I'm gonna blow ya brains out you cocksuckers!
You're not going to do anything.
Black Benjie died for peace and if you take revenge and declare war, n will have been in vain.
His mission was already in vain. These motherfuckers killed Black Benjie. And you want to save this stupid son of a bitch who killed one of us?

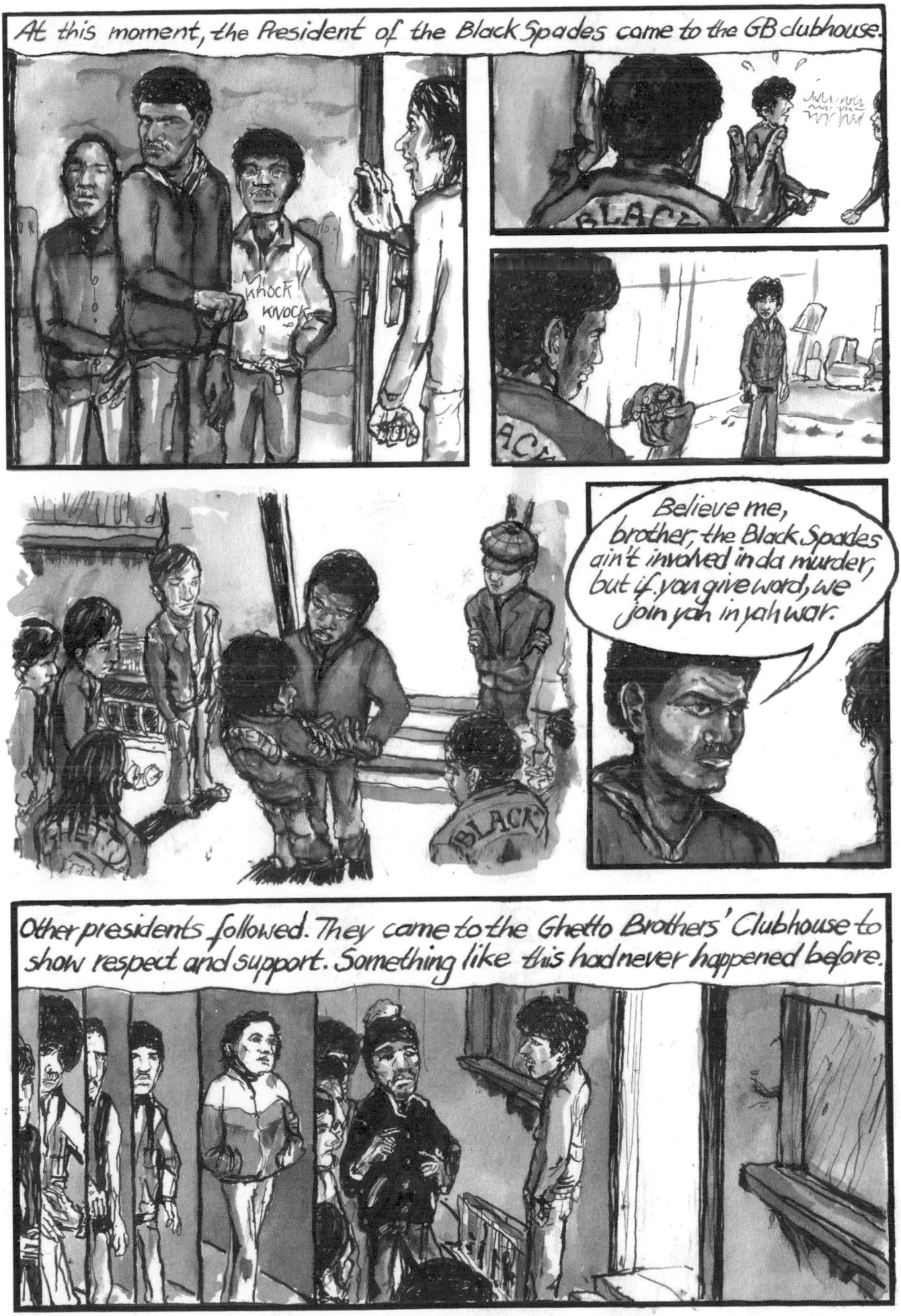
At this moment, the President of the Black Spades came to the GB clubhouse.
KNOCK KNOCK
BLACK
Believe me, brother, the Black Spades ain't involved in da murder, but if you give word, we join yah in yah war.
BLACK
Other presidents followed. They came to the Ghetto Brothers' Clubhouse to show respect and support. Something like this had never happened before.

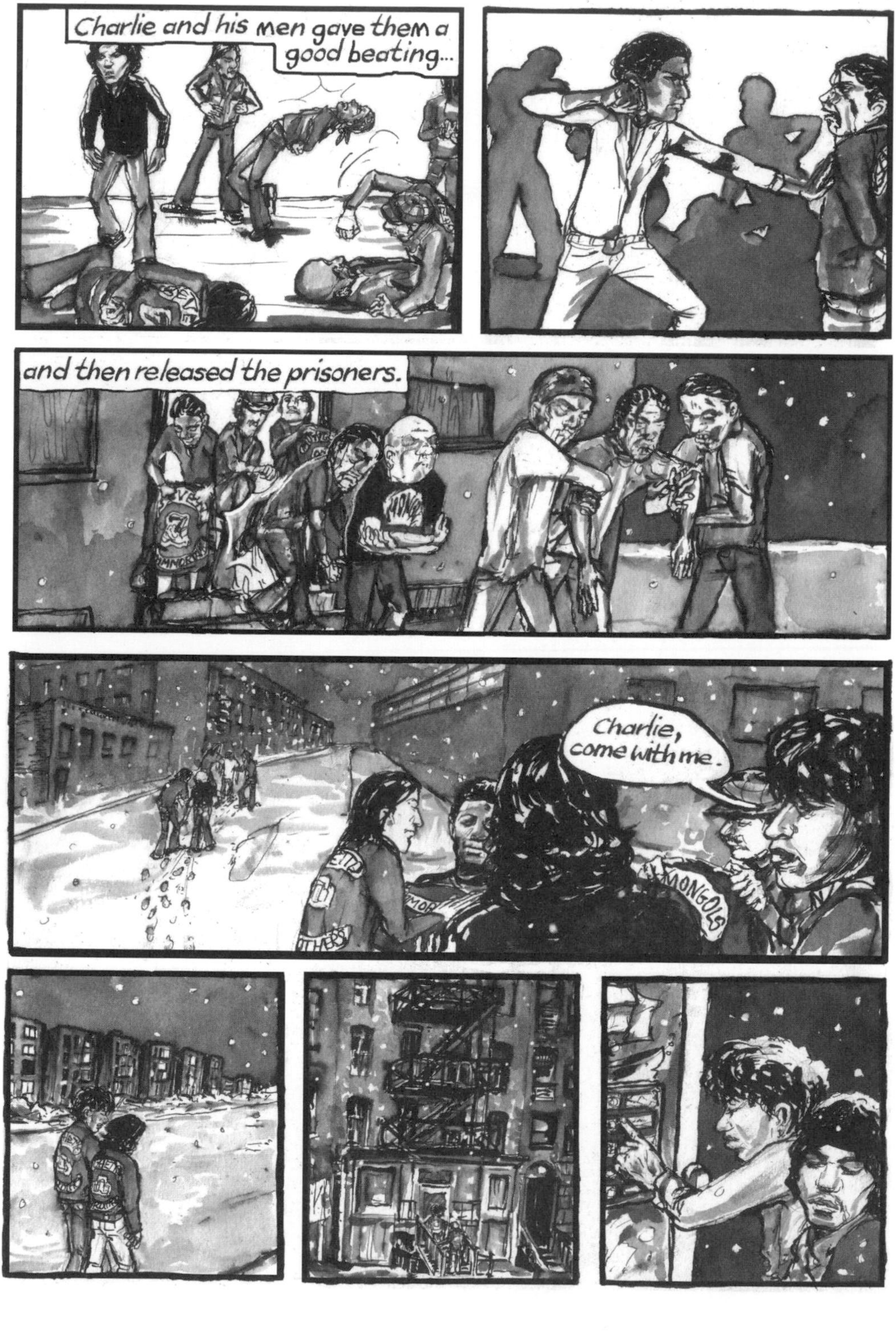
Charlie and his men gave them a good beating...
and then released the prisoners.
Charlie, come with me.
MONGOLS

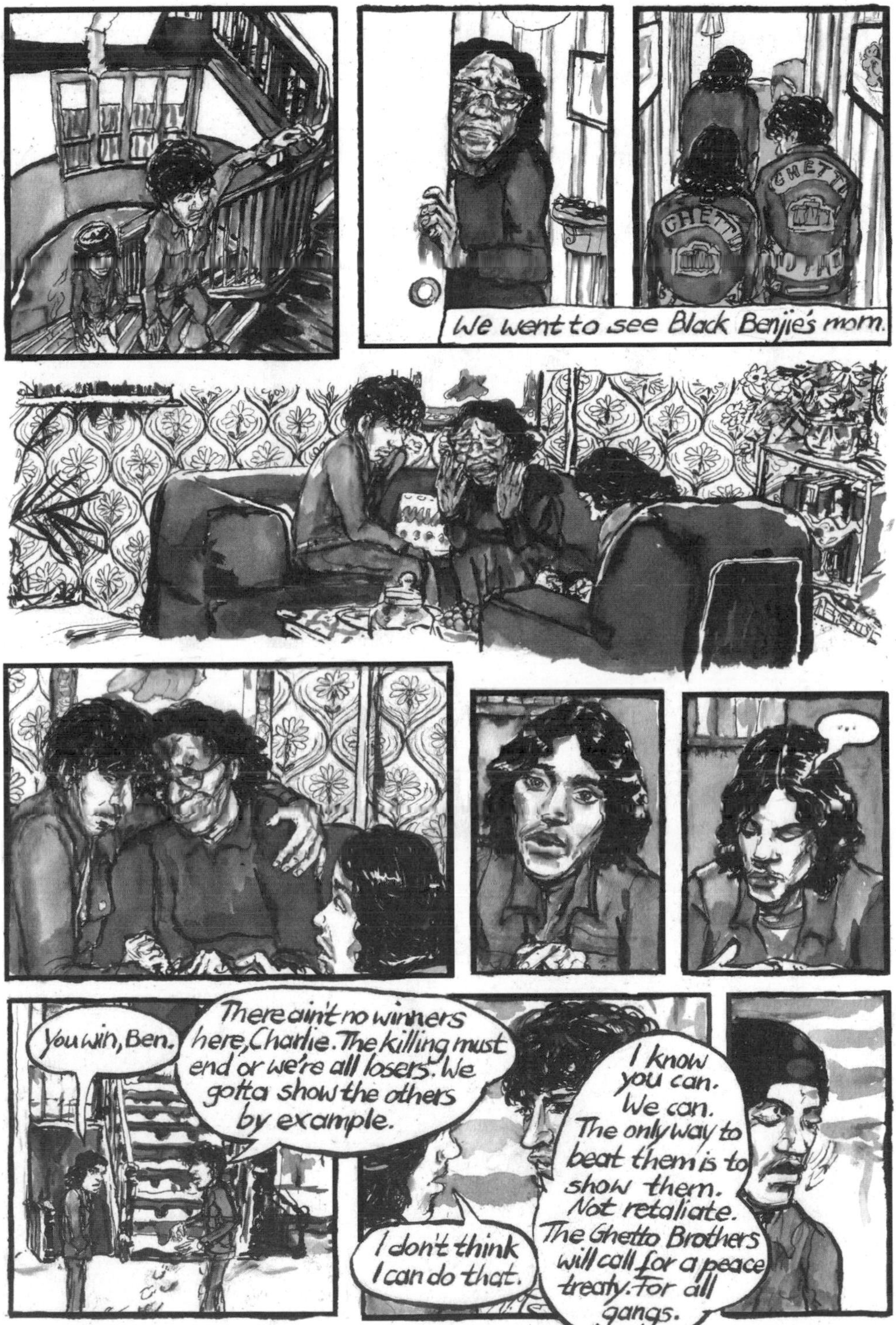
We went to see Black Benjie's mom.
...
You win, Ben.
There ain't no winners here, Charlie. The killing must end or we're all losers. We gotta show the others by example.
I don't think I can do that.
I know you can. We can. The only way to beat them is to show them. Not retaliate. The Ghetto Brothers will call for a peace treaty. For all gangs.

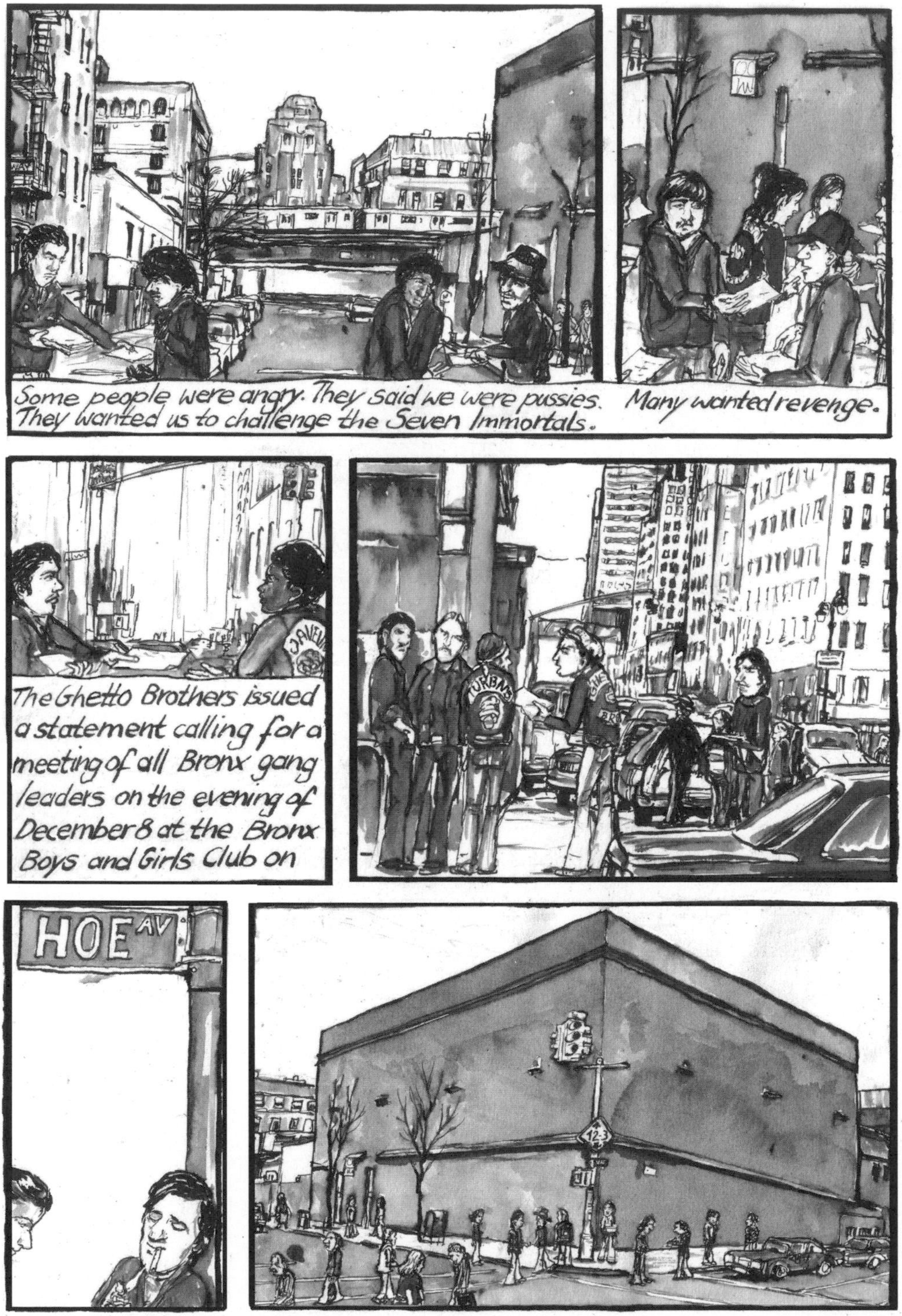
Some people were angry. They said we were pussies. They wanted us to challenge the Seven Immortals.
Many wanted revenge.
The Ghetto Brothers issued a statement calling for a meeting of all Bronx gang leaders on the evening of December 8 at the Bronx Boys and Girls Club on
HOE AV

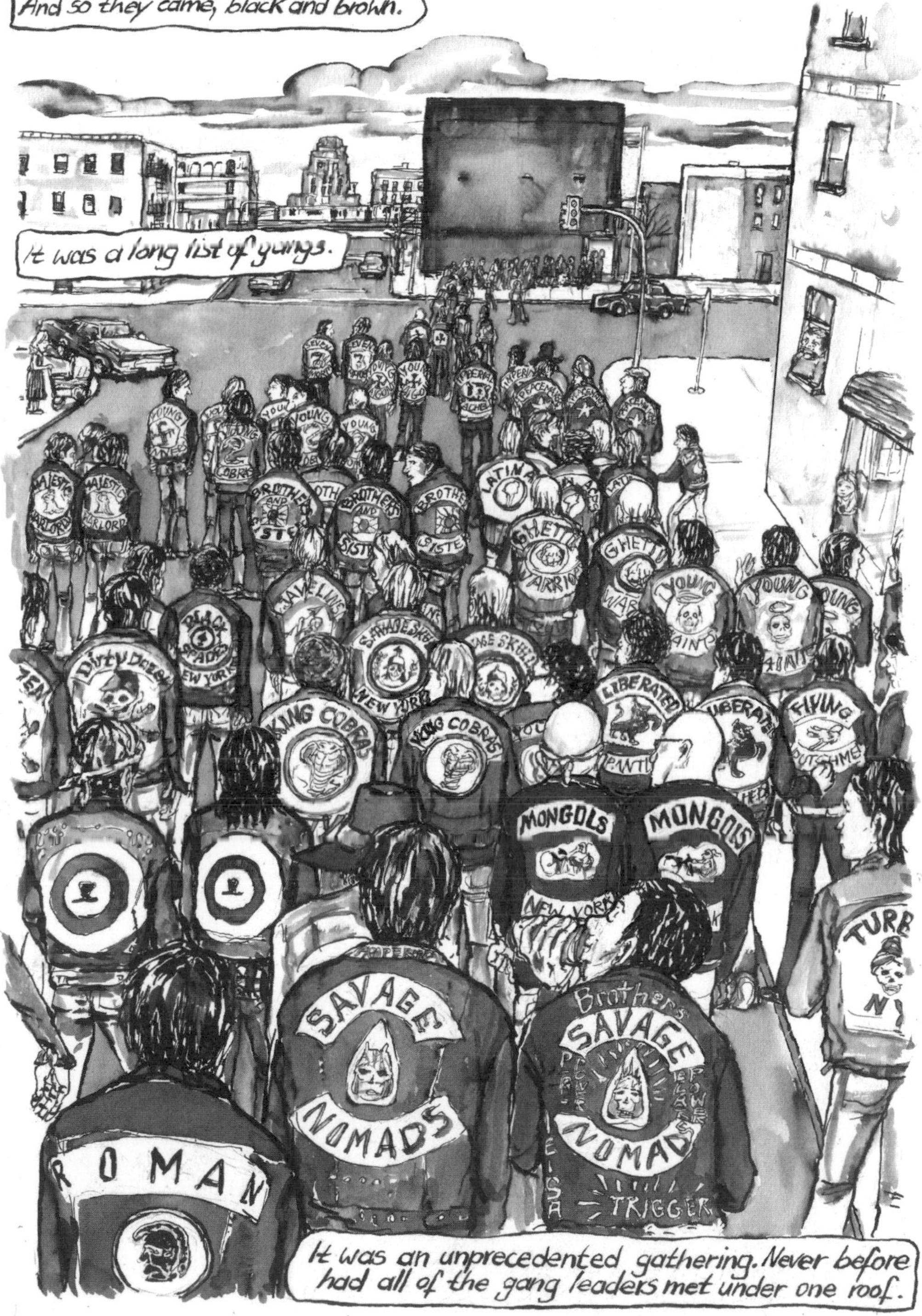

And so they came, black and brown.
It was a long list of gangs.
SAVAGE NOMADS
Brothers
SAVAGE NOMADS
TRIGGER
ROMAN
MONGOLS
MONGOLS
NEW YORK
KING COBRAS
KING COBRAS
LIBERATED
FLYING DUTCHMEN
BLACK SPADES NEW YORK
SAVAGE SKULLS NEW YORK
GHETTO WARRIORS
YOUNG SAINTS
BROTHERS AND SISTERS
MAJESTIC WARLORDS
YOUNG COBRAS
It was an unprecedented gathering. Never before had all of the gang leaders met under one roof.

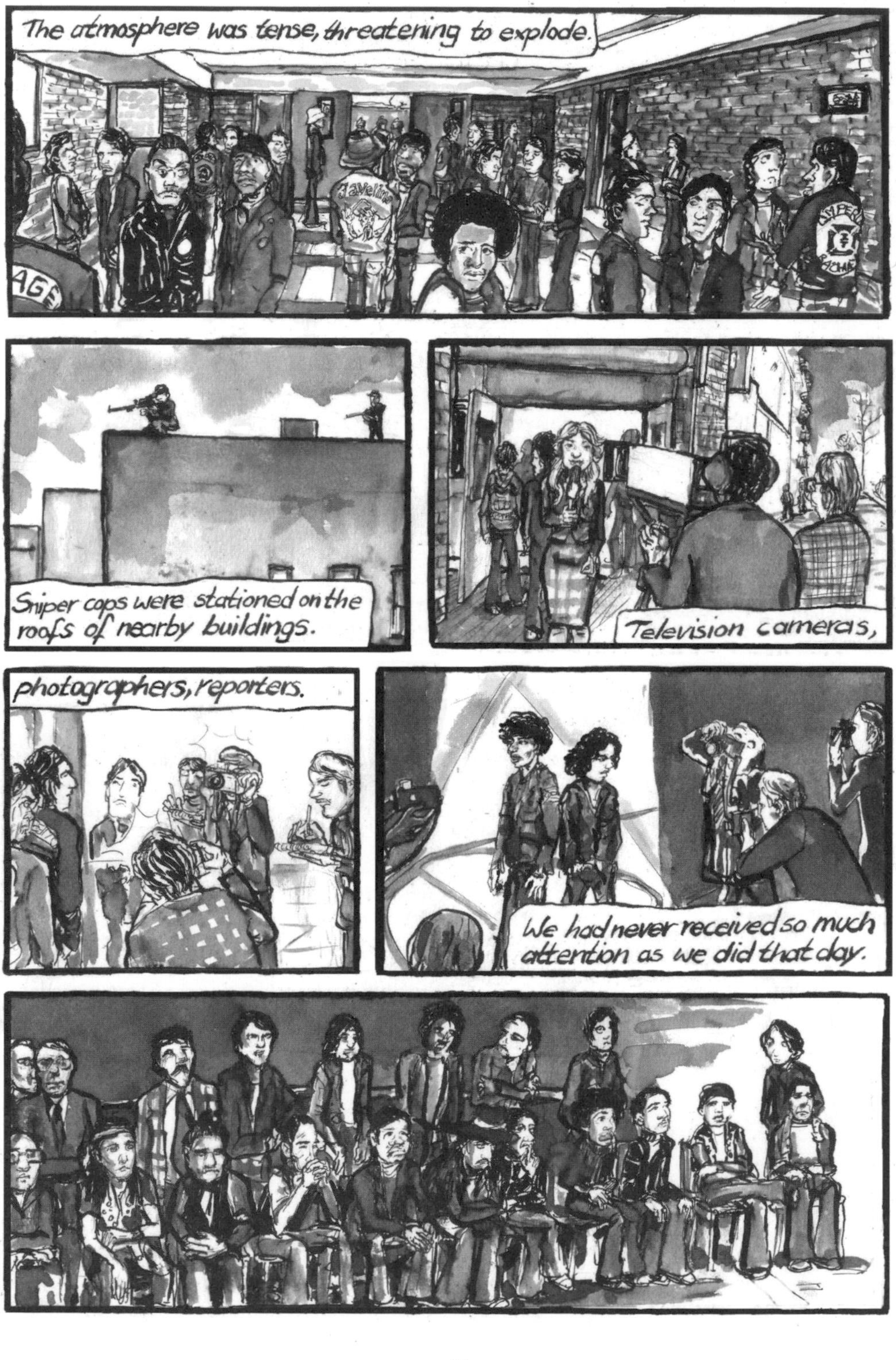
The atmosphere was tense, threatening to explode.
Sniper cops were stationed on the roofs of nearby buildings.
Television cameras,
photographers, reporters.
We had never received so much attention as we did that day.

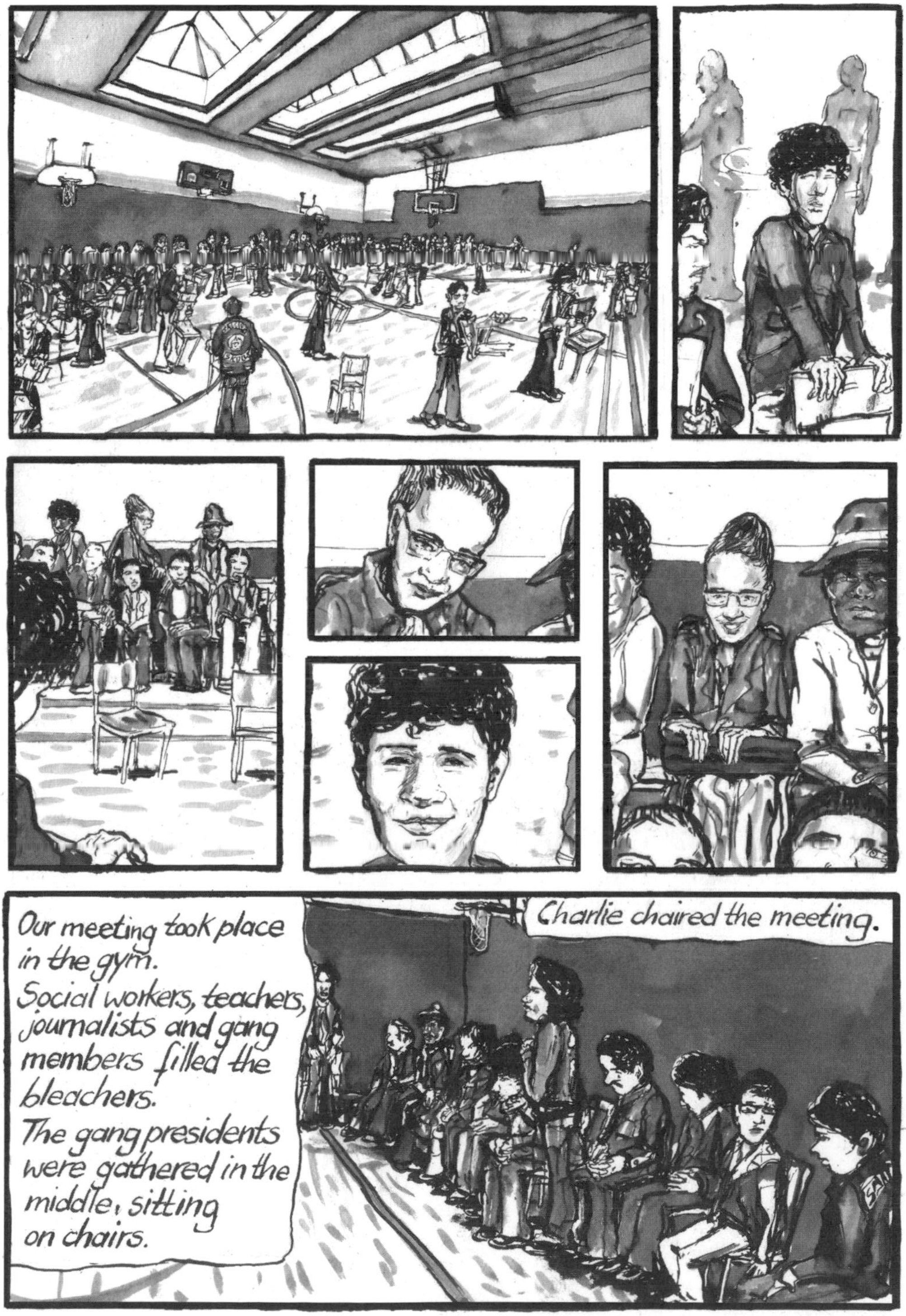
Our meeting took place in the gym.
Social workers, teachers, journalists and gang members filled the bleachers.
The gang presidents were gathered in the middle, sitting on chairs.
Charlie chaired the meeting.

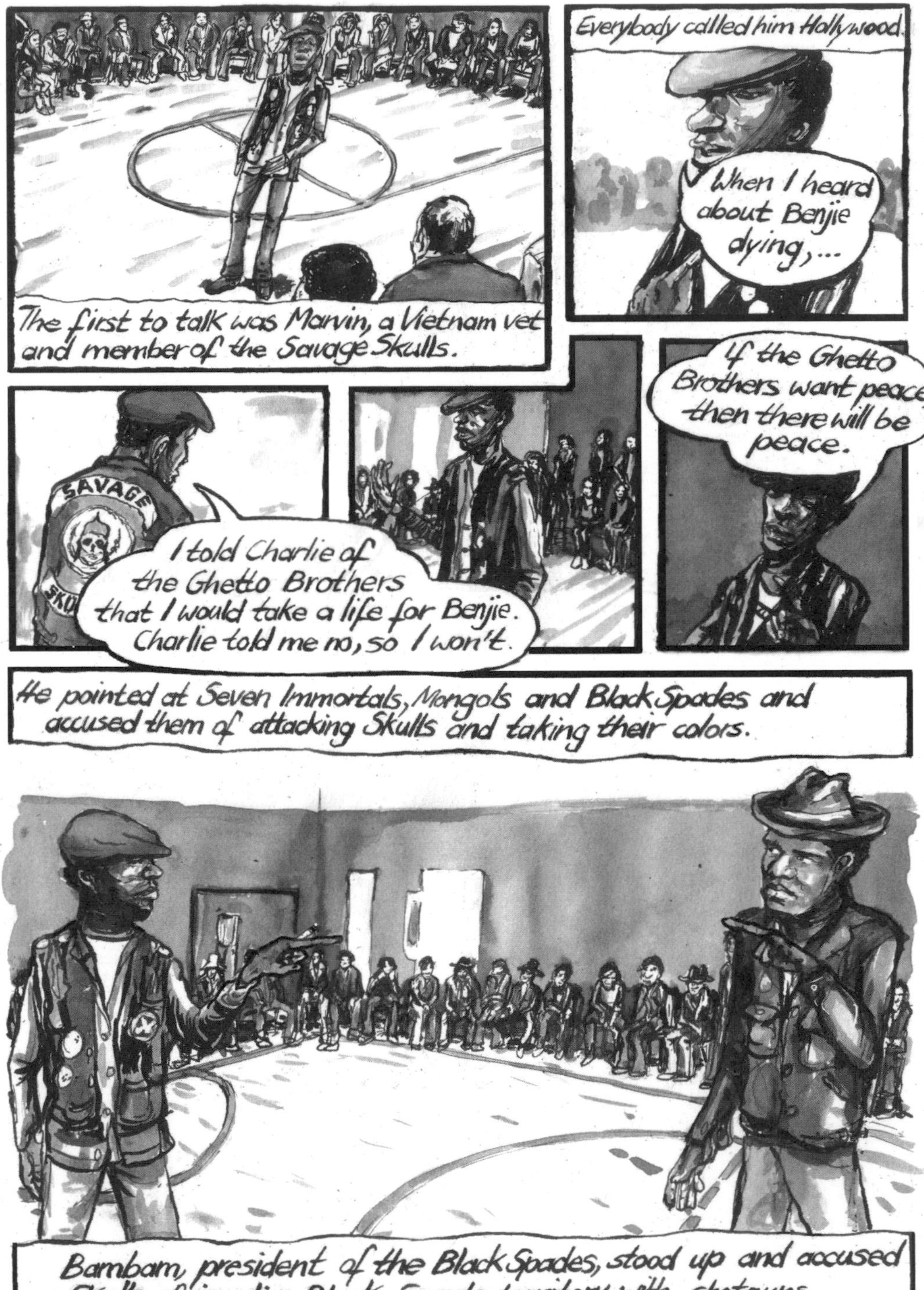
The first to talk was Marvin, a Vietnam vet and member of the Savage Skulls.
Everybody called him Hollywood.
When I heard about Benjie dying,...
SAVAGE
I told Charlie of the Ghetto Brothers that I would take a life for Benjie. Charlie told me no, so I won't.
If the Ghetto Brothers want peace, then there will be peace.
He pointed at Seven Immortals, Mongols and Black Spades and accused them of attacking Skulls and taking their colors.
Bambam, president of the Black Spades, stood up and accused Skulls of invading Black Spade territory with shotguns.

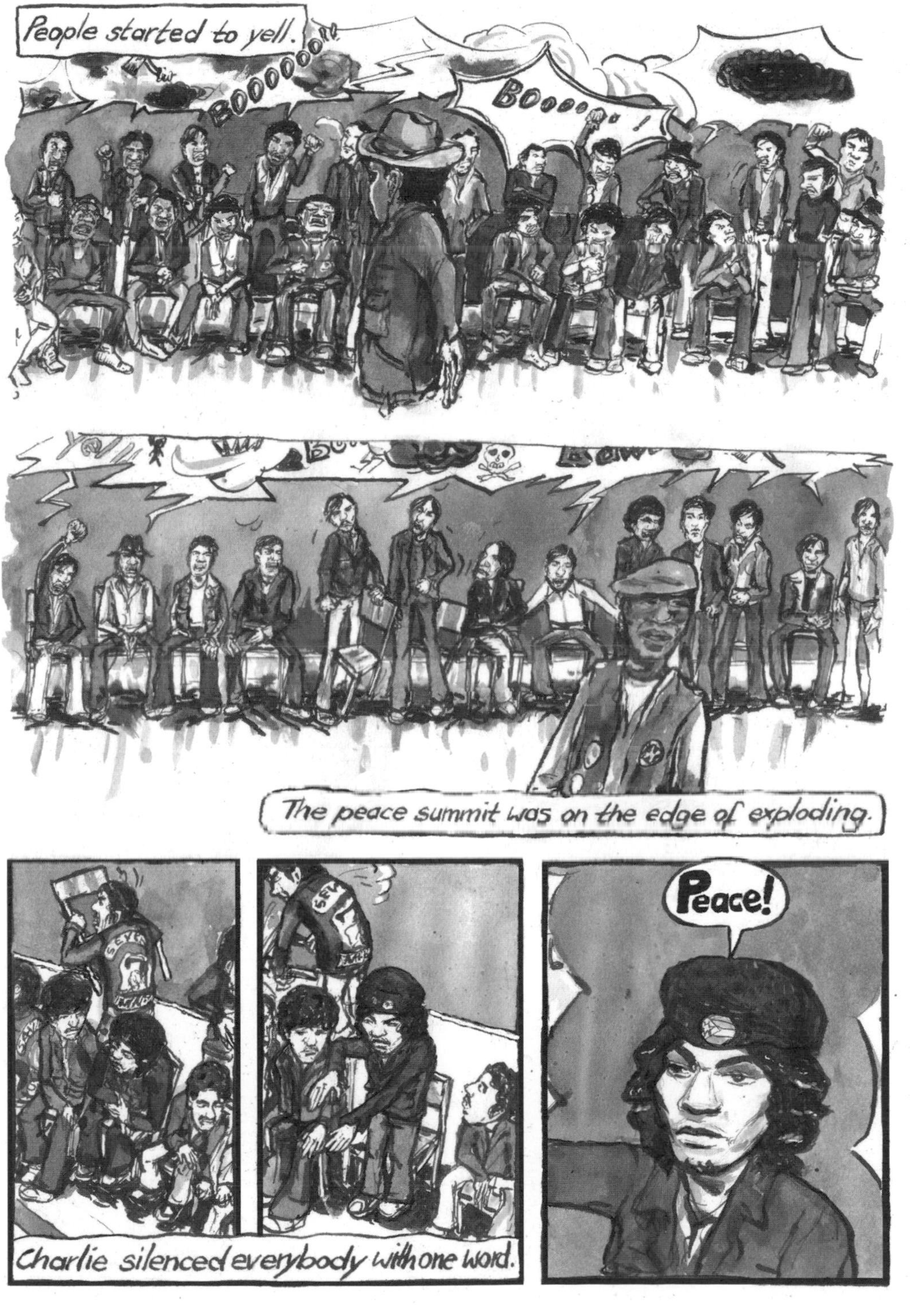
People started to yell.
BOOOOOOO!!
Booooo..!
The peace summit was on the edge of exploding.
Charlie silenced everybody with one word.
Peace!

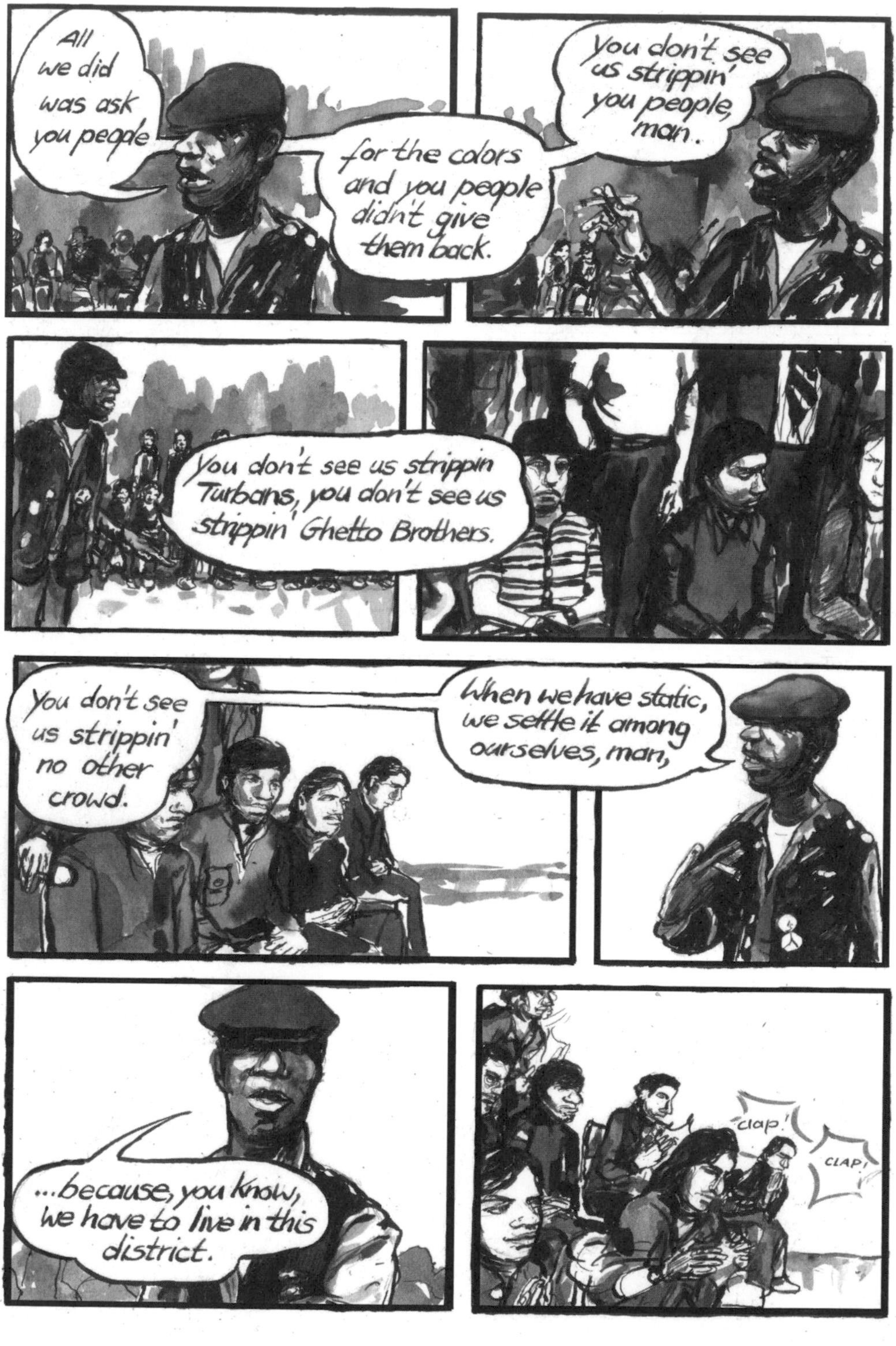

All we did was ask you people
for the colors and you people didn't give them back.
You don't see us strippin' you people, man.
You don't see us strippin Turbans, you don't see us strippin' Ghetto Brothers.
You don't see us strippin' no other crowd.
When we have static, we settle it among ourselves, man,
...because, you know, we have to live in this district.
clap!
CLAP!

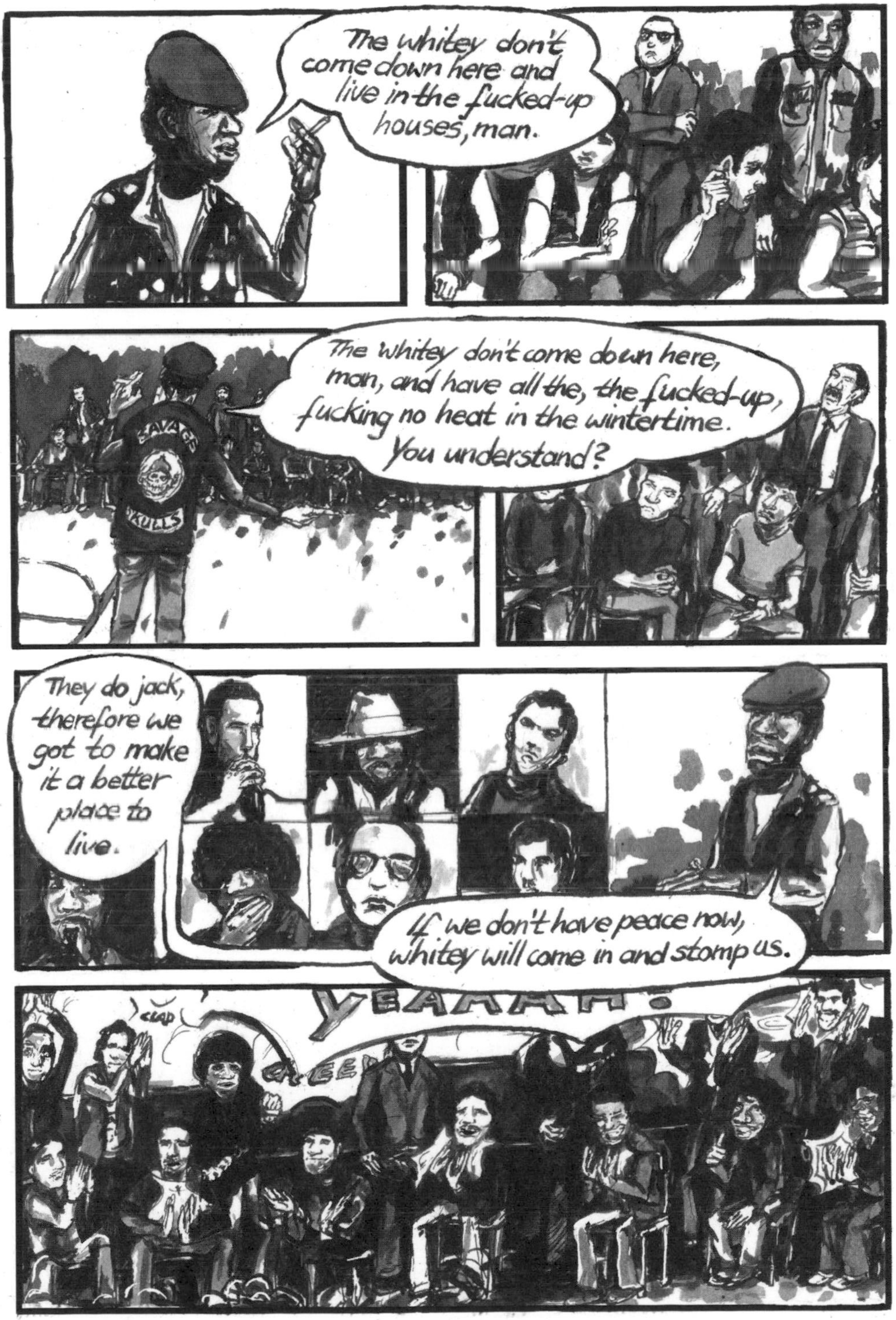
The whitey don't come down here and live in the fucked-up houses, man.
The whitey don't come down here, man, and have all the, the fucked-up, fucking no heat in the wintertime. You understand?
They do jack, therefore we got to make it a better place to live.
If we don't have peace now, whitey will come in and stomp us.
YEAAAAH!
CLAP

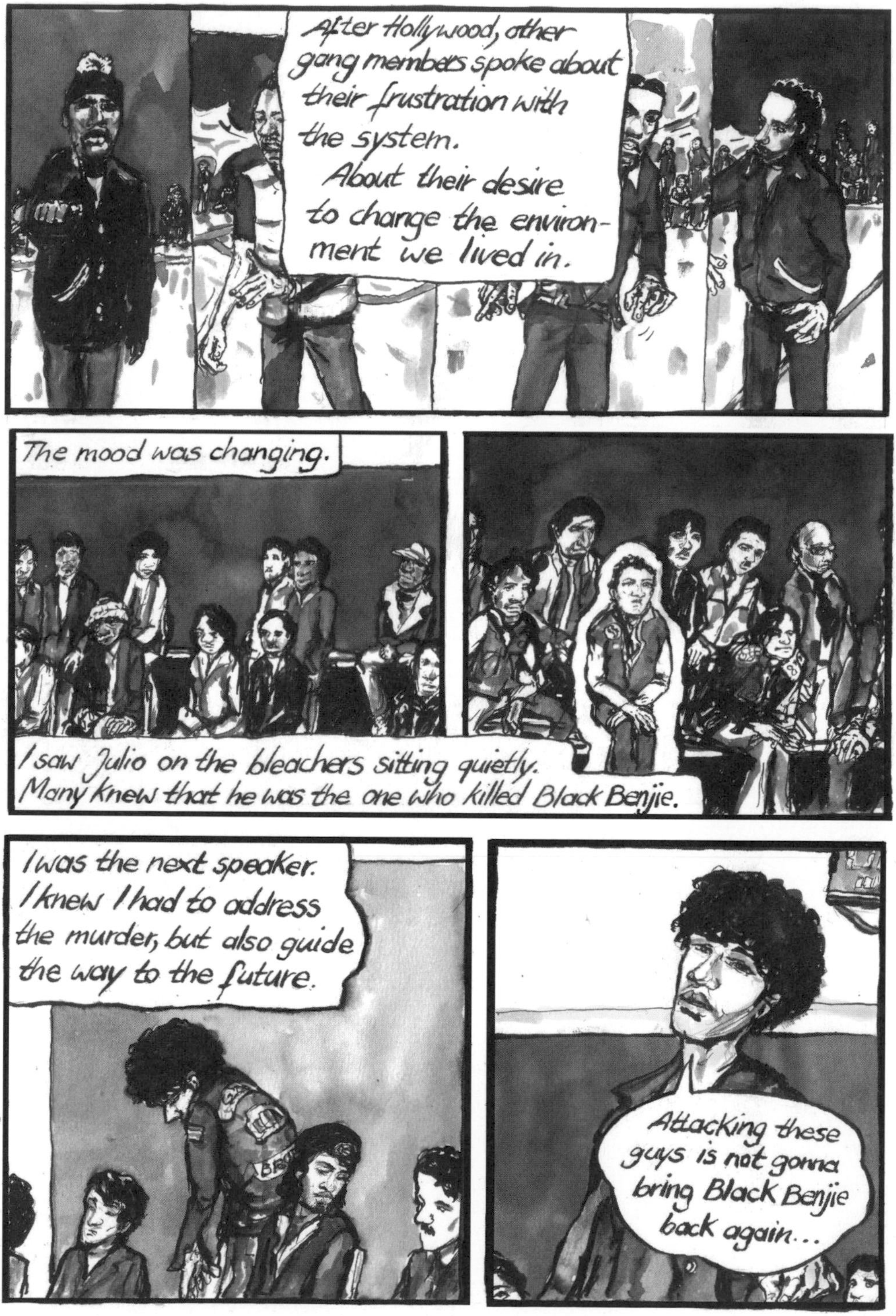
After Hollywood, other gang members spoke about their frustration with the system.
About their desire to change the environment we lived in.
The mood was changing.
I saw Julio on the bleachers sitting quietly.
Many knew that he was the one who killed Black Benjie.
I was the next speaker.
I knew I had to address the murder, but also guide the way to the future.
Attacking these guys is not gonna bring Black Benjie back again...

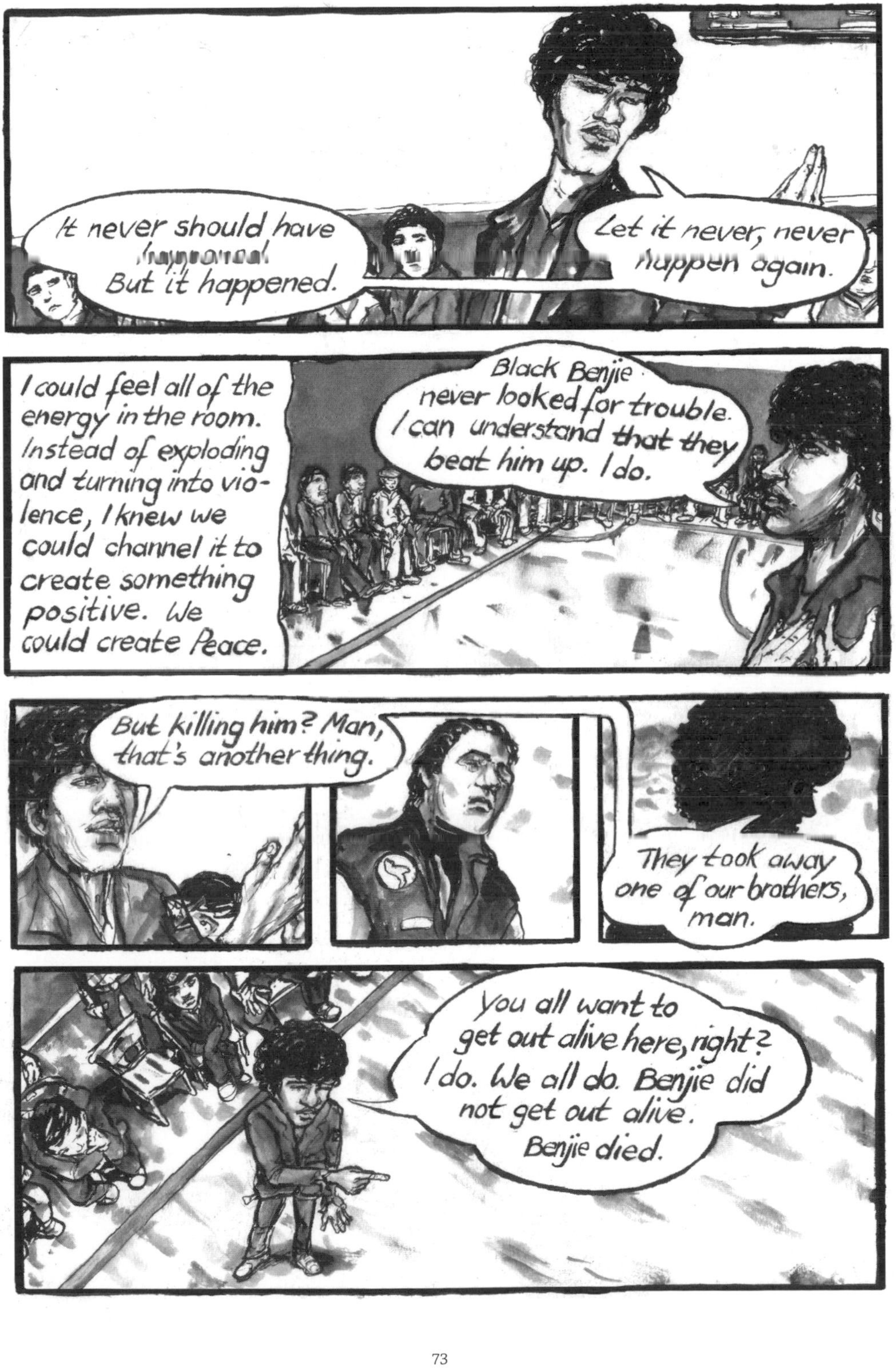
It never should have happened. But it happened.
Let it never, never happen again.
I could feel all of the energy in the room. Instead of exploding and turning into violence, I knew we could channel it to create something positive. We could create Peace.
Black Benjie never looked for trouble. I can understand that they beat him up. I do.
But killing him? Man, that's another thing.
They took away one of our brothers, man.
You all want to get out alive here, right? I do. We all do. Benjie did not get out alive. Benjie died.

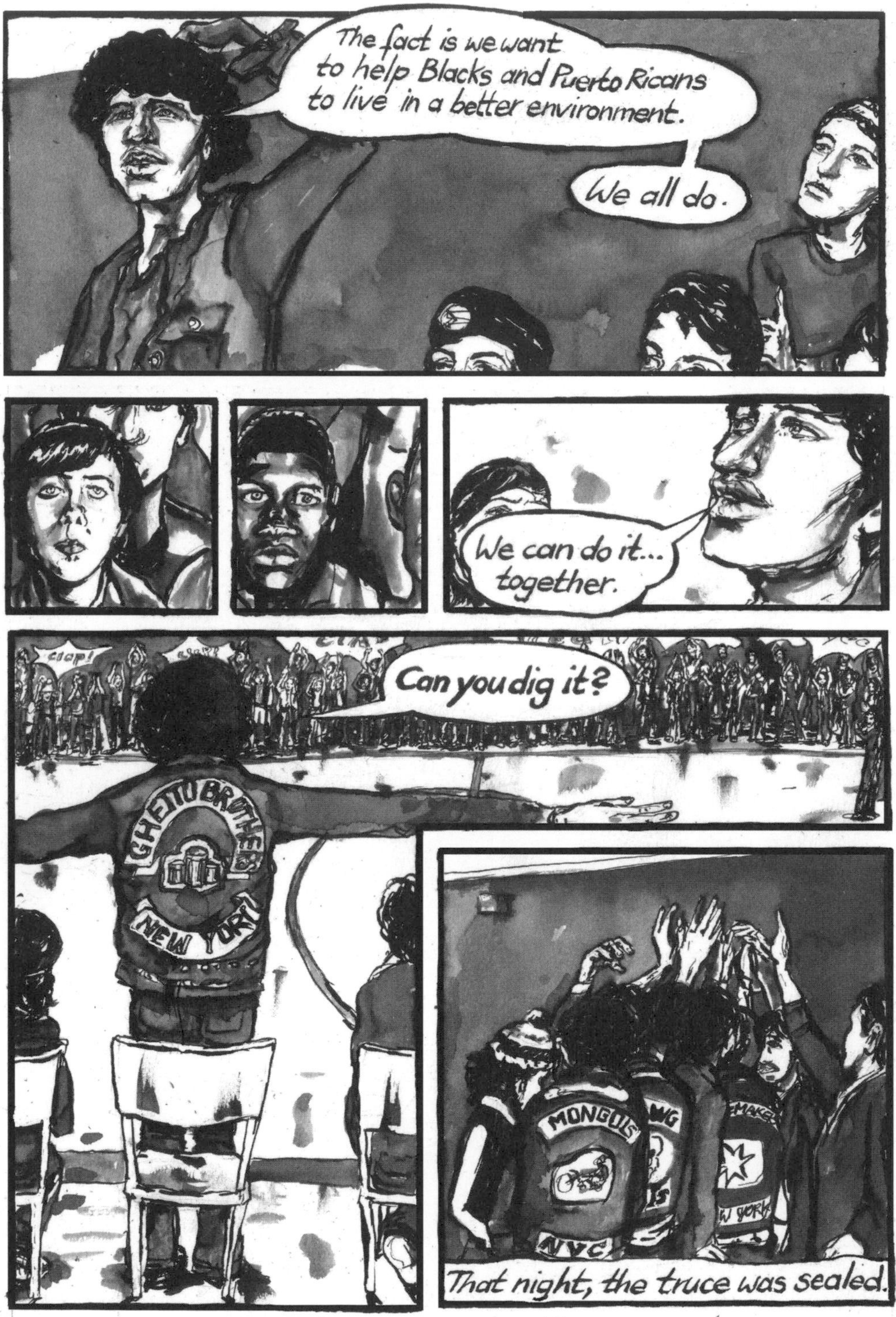

The fact is we want to help Blacks and Puerto Ricans to live in a better environment.
We all do.
We can do it... together.
clap!
Can you dig it?
GHETTO BROTHERS
NEW YORK
MONGOLS
NYC
W YORK
That night, the truce was sealed.

To All Brothers and Sisters:

We realize that we are all brothers living in the same neighborhoods and having the same problems.

We also realize that fighting amongst ourselves will not solve our common problems.

If we are to build up our community to be a better place for our families and ourselves we must work together. We who have signed this treaty pledge peace and unity for all. All of us who have signed this peace will be known from now on as The Family.

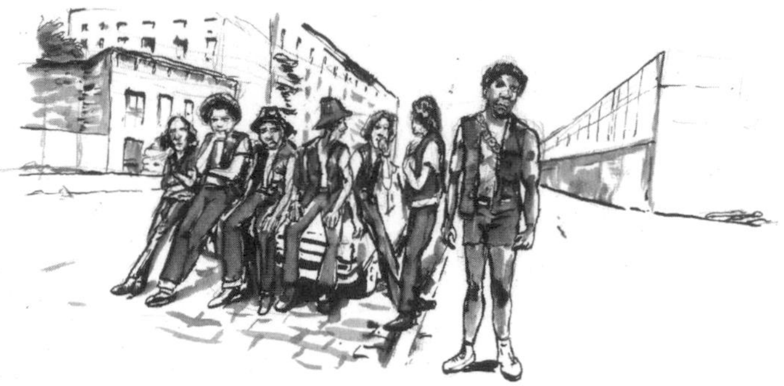

The terms of the Peace are as follows:

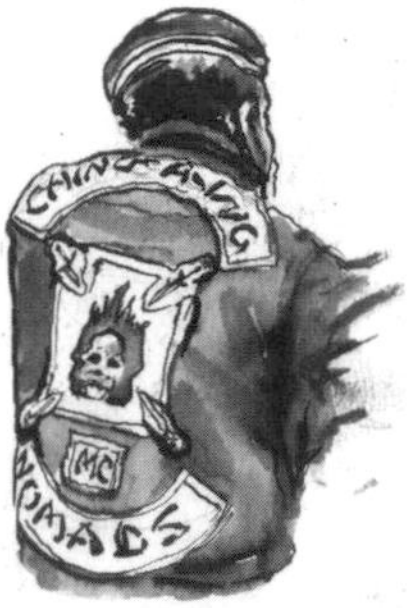
MC
NOMADS

1. All groups are to respect each other - cliques, individual members and their women. Each member clique of the Family will be able to wear their colors in other member cliques' turf without being bothered. They are to remember in whose turf they are and respect that turf as if it were their own.

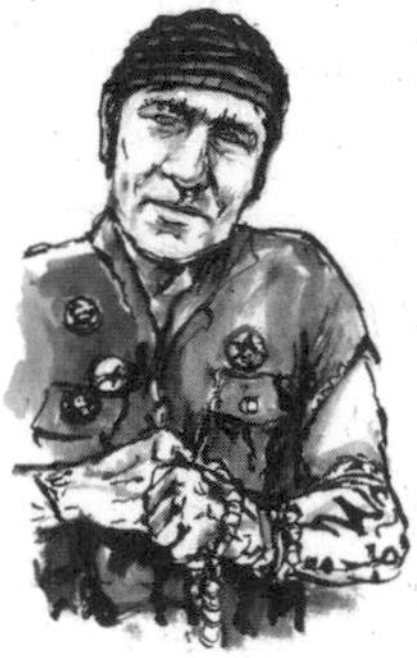

2. If any clique has a gripe against another clique the presidents of each are to meet together to talk it out. If one member of a clique has a beef with a member of another clique, the two are to talk it over. If that does not solve it then they will both fight it out between themselves, after that, it is considered finished. If there are any rumors about cliques going down on each other, the leaders of these groups shall meet and talk it out.

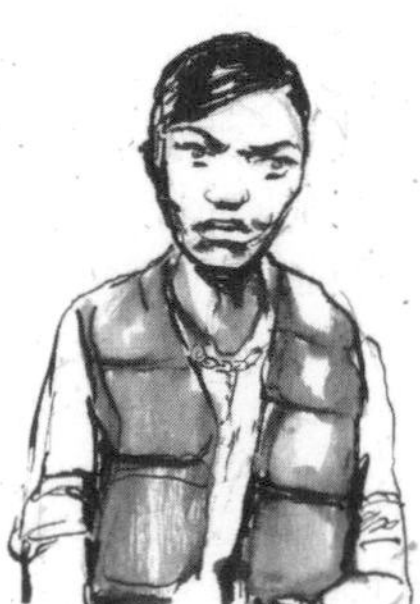

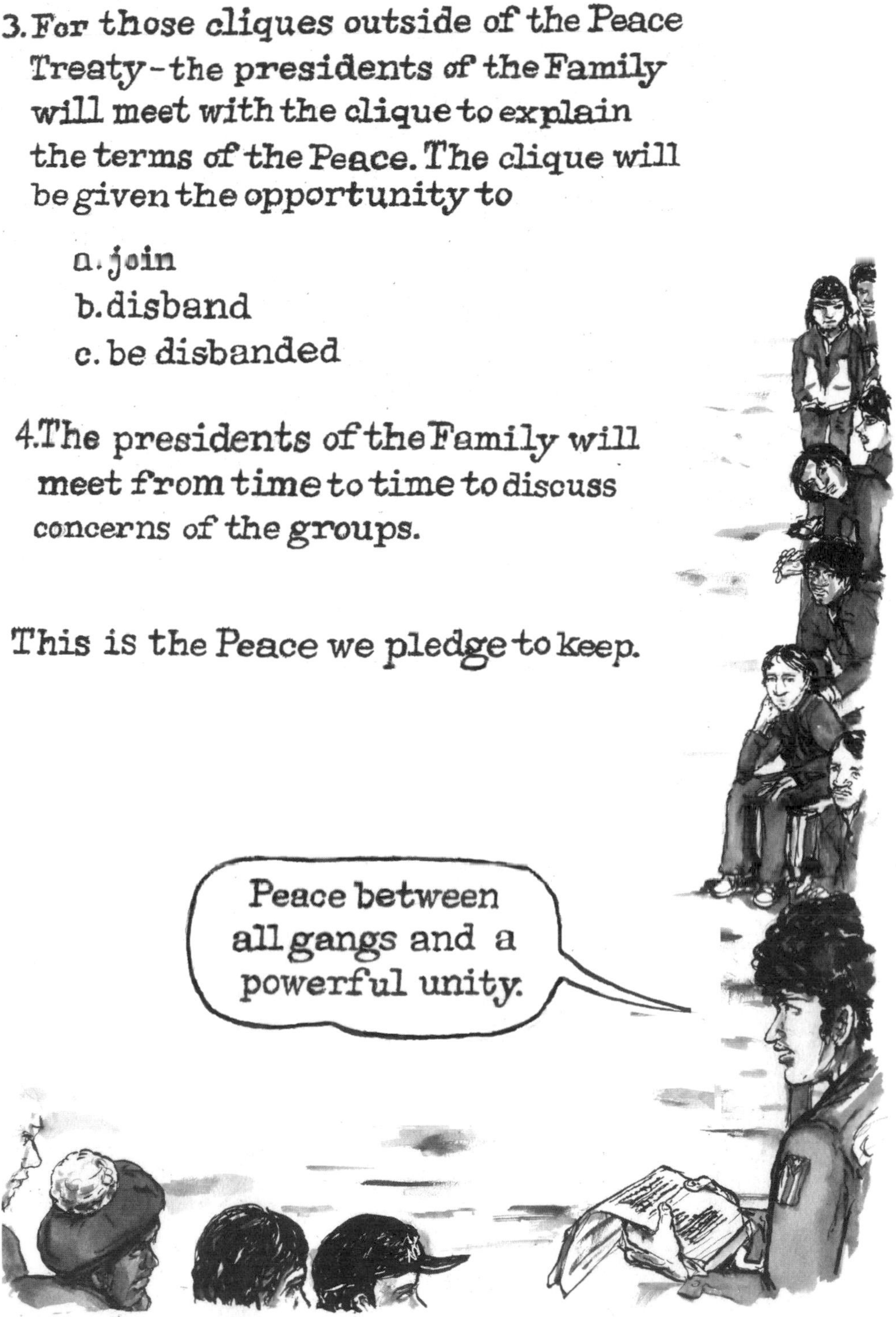

3. For those cliques outside of the Peace Treaty - the presidents of the Family will meet with the clique to explain the terms of the Peace. The clique will be given the opportunity to
a. join
b. disband
c. be disbanded
4. The presidents of the Family will meet from time to time to discuss concerns of the groups.
This is the Peace we pledge to keep.
Peace between all gangs and a powerful unity.

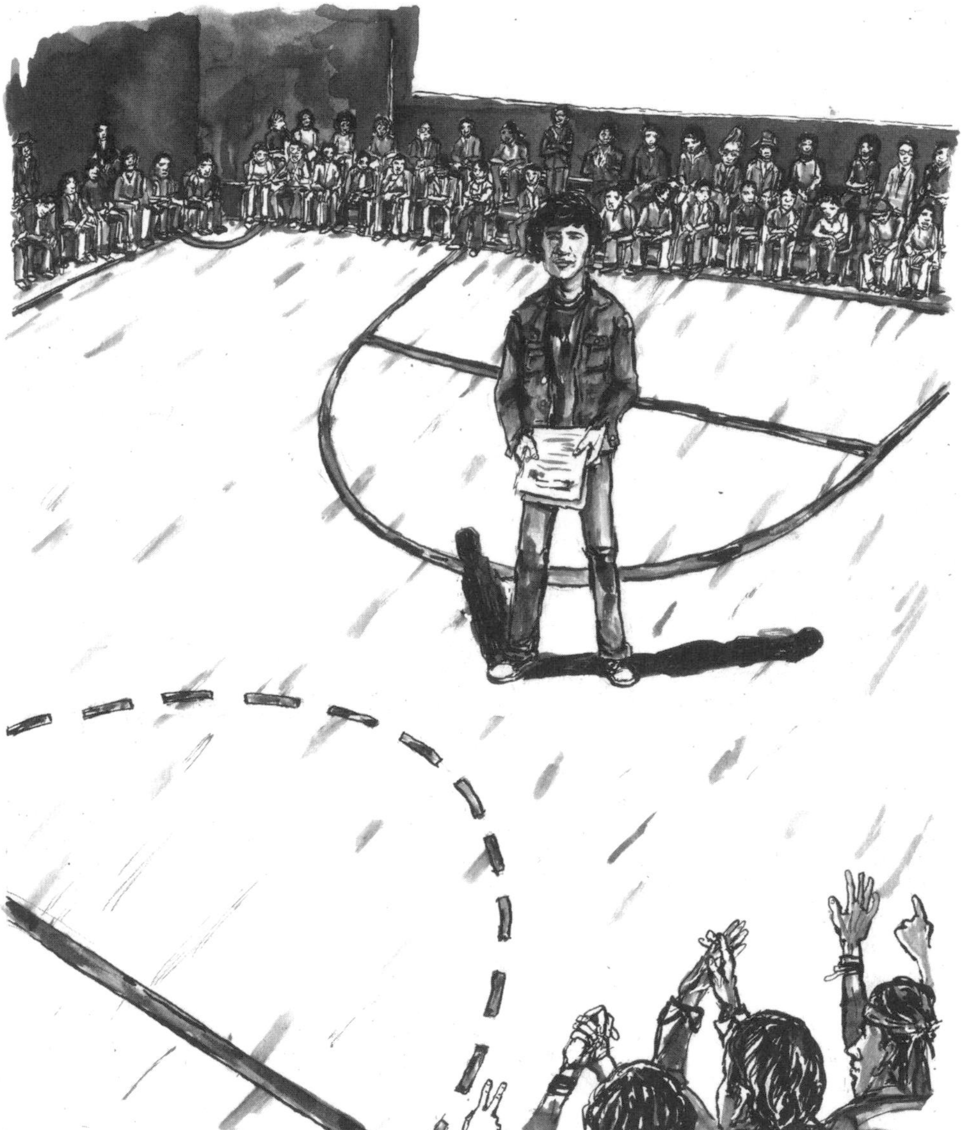

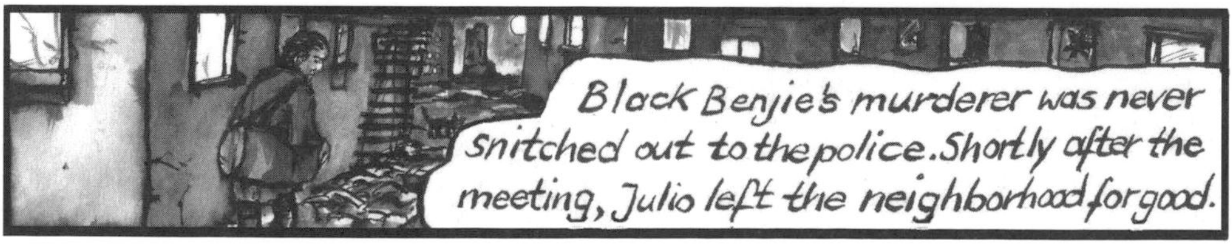
Black Benjie's murderer was never snitched out to the police. Shortly after the meeting, Julio left the neighborhood for good.

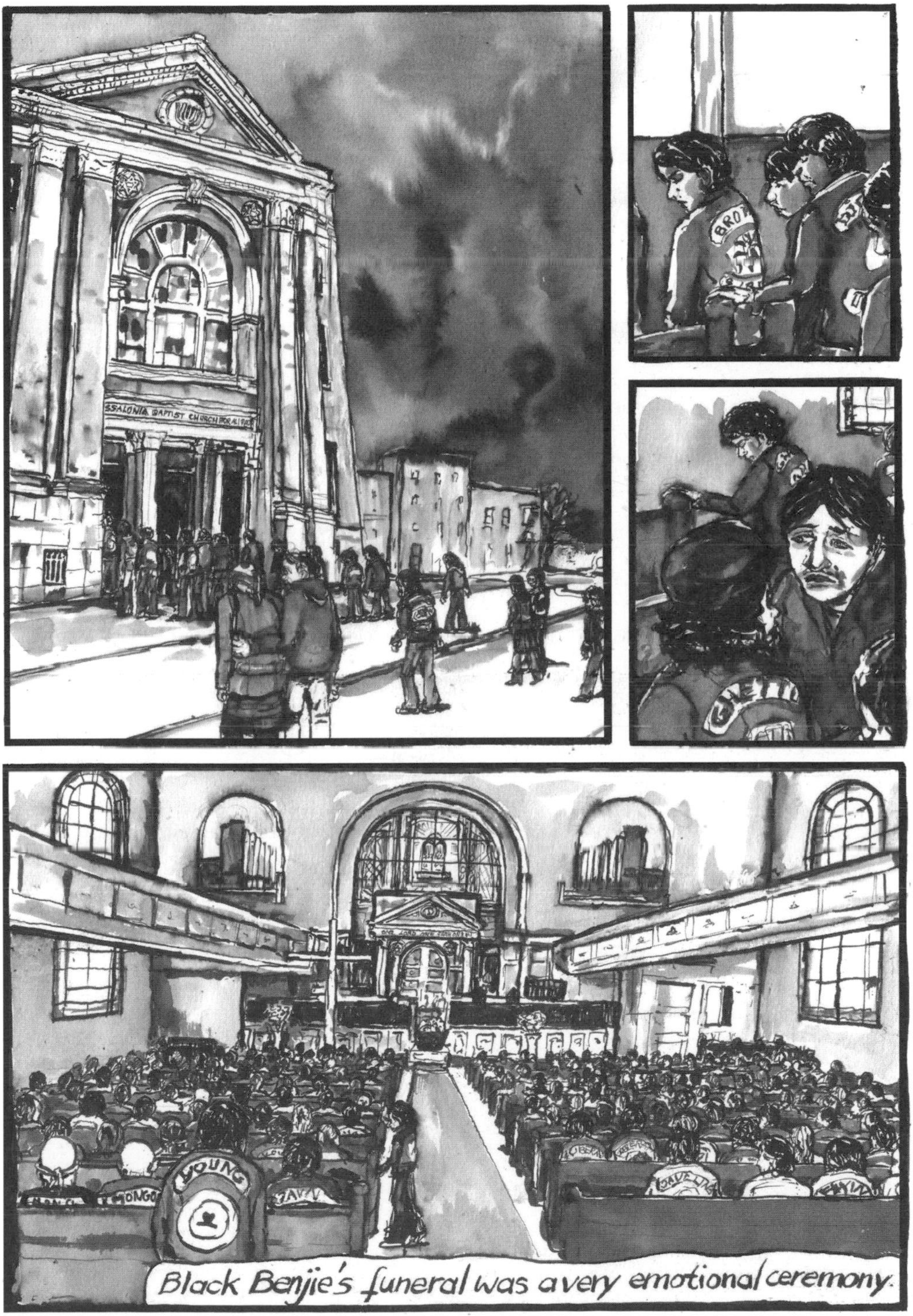
YOUNG
Black Benjie's funeral was a very emotional ceremony.

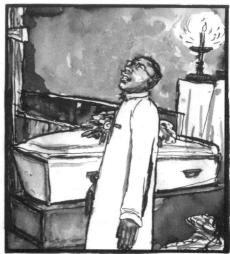

Nothing was the same anymore after Black Benjie's death.

The neighborhood changed.

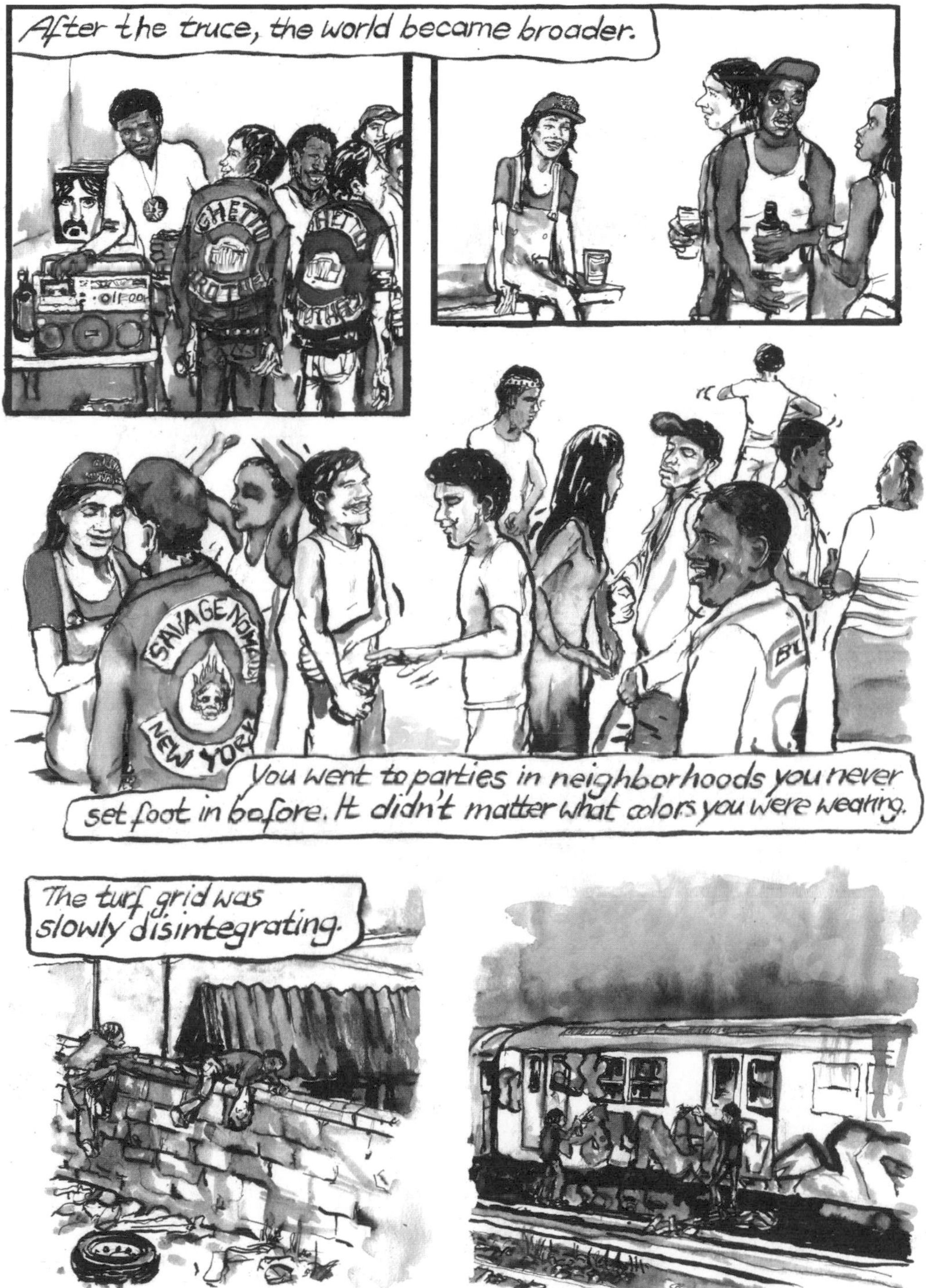
After the truce, the world became broader.
GHETTO BROTHERS
GHETTO BROTHERS
SAVAGE NOMADS NEW YORK
You went to parties in neighborhoods you never set foot in before. It didn't matter what colors you were wearing.
The turf grid was slowly disintegrating.

CROTONA PARK
ONE WAY
CROTONA PARK
chr-
chr-
r-...
Former warlords became DJ's, and gangbangers battled on the dance floor,
showing off their dance moves combined with martial arts skills.

In the East...

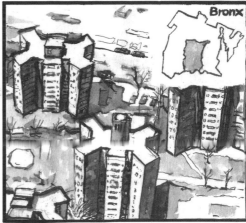

Bronx

...inspired by the truce, the warlord of the Black Spades decided to turn the gang into something positive.

The Black Spades...

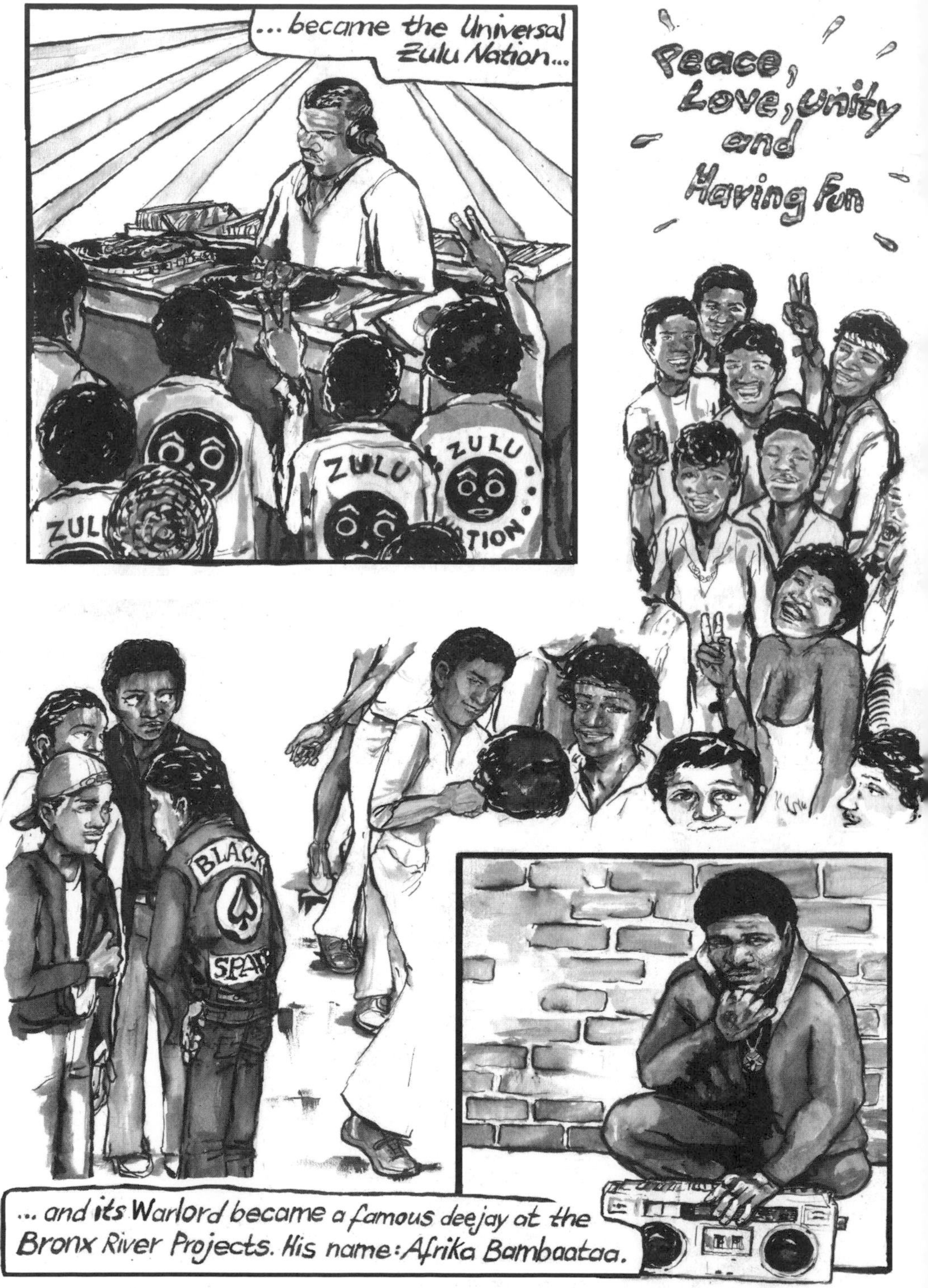

...became the Universal Zulu Nation...
Peace, Love, unity and Having Fun
... and its Warlord became a famous deejay at the Bronx River Projects. His name: Afrika Bambaataa.

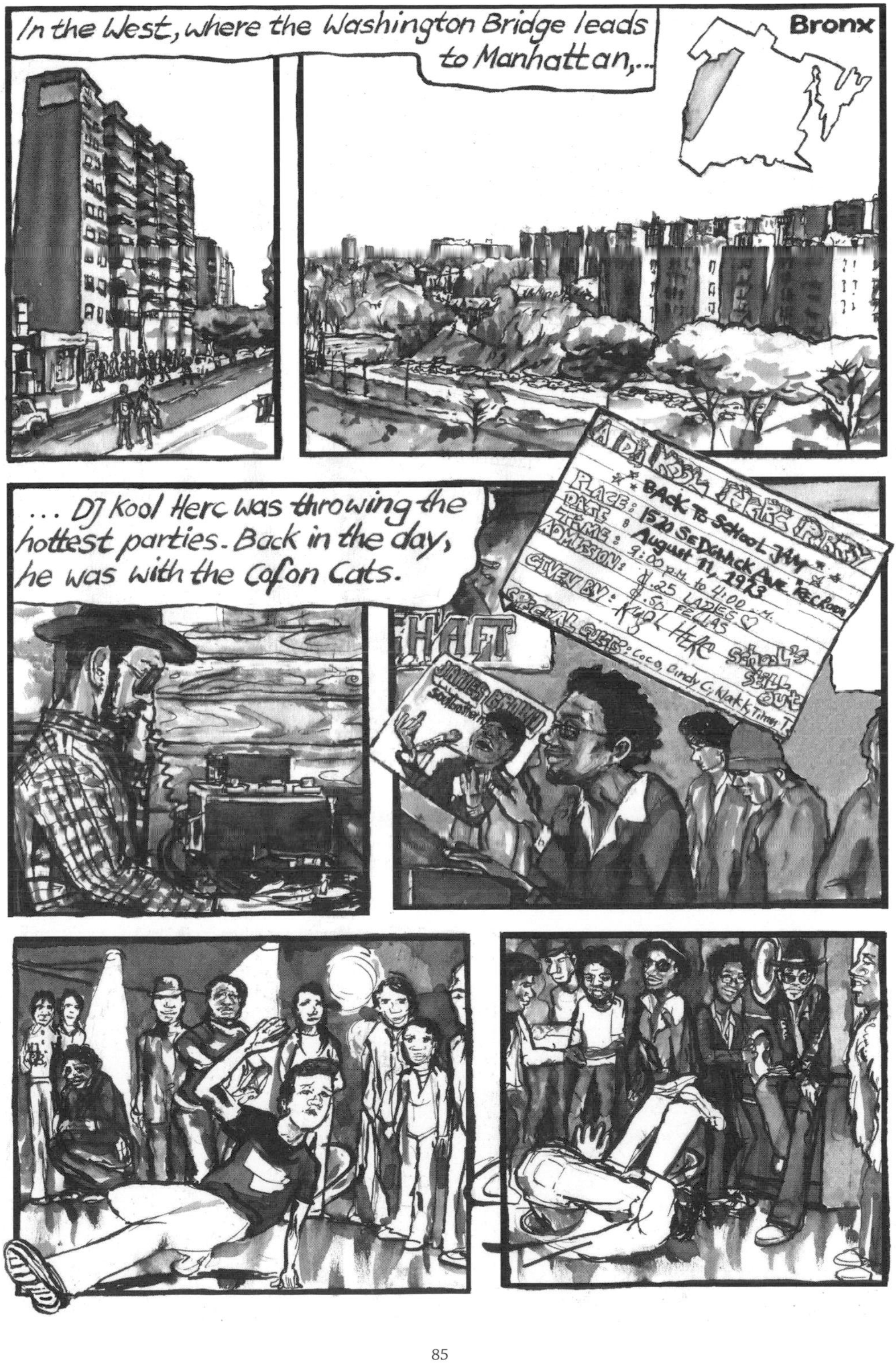
In the West, where the Washington Bridge leads to Manhattan,...
Bronx
... DJ Kool Herc was throwing the hottest parties. Back in the day, he was with the Cofon Cats.
BACK TO SCHOOL JAM
PLACE: 1520 SEDGWICK AVE. REC ROOM
DATE: August 11, 1973
TIME: 9:00 p.m. to 4:00
ADMISSION: $.25 LADIES
$.50 FELLAS
GIVEN BY: KOOL HERC
SPECIAL GUESTS: Coco, Cindy C,
School's Still Out
JAMES BROWN

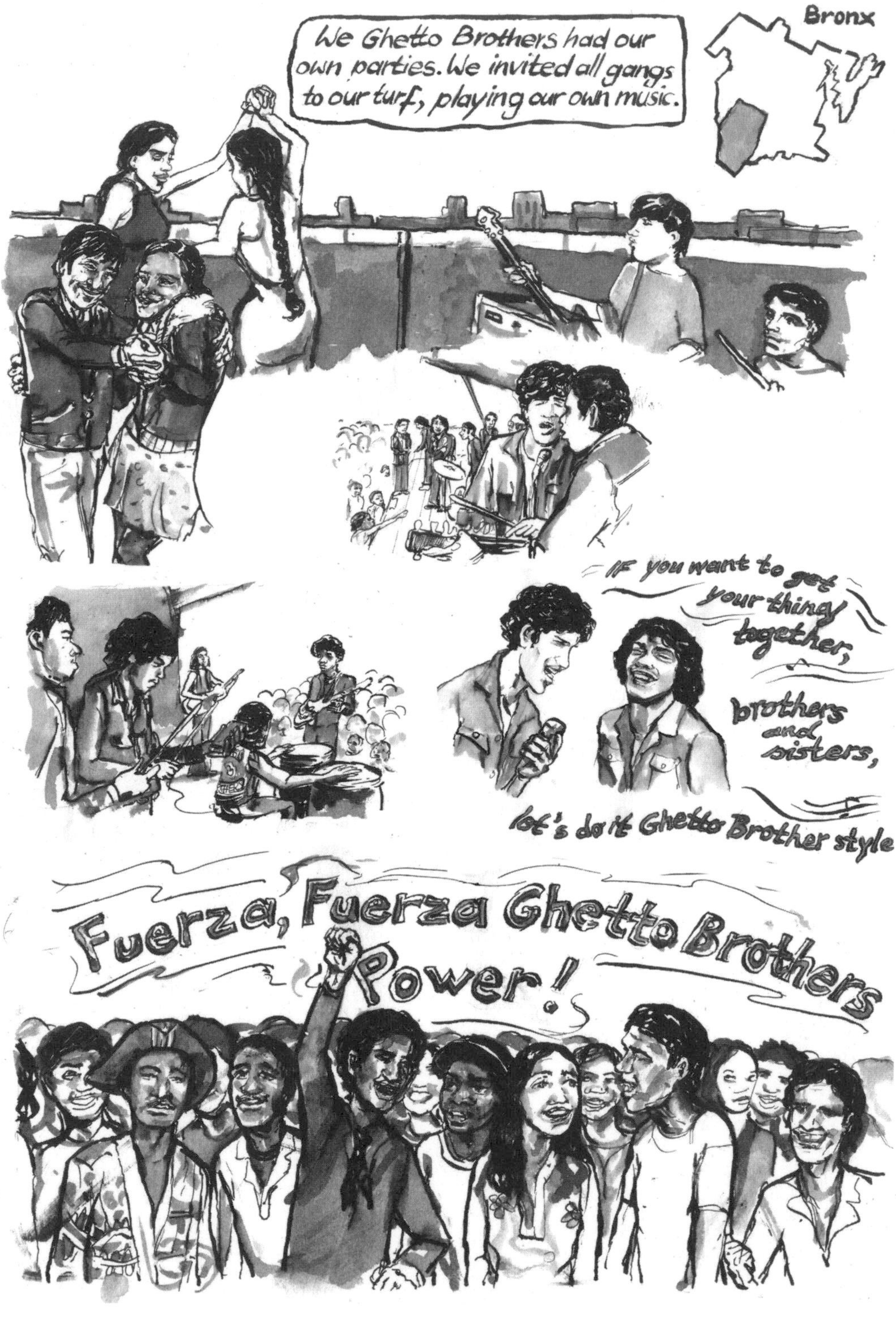
We Ghetto Brothers had our own parties. We invited all gangs to our turf, playing our own music.
Bronx
If you want to get your thing together,
brothers and sisters,
let's do it Ghetto Brother style
Fuerza, Fuerza Ghetto Brothers Power!

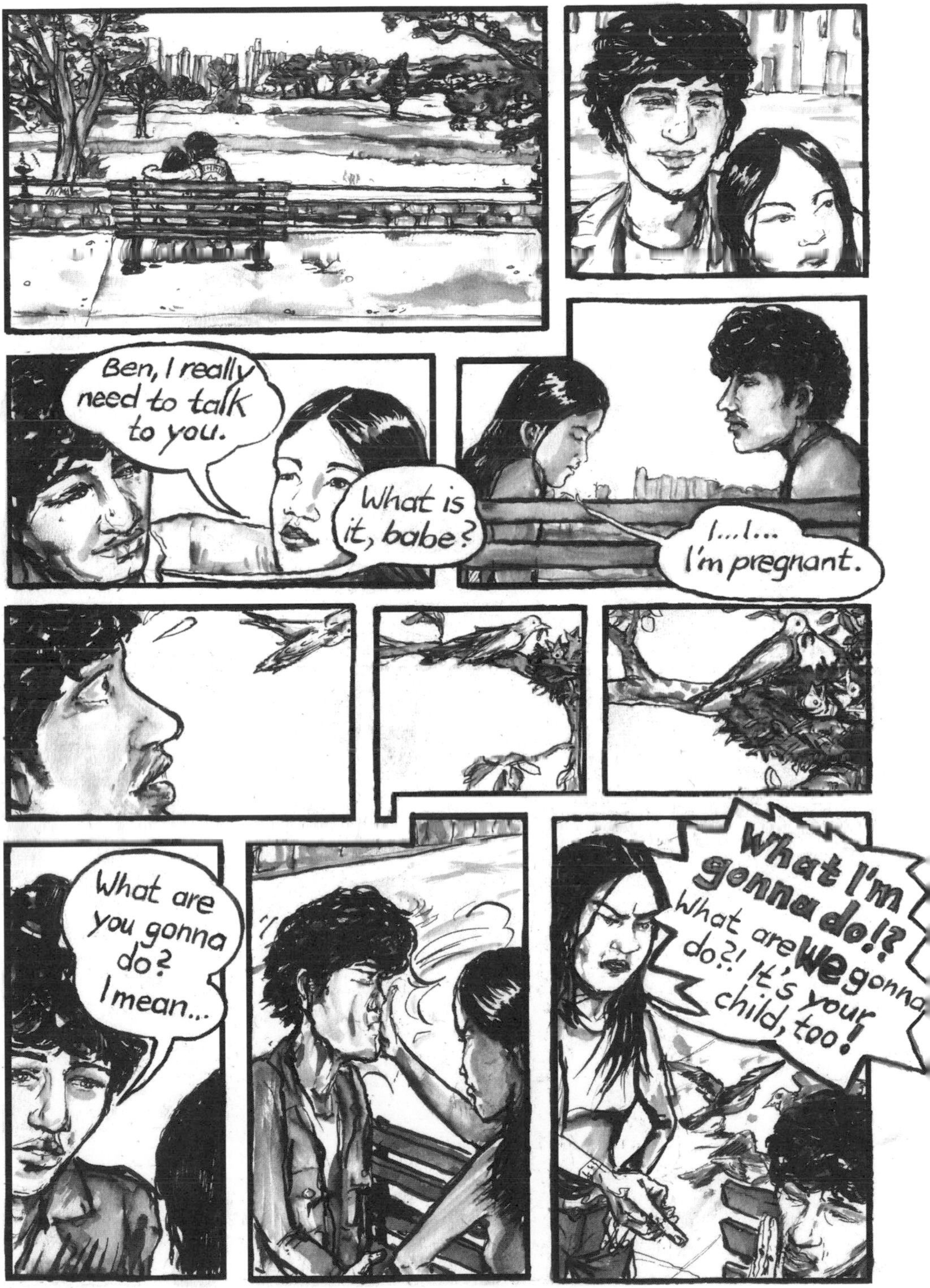
Ben, I really need to talk to you.
What is it, babe?
I... I... I'm pregnant.
What are you gonna do? I mean...
What I'm gonna do!? What are WE gonna do?! It's your child, too!

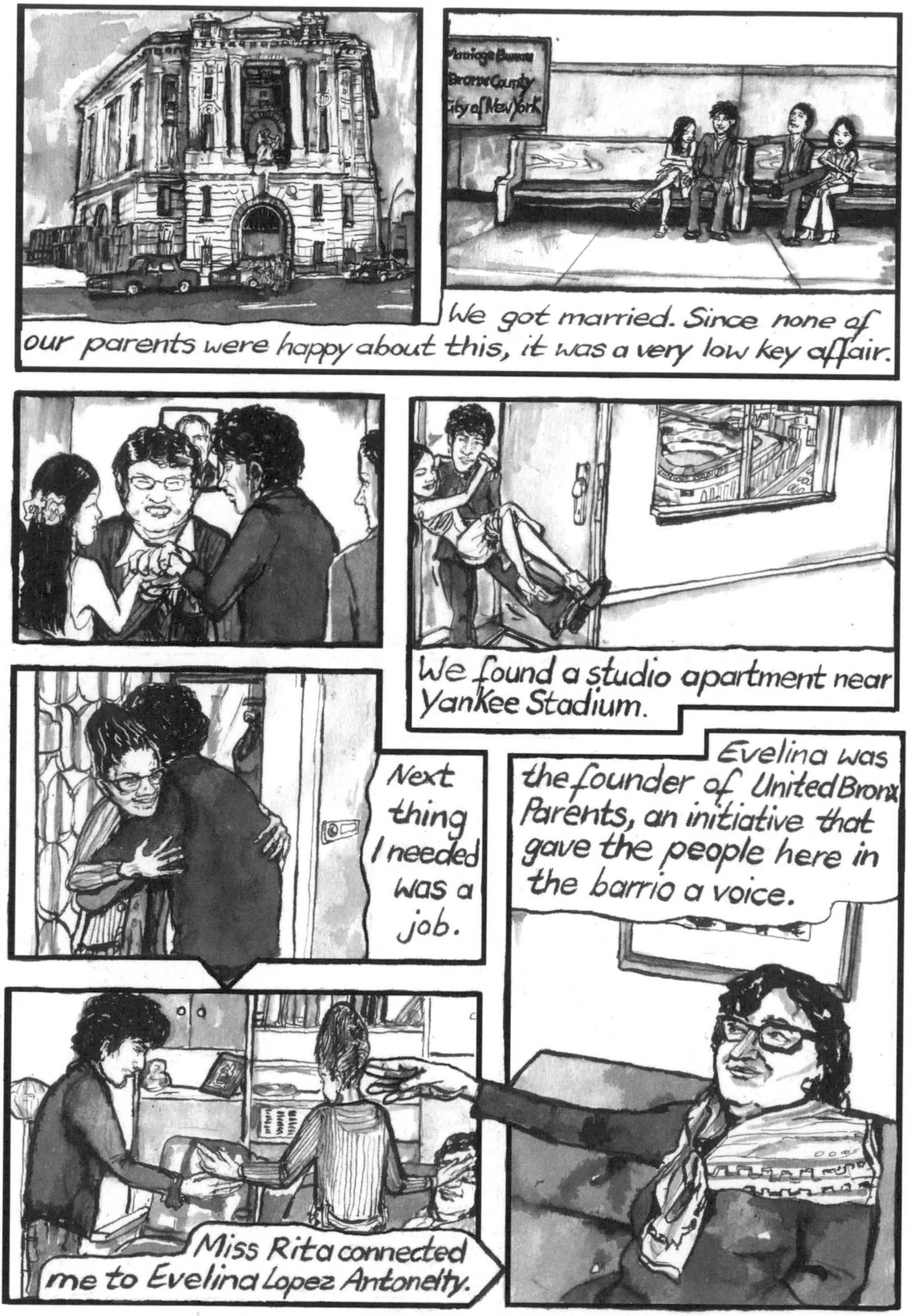

Marriage Bureau
Bronx County
City of New York
We got married. Since none of our parents were happy about this, it was a very low key affair.
We found a studio apartment near Yankee Stadium.
Next thing I needed was a job.
Evelina was the founder of United Bronx Parents, an initiative that gave the people here in the barrio a voice.
Miss Rita connected me to Evelina Lopez Antonetty.

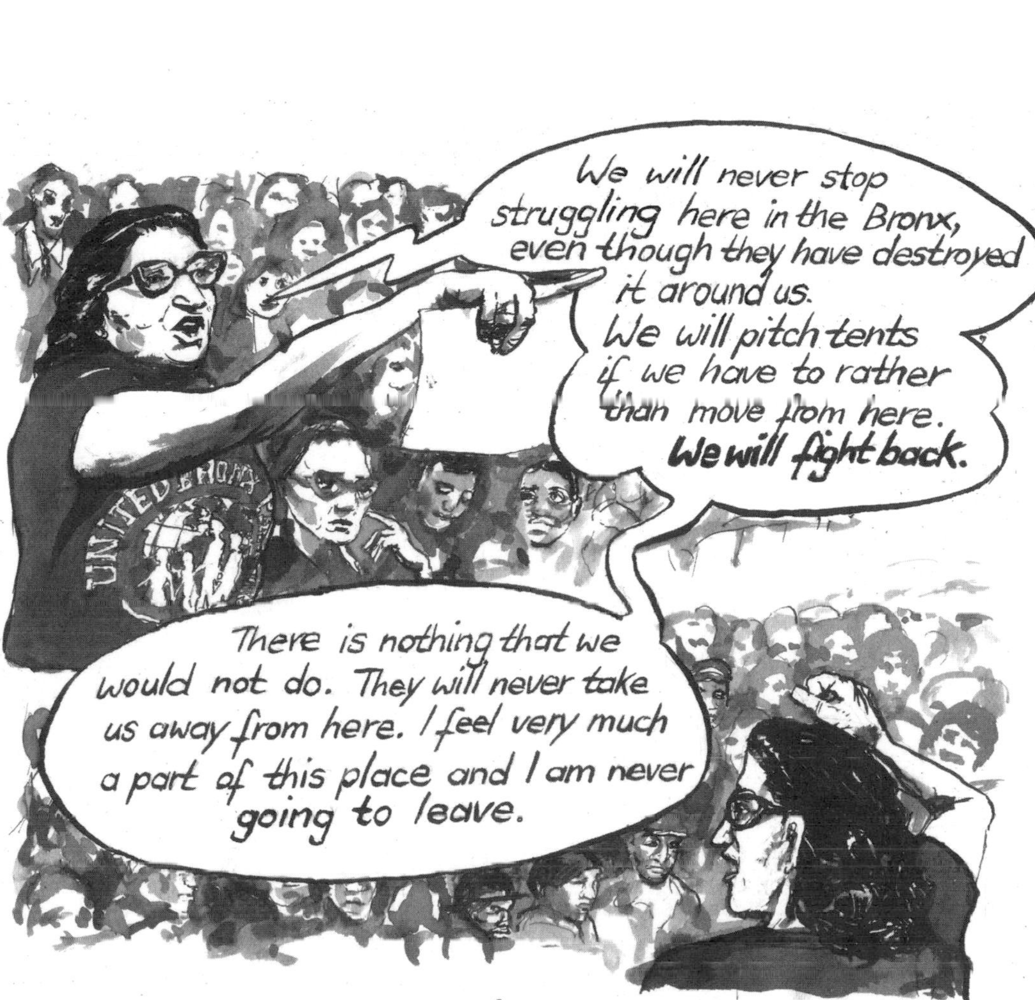
We will never stop struggling here in the Bronx, even though they have destroyed it around us. We will pitch tents if we have to rather than move from here. **We will fight back.**
There is nothing that we would not do. They will never take us away from here. I feel very much a part of this place and I am never going to leave.
UNITED BRONX

The United Bronx Parents pushed for bilingual education programs in schools, minority hiring, parent training, and began to develop new service offerings in the Bronx, including emergency food programs.

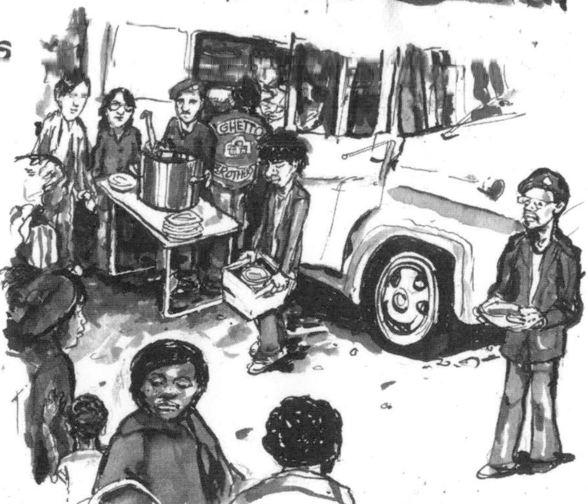
GHETTO
BROTHERS

My connection to the Ghetto Brothers was a win-win situation.

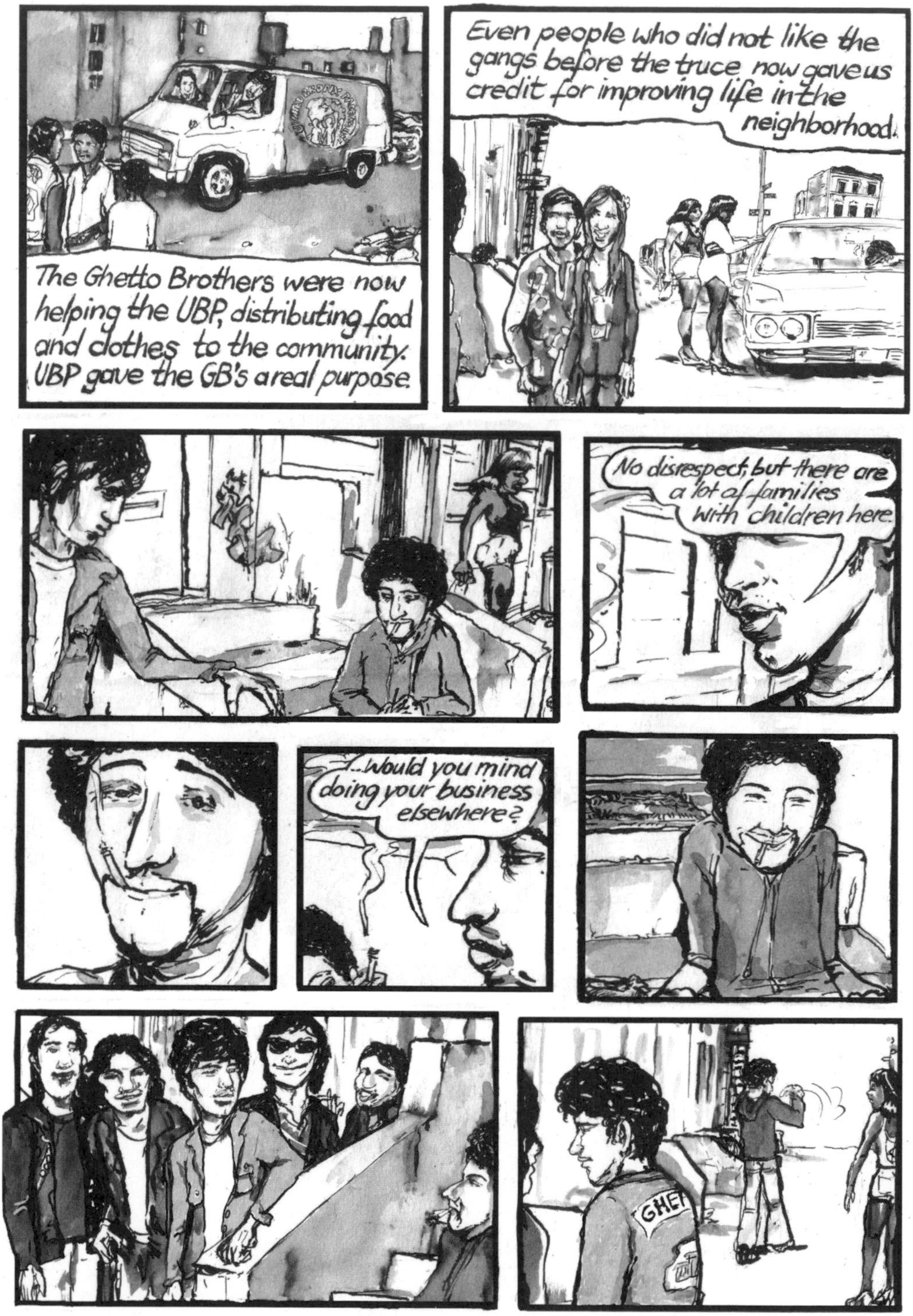
The Ghetto Brothers were now helping the UBP, distributing food and clothes to the community. UBP gave the GB's a real purpose.
Even people who did not like the gangs before the truce now gave us credit for improving life in the neighborhood.
No disrespect, but there are a lot of families with children here.
...Would you mind doing your business elsewhere?
GHET

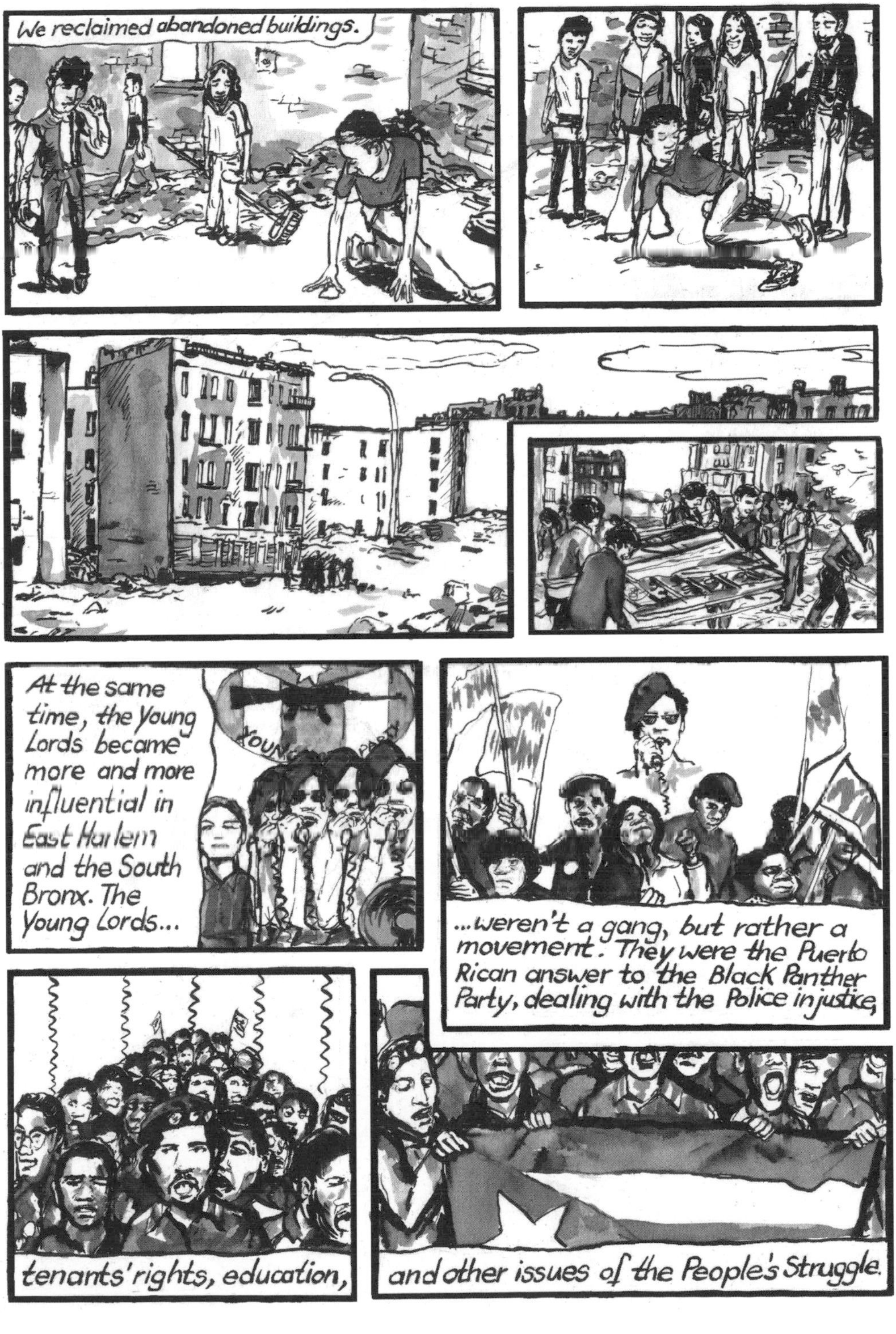
We reclaimed abandoned buildings.
At the same time, the Young Lords became more and more influential in East Harlem and the South Bronx. The Young Lords...
...weren't a gang, but rather a movement. They were the Puerto Rican answer to the Black Panther Party, dealing with the Police injustice,
tenants' rights, education,
and other issues of the People's Struggle.

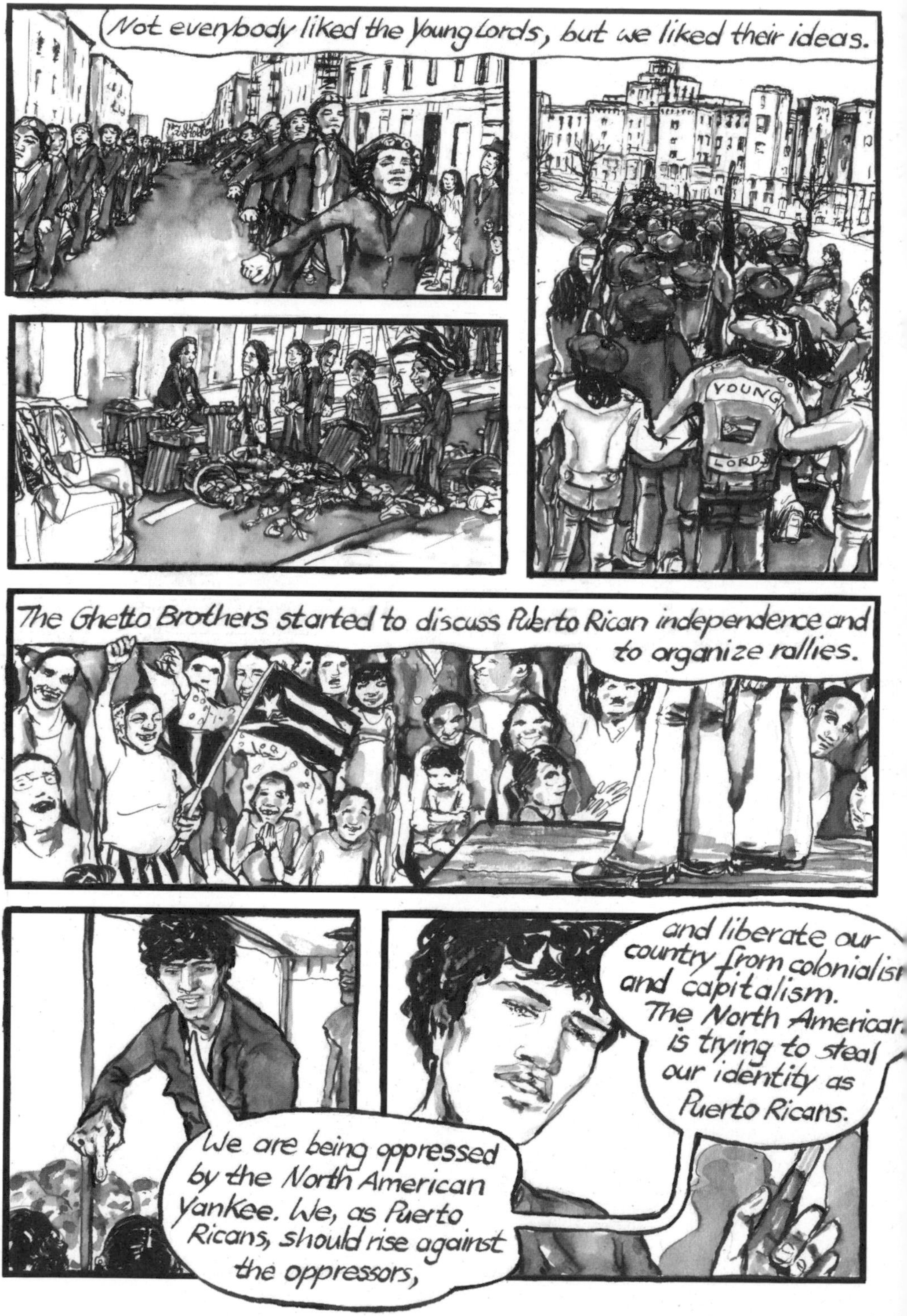
Not everybody liked the Young Lords, but we liked their ideas.
YOUNG
LORDS
The Ghetto Brothers started to discuss Puerto Rican independence and to organize rallies.
We are being oppressed by the North American Yankee. We, as Puerto Ricans, should rise against the oppressors,
and liberate our country from colonialis and capitalism. The North American is trying to steal our identity as Puerto Ricans.

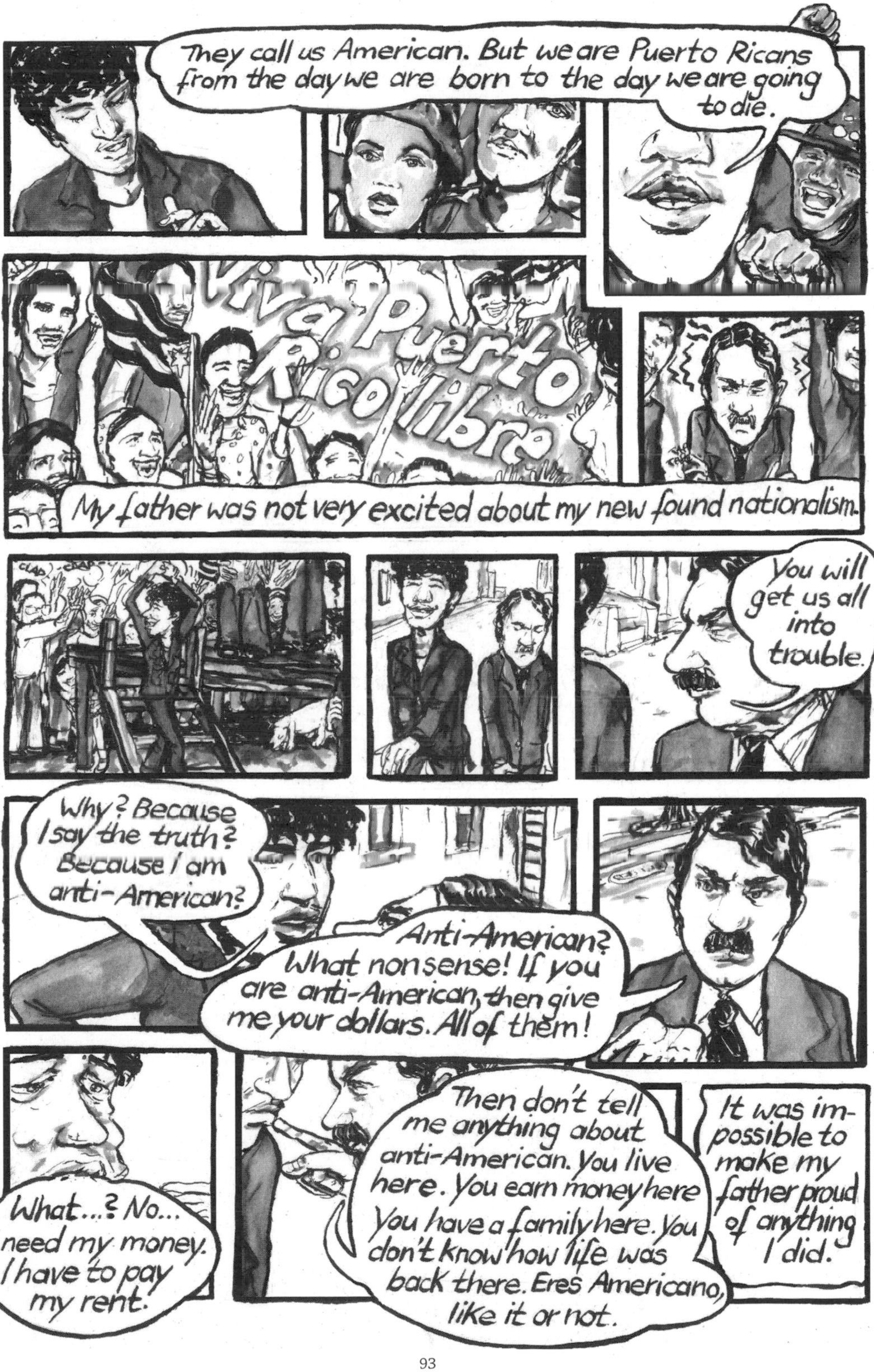

They call us American. But we are Puerto Ricans from the day we are born to the day we are going to die.
Viva Puerto Rico libre
My father was not very excited about my new found nationalism.
You will get us all into trouble.
Why? Because I say the truth? Because I am anti-American?
Anti-American? What nonsense! If you are anti-American, then give me your dollars. All of them!
What...? No... I need my money. I have to pay my rent.
Then don't tell me anything about anti-American. You live here. You earn money here You have a family here. You don't know how life was back there. Eres Americano, like it or not.
It was impossible to make my father proud of anything I did.

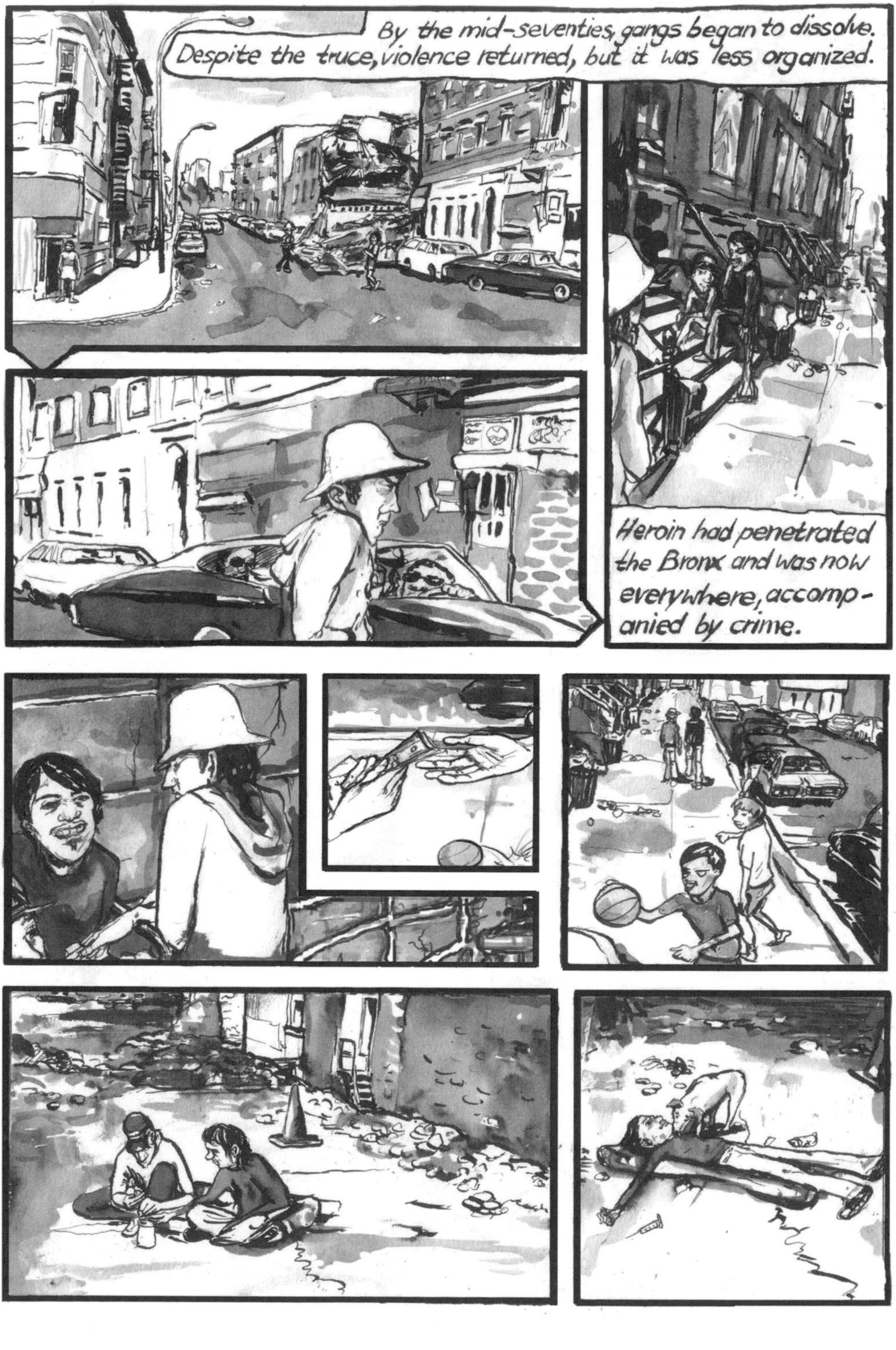
By the mid-seventies, gangs began to dissolve. Despite the truce, violence returned, but it was less organized.
Heroin had penetrated the Bronx and was now everywhere, accompanied by crime.

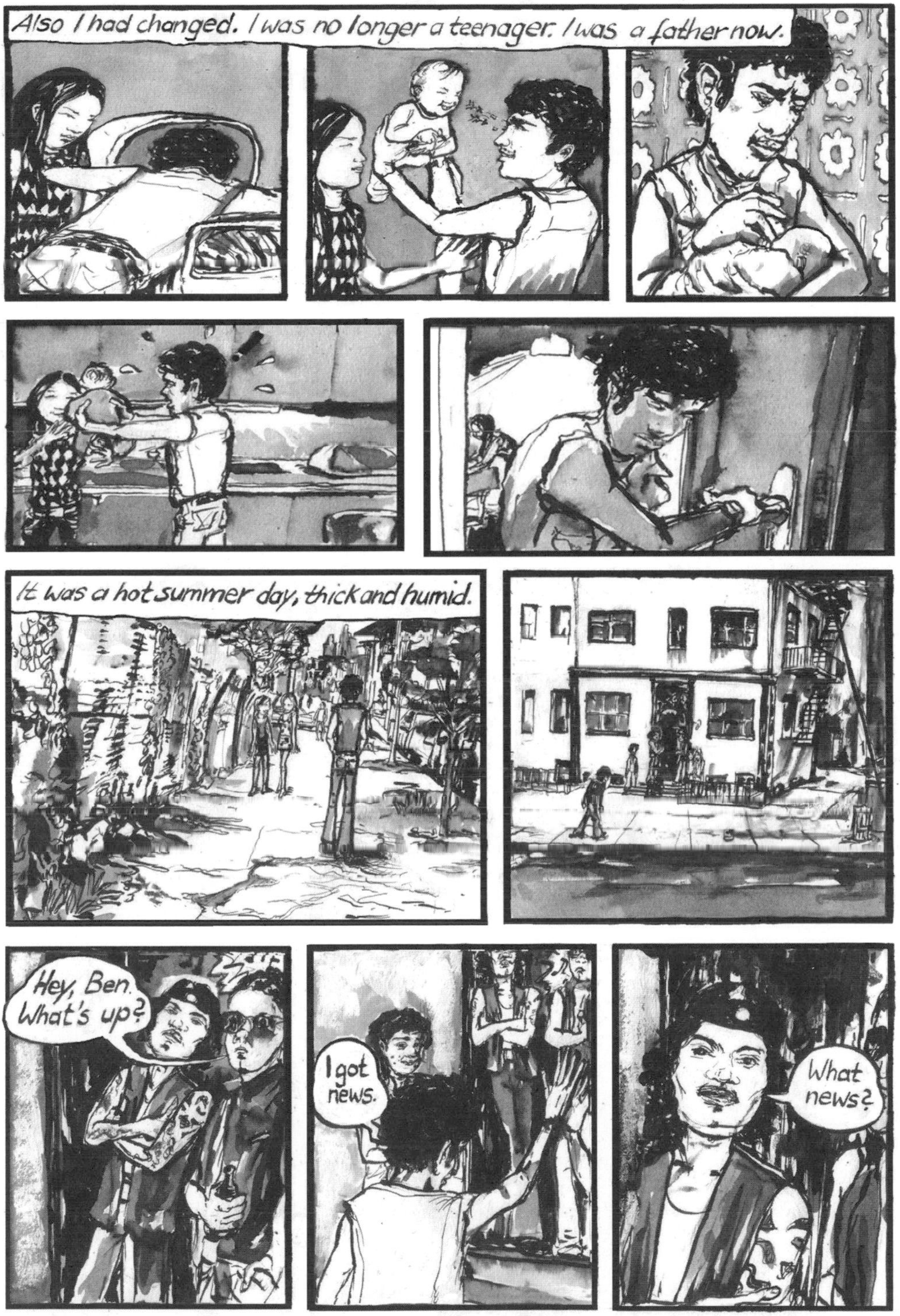
Also I had changed. I was no longer a teenager. I was a father now.
It was a hot summer day, thick and humid.
Hey, Ben. What's up?
I got news.
What news?

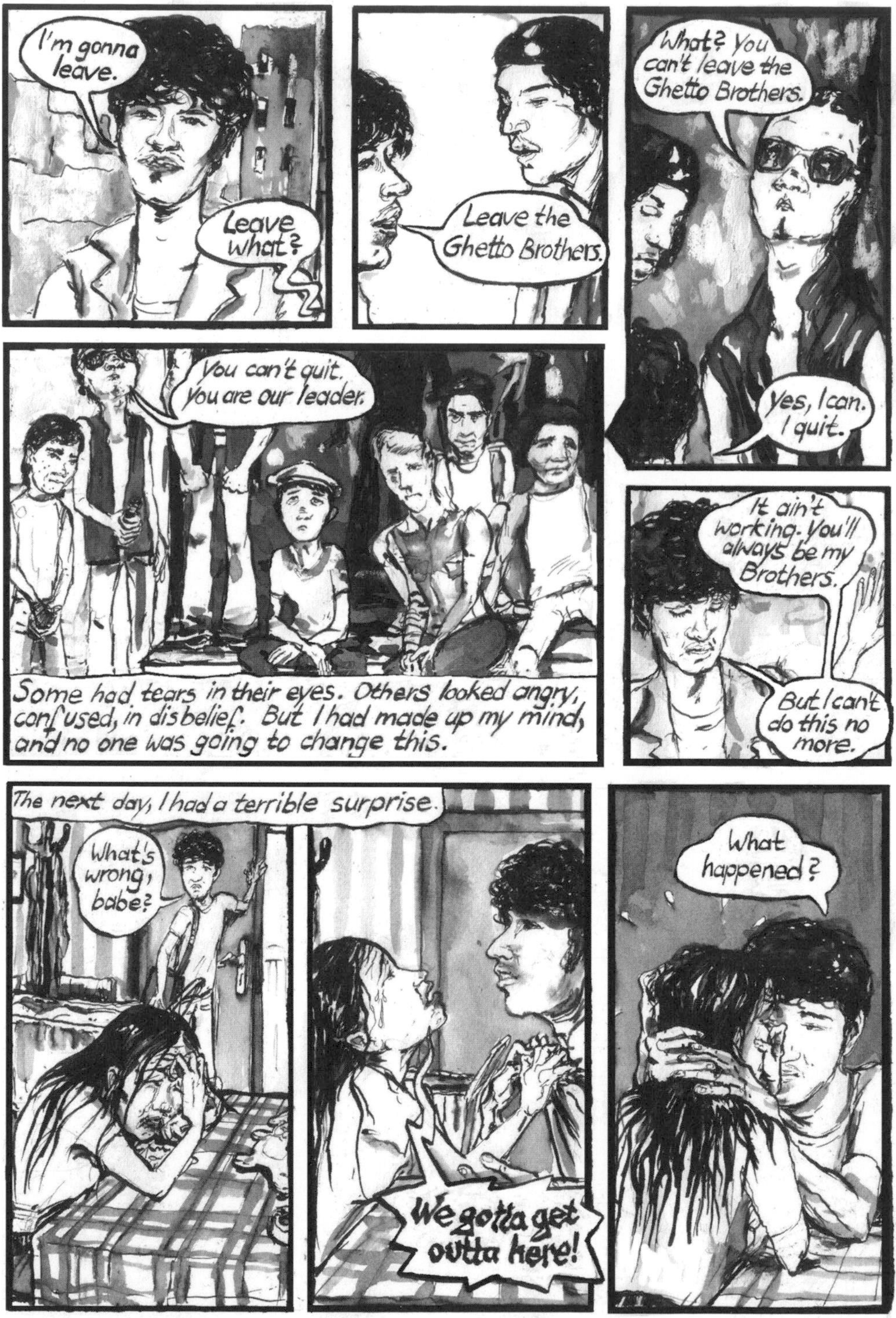
I'm gonna leave.
Leave what?
Leave the Ghetto Brothers.
What? You can't leave the Ghetto Brothers.
Yes, I can. I quit.
You can't quit. You are our leader.
Some had tears in their eyes. Others looked angry, confused, in disbelief. But I had made up my mind, and no one was going to change this.
It ain't working. You'll always be my Brothers.
But I can't do this no more.
The next day, I had a terrible surprise.
What's wrong, babe?
We gotta get outta here!
What happened?

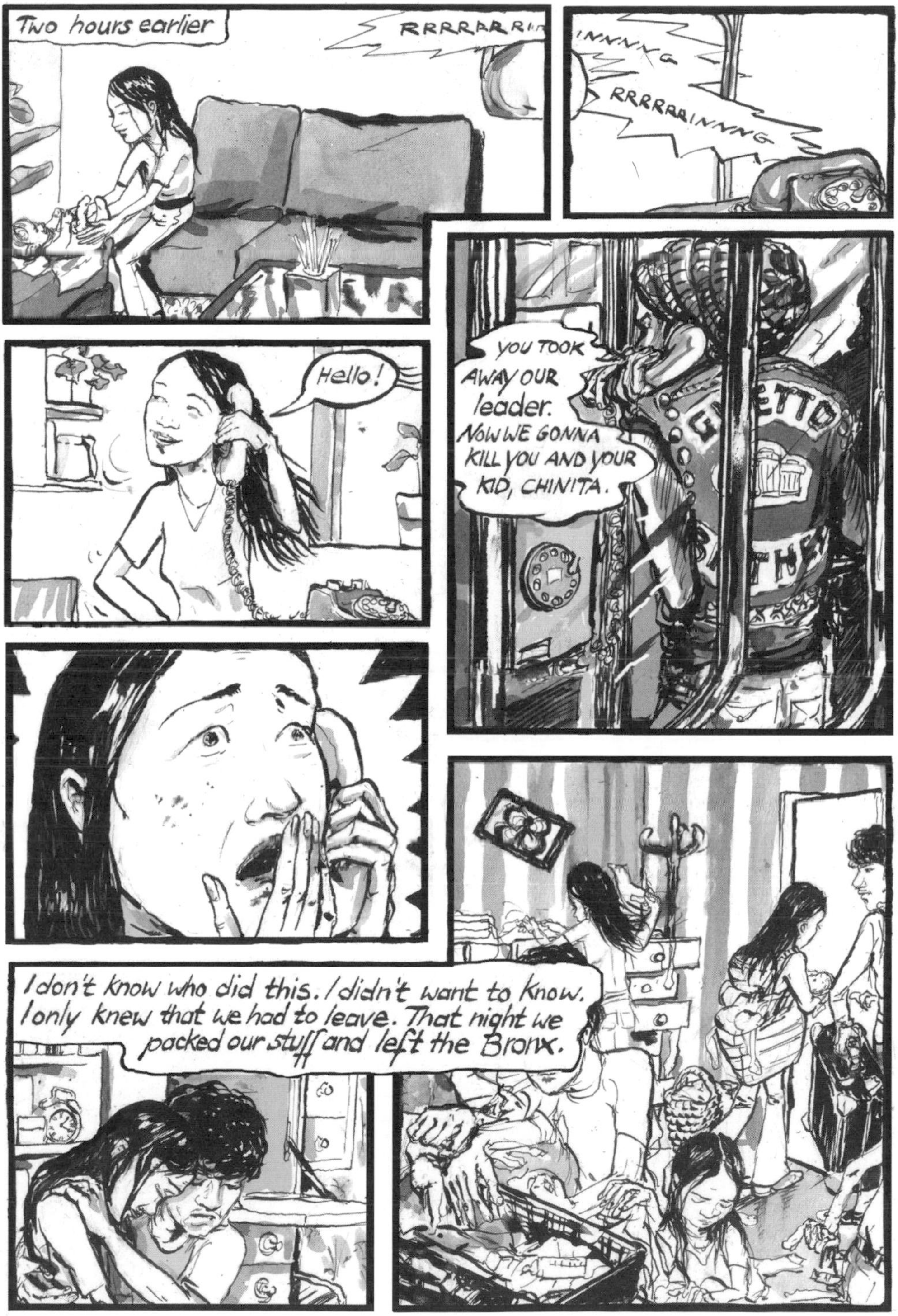
Two hours earlier
RRRRARRRINNNNG
RRRRRRINNNNG
Hello!
YOU TOOK AWAY OUR leader. NOW WE GONNA KILL YOU AND YOUR KID, CHINITA.
I don't know who did this. I didn't want to know. I only knew that we had to leave. That night we packed our stuff and left the Bronx.

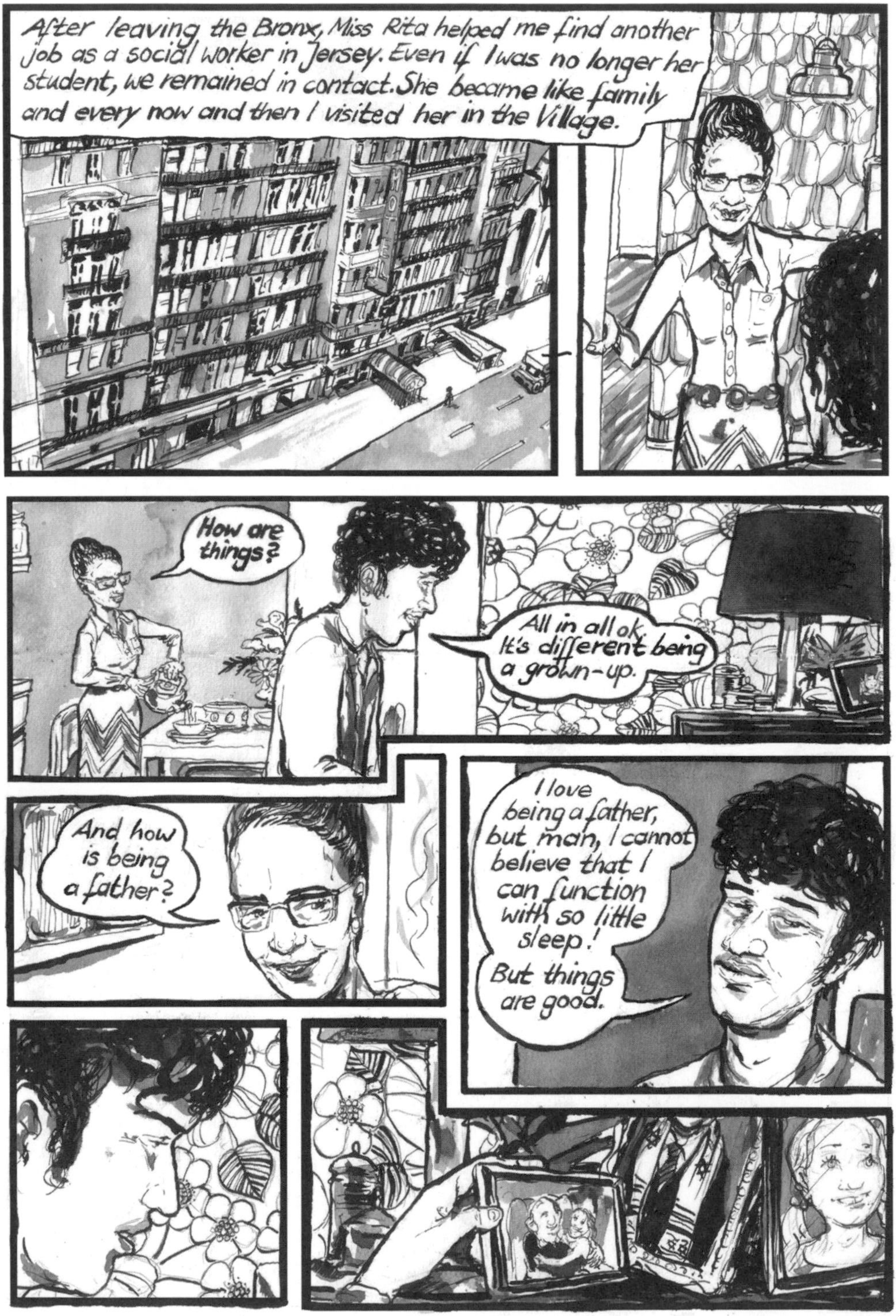
After leaving the Bronx, Miss Rita helped me find another job as a social worker in Jersey. Even if I was no longer her student, we remained in contact. She became like family and every now and then I visited her in the Village.
How are things?
All in all ok. It's different being a grown-up.
And how is being a father?
I love being a father, but man, I cannot believe that I can function with so little sleep! But things are good.

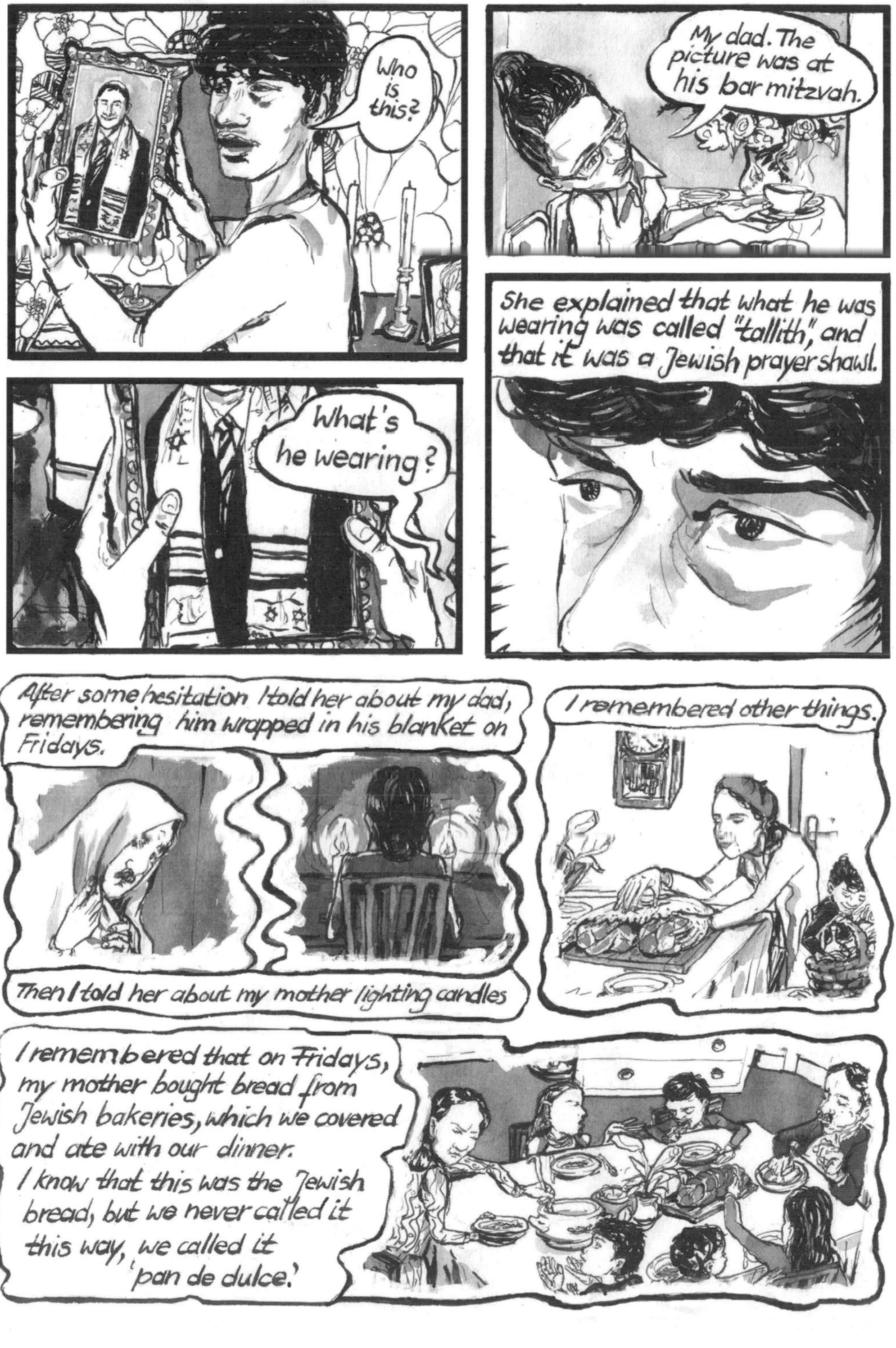
Who is this?
My dad. The picture was at his bar mitzvah.
What's he wearing?
She explained that what he was wearing was called "tallith," and that it was a Jewish prayer shawl.
After some hesitation I told her about my dad, remembering him wrapped in his blanket on Fridays.
Then I told her about my mother lighting candles
I remembered other things.
I remembered that on Fridays, my mother bought bread from Jewish bakeries, which we covered and ate with our dinner.
I know that this was the Jewish bread, but we never called it this way, we called it 'pan de dulce.'

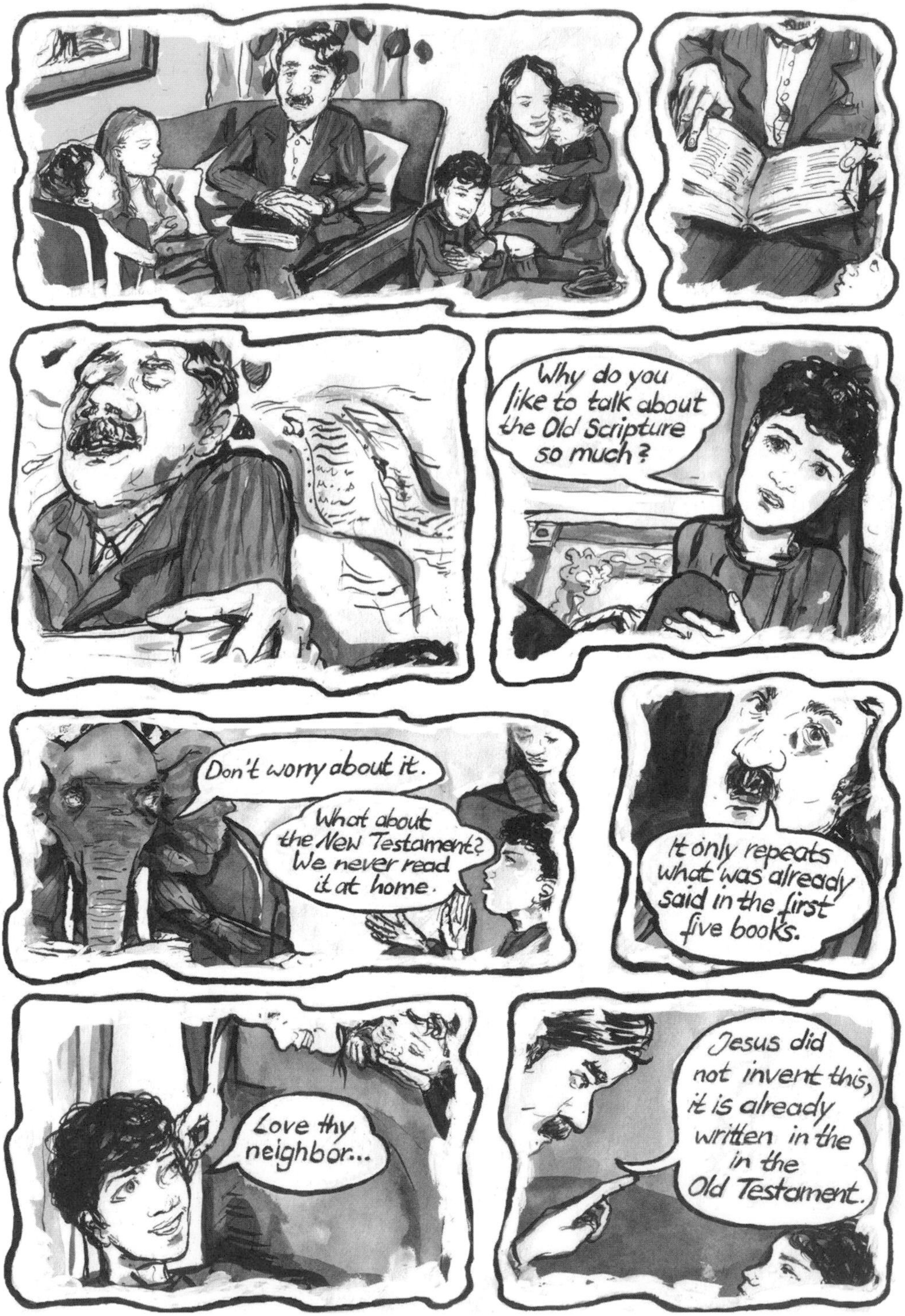
Why do you like to talk about the Old Scripture so much?
Don't worry about it.
What about the New Testament? We never read it at home.
It only repeats what was already said in the first five books.
Love thy neighbor...
Jesus did not invent this, it is already written in the in the Old Testament.

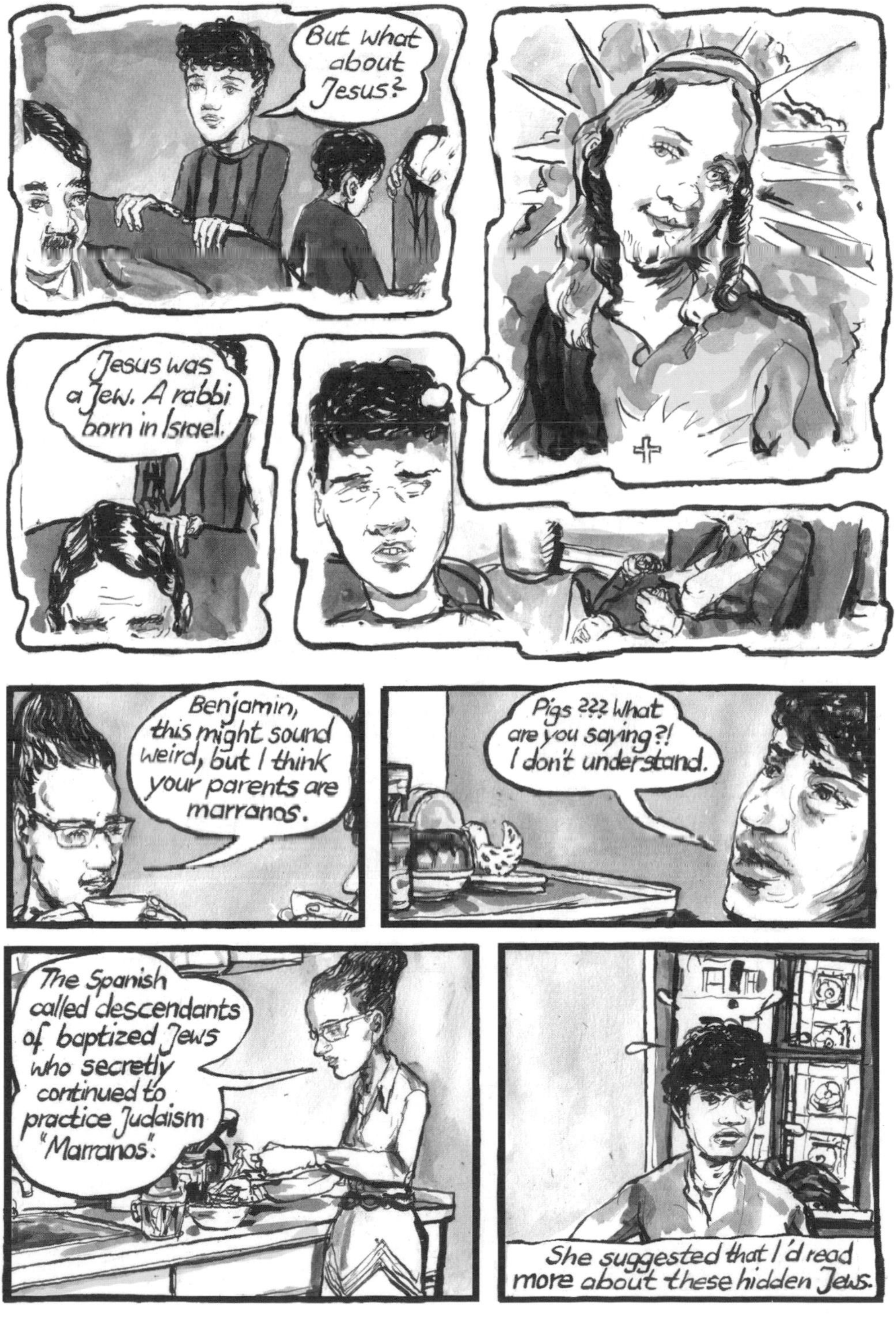
But what about Jesus?
Jesus was a Jew. A rabbi born in Israel.
Benjamin, this might sound weird, but I think your parents are marranos.
Pigs ??? What are you saying?! I don't understand.
The Spanish called descendants of baptized Jews who secretly continued to practice Judaism "Marranos".
She suggested that I'd read more about these hidden Jews.

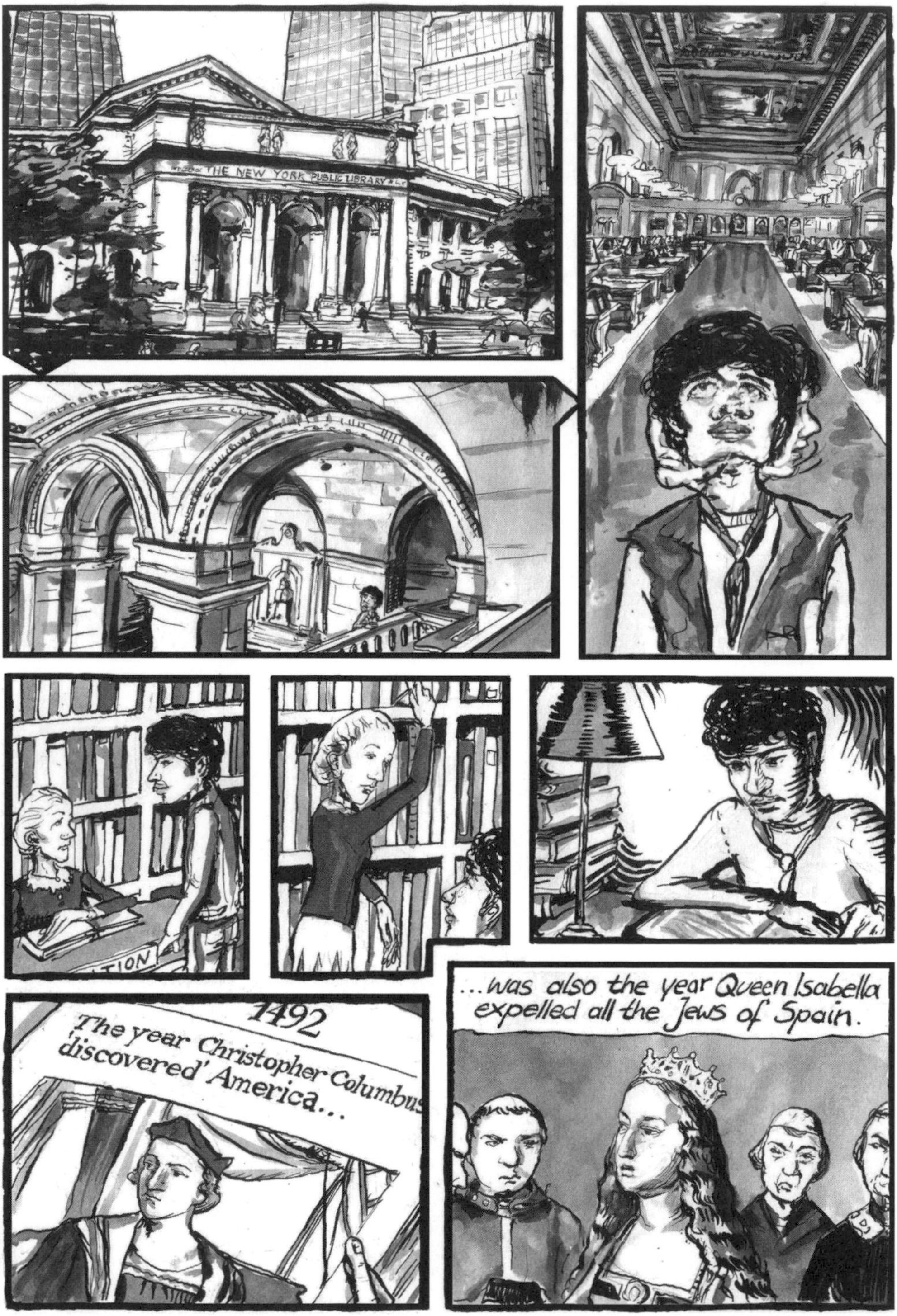
THE NEW YORK PUBLIC LIBRARY
1492
The year Christopher Columbus 'discovered' America...
...was also the year Queen Isabella expelled all the Jews of Spain.

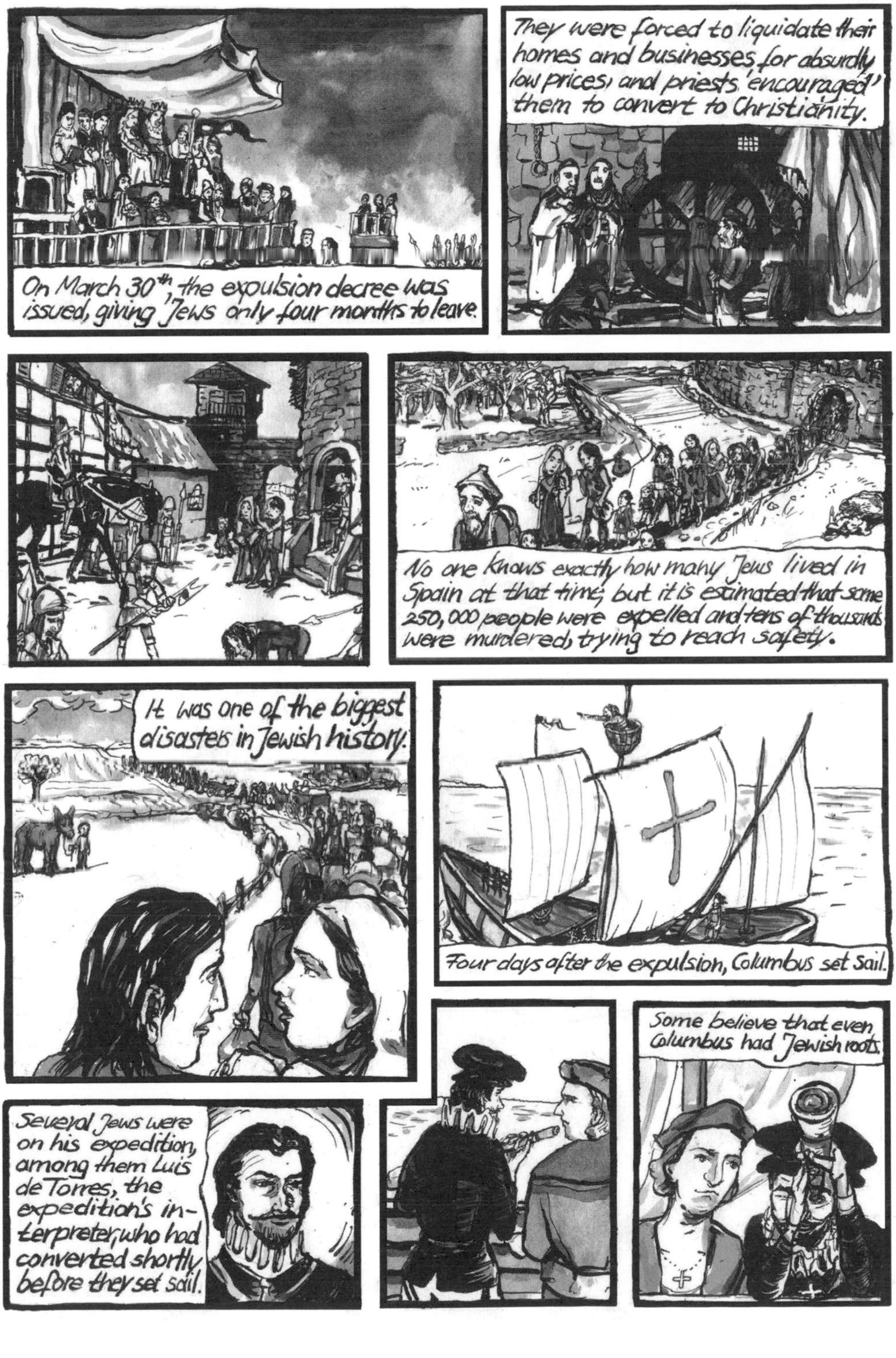
On March 30th, the expulsion decree was issued, giving Jews only four months to leave.
They were forced to liquidate their homes and businesses for absurdly low prices, and priests 'encouraged' them to convert to Christianity.
No one knows exactly how many Jews lived in Spain at that time; but it is estimated that some 250,000 people were expelled and tens of thousands were murdered, trying to reach safety.
It was one of the biggest disasters in Jewish history.
Four days after the expulsion, Columbus set sail.
Some believe that even Columbus had Jewish roots.
Several Jews were on his expedition, among them Luis de Torres, the expedition's interpreter, who had converted shortly before they set sail.

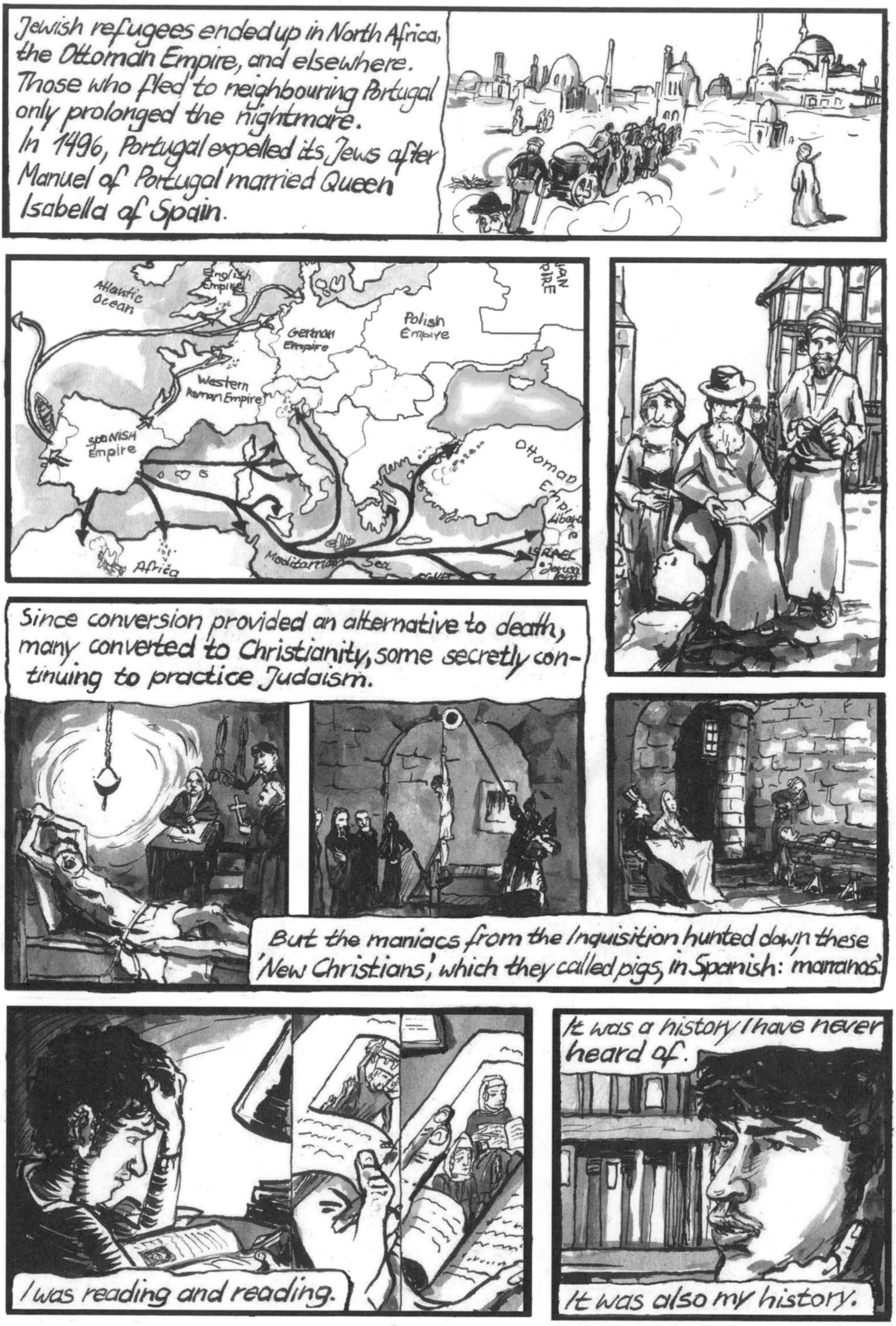
Jewish refugees ended up in North Africa, the Ottoman Empire, and elsewhere. Those who fled to neighbouring Portugal only prolonged the nightmare.
In 1496, Portugal expelled its Jews after Manuel of Portugal married Queen Isabella of Spain.
English Empire
Atlantic Ocean
German Empire
Polish Empire
Western Roman Empire
Spanish Empire
Ottoman Empire
Africa
ISRAEL
Since conversion provided an alternative to death, many converted to Christianity, some secretly continuing to practice Judaism.
But the maniacs from the Inquisition hunted down these 'New Christians,' which they called pigs, in Spanish: 'marranos.'
I was reading and reading.
It was a history I have never heard of.
It was also my history.

Mama, aquí está Benjamin.

I called my parents, only to find out the bad news.

¿Qué pasó?

My father was in the hospital.

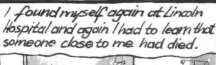

I found myself again at Lincoln Hospital and again I had to learn that someone close to me had died.

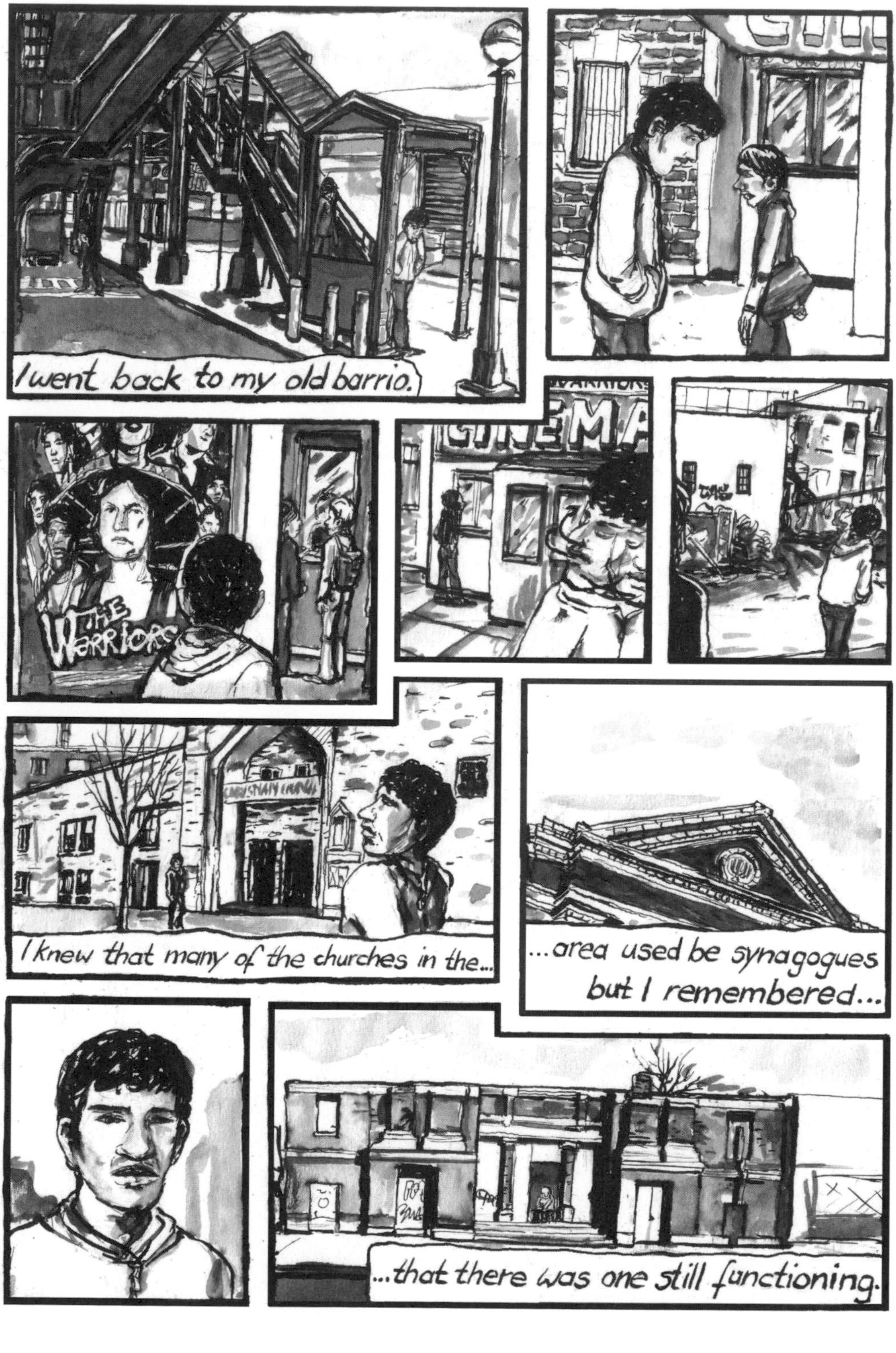
I went back to my old barrio.
WARRIORS
CINEMA
THE WARRIORS
I knew that many of the churches in the...
...area used be synagogues but I remembered...
...that there was one still functioning.

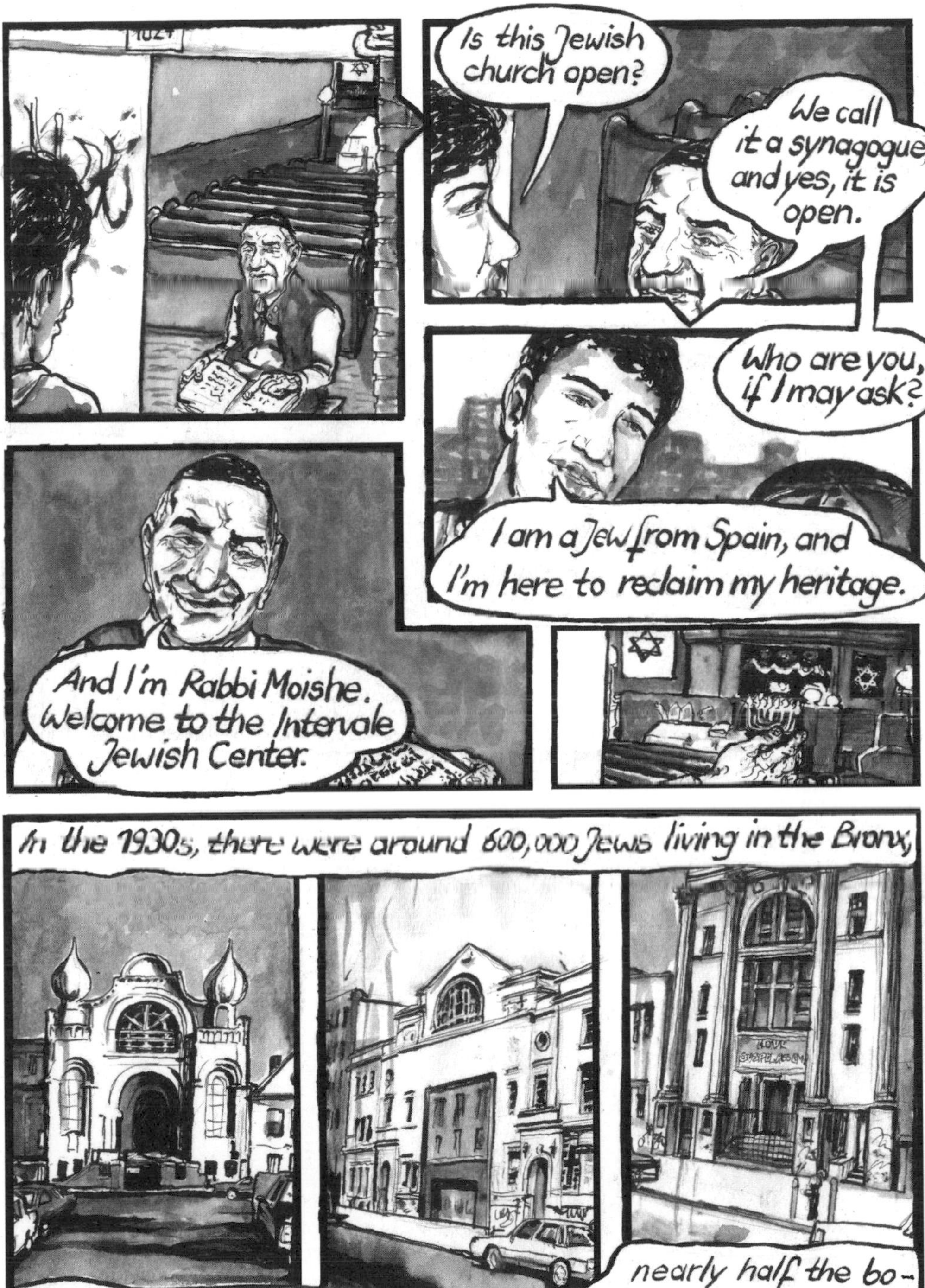

Is this Jewish church open?
We call it a synagogue, and yes, it is open.
Who are you, if I may ask?
I am a Jew from Spain, and I'm here to reclaim my heritage.
And I'm Rabbi Moishe. Welcome to the Intervale Jewish Center.
In the 1930s, there were around 600,000 Jews living in the Bronx,
nearly half the bo-
rough's population. On every corner one could find a synagogue.

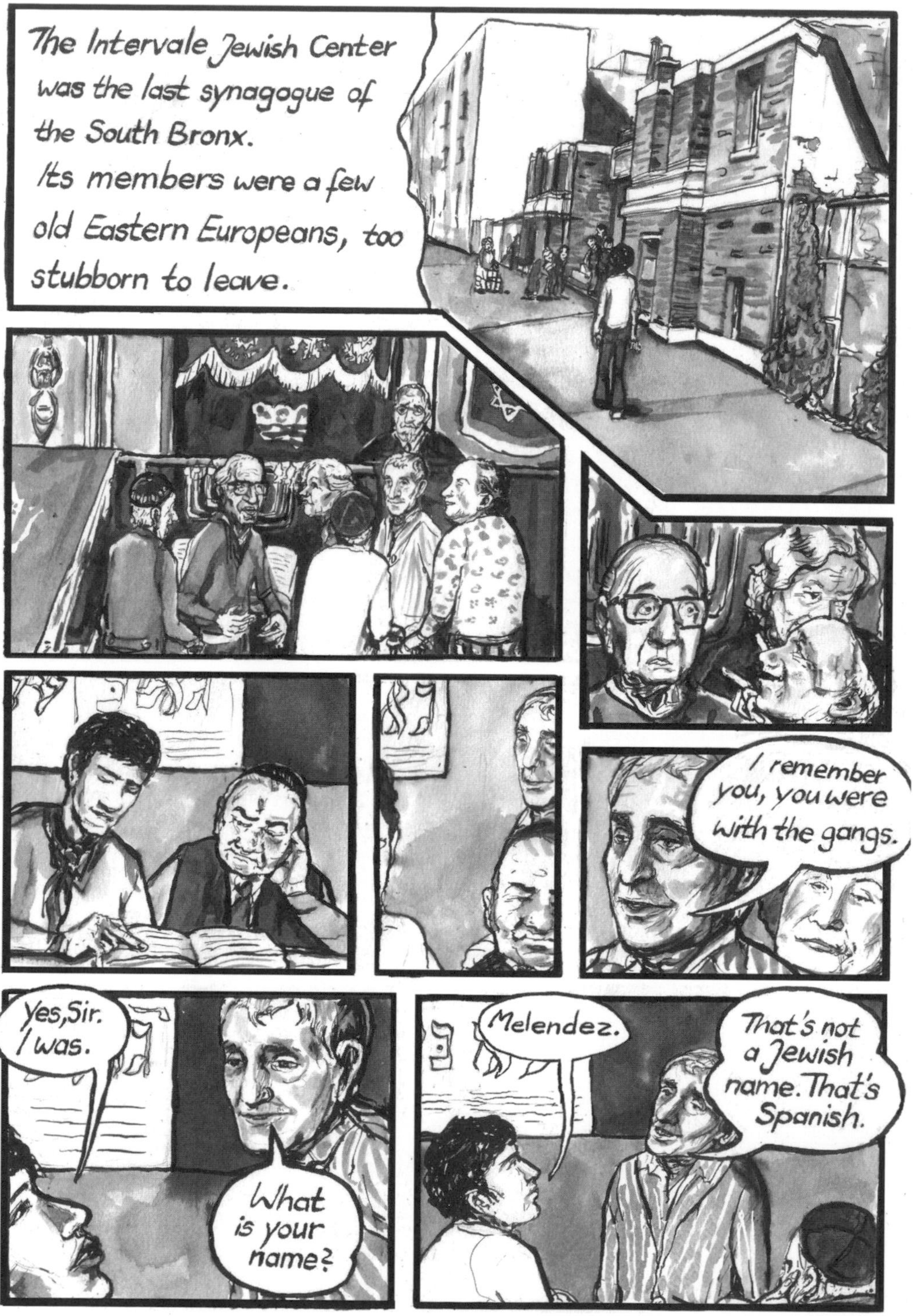
The Intervale Jewish Center was the last synagogue of the South Bronx.
Its members were a few old Eastern Europeans, too stubborn to leave.
I remember you, you were with the gangs.
Yes, Sir. I was.
What is your name?
Melendez.
That's not a Jewish name. That's Spanish.

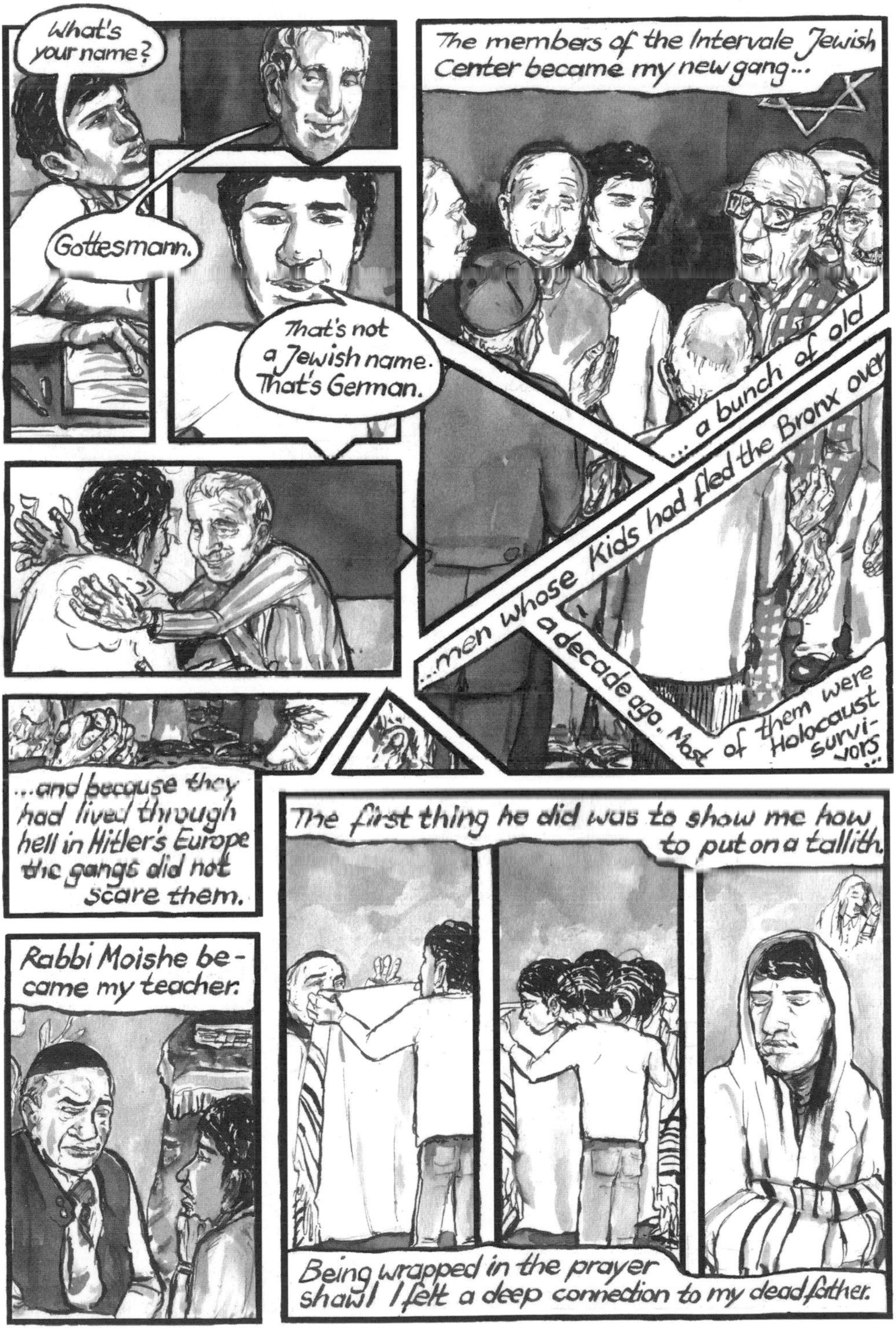
What's your name?
Gottesmann.
That's not a Jewish name. That's German.
The members of the Intervale Jewish Center became my new gang...
...a bunch of old
...men whose kids had fled the Bronx over
a decade ago. Most of them were Holocaust survivors...
...and because they had lived through hell in Hitler's Europe the gangs did not scare them.
The first thing he did was to show me how to put on a tallith.
Rabbi Moishe became my teacher.
Being wrapped in the prayer shawl I felt a deep connection to my dead father.

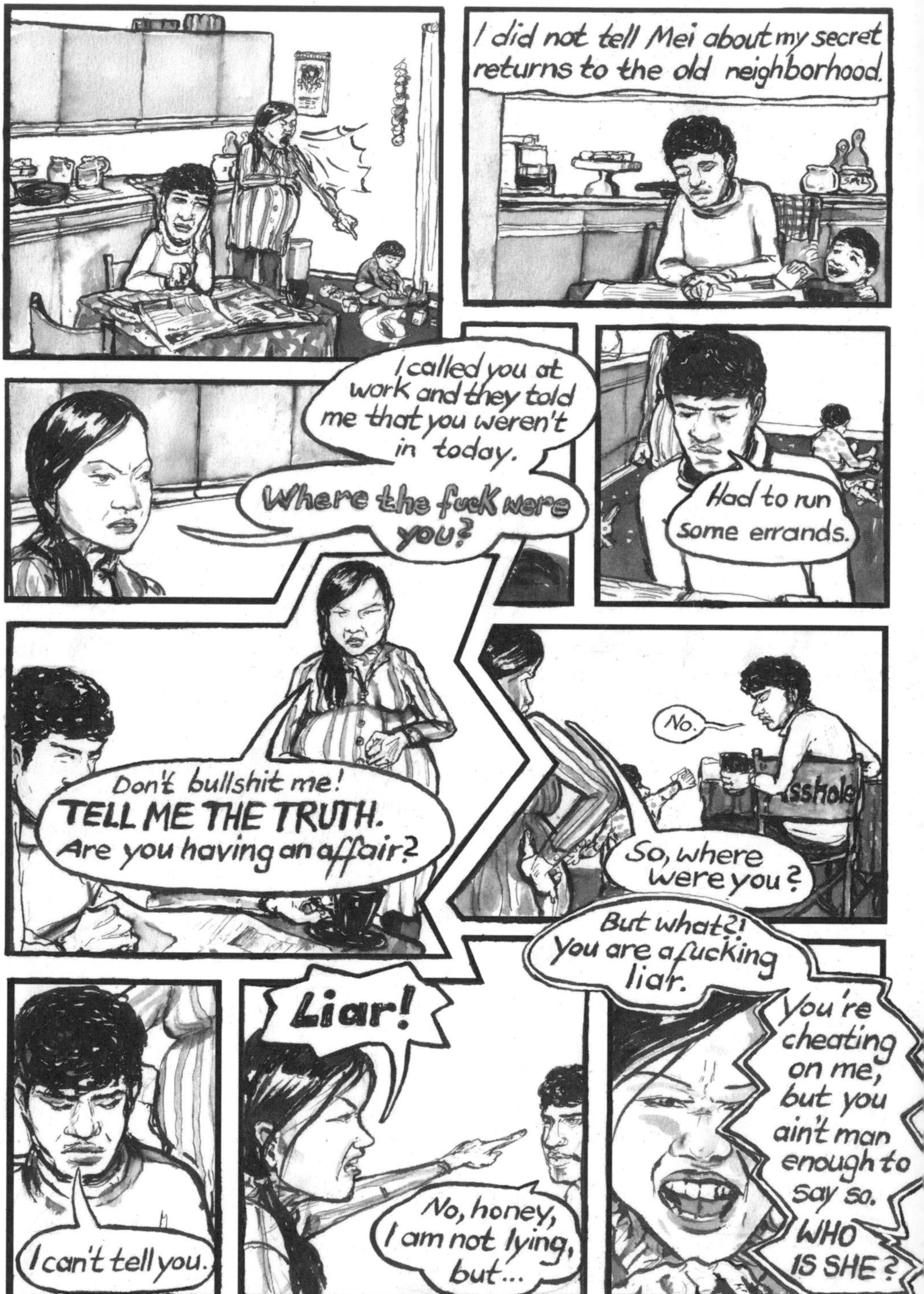

I did not tell Mei about my secret returns to the old neighborhood.
I called you at work and they told me that you weren't in today.
Where the fuck were you?
Had to run some errands.
Don't bullshit me!
TELL ME THE TRUTH.
Are you having an affair?
No.
Asshole
So, where were you?
I can't tell you.
Liar!
No, honey, I am not lying, but...
But what?! You are a fucking liar.
You're cheating on me, but you ain't man enough to say so.
WHO IS SHE?

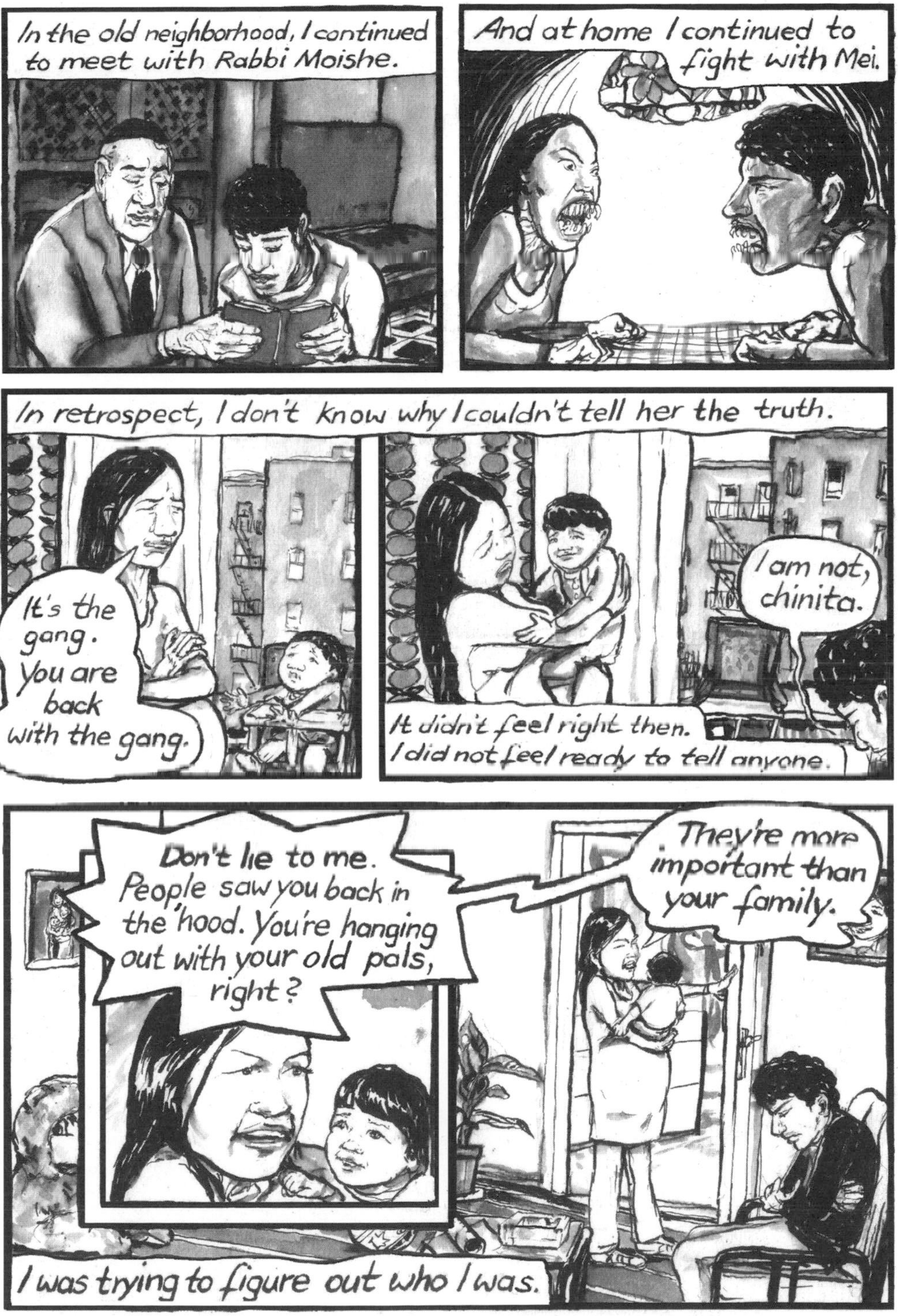

In the old neighborhood, I continued to meet with Rabbi Moishe.
And at home I continued to fight with Mei.
In retrospect, I don't know why I couldn't tell her the truth.
It's the gang. You are back with the gang.
I am not, chinita.
It didn't feel right then. I did not feel ready to tell anyone.
Don't lie to me. People saw you back in the 'hood. You're hanging out with your old pals, right?
They're more important than your family.
I was trying to figure out who I was.

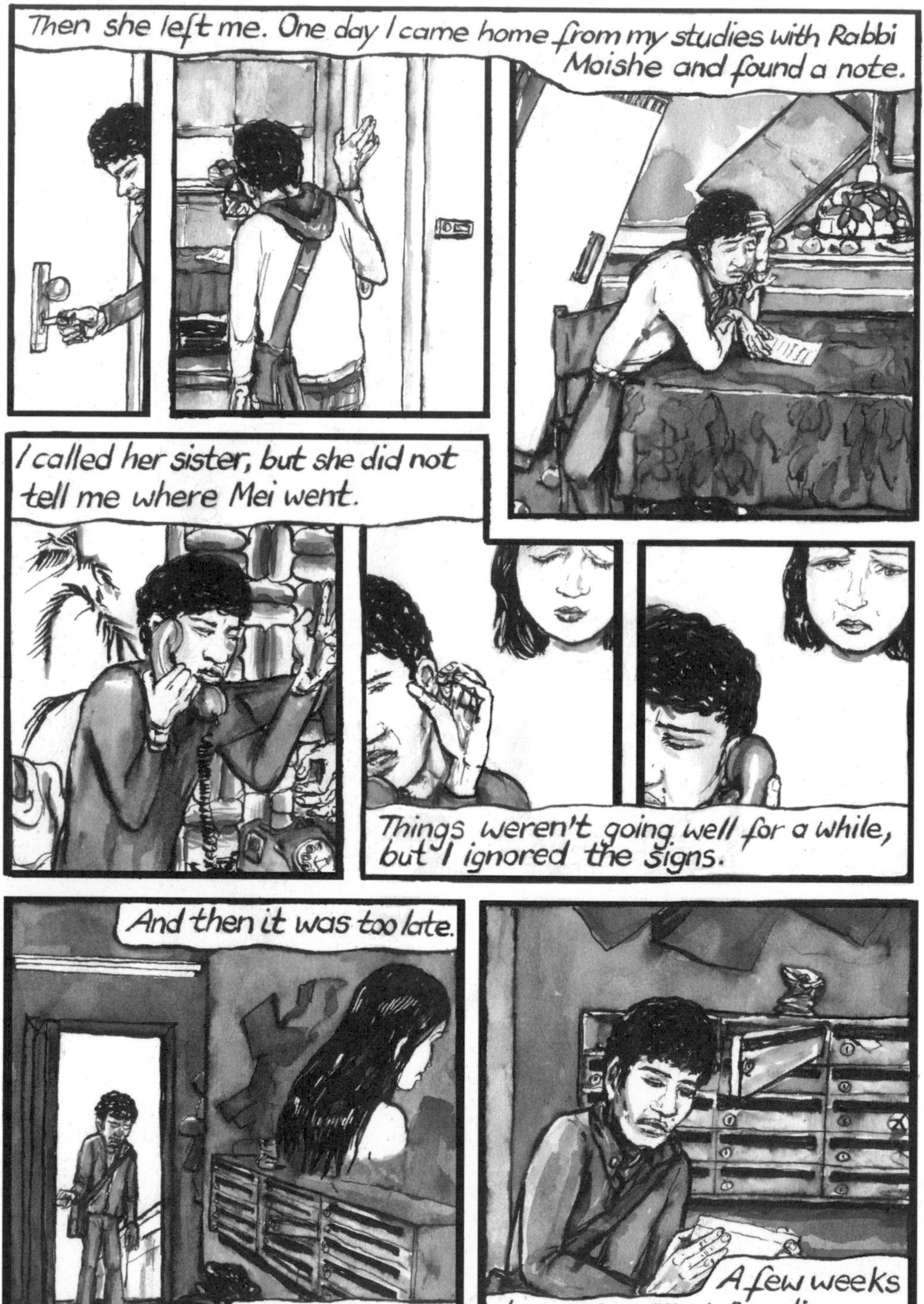
Then she left me. One day I came home from my studies with Rabbi Moishe and found a note.
I called her sister, but she did not tell me where Mei went.
Things weren't going well for a while, but I ignored the signs.
And then it was too late.
She was gone.
A few weeks later she filed for divorce.

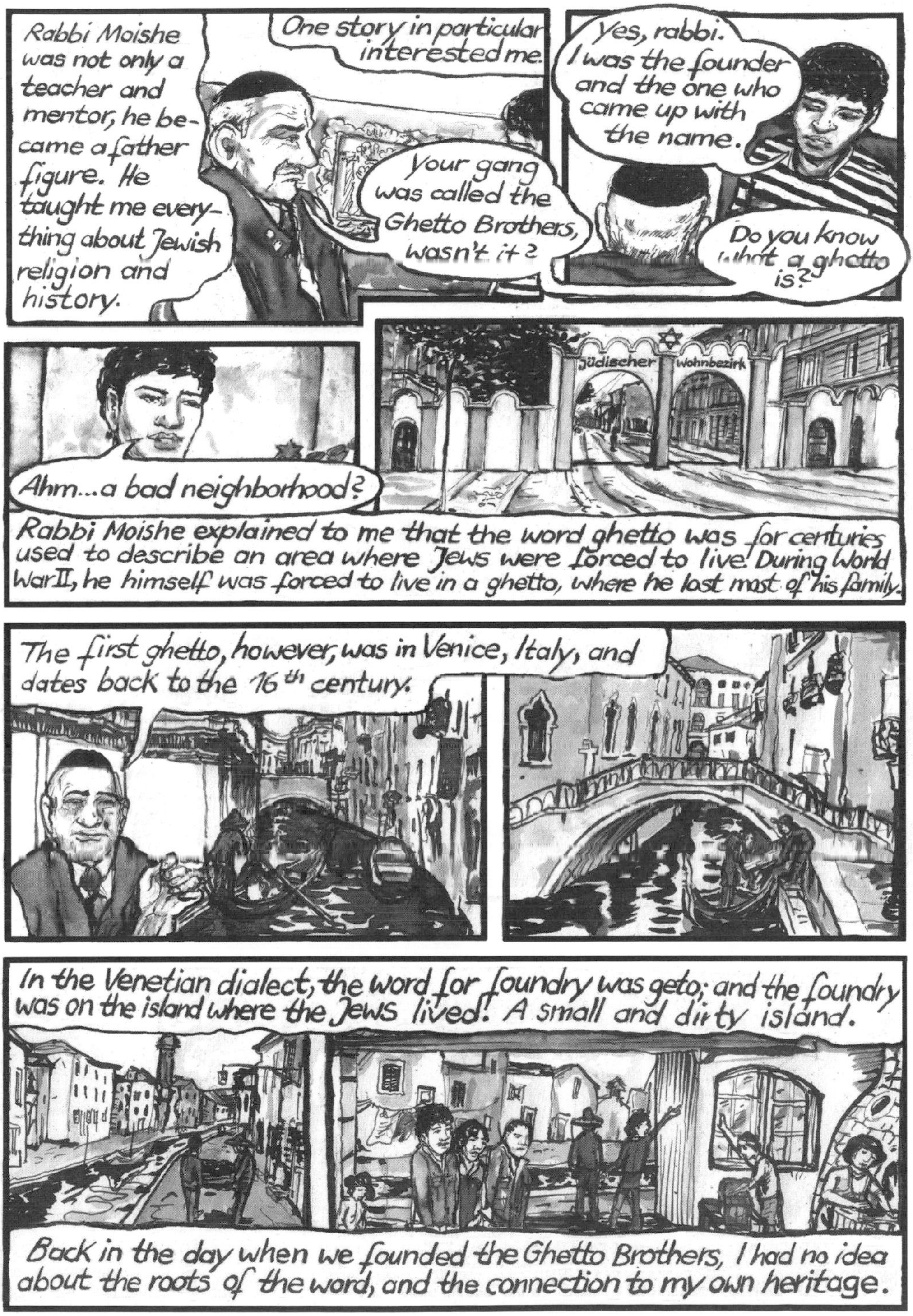
Rabbi Moishe was not only a teacher and mentor, he became a father figure. He taught me everything about Jewish religion and history.
One story in particular interested me.
Your gang was called the Ghetto Brothers, wasn't it?
Yes, rabbi. I was the founder and the one who came up with the name.
Do you know what a ghetto is?
Ahm...a bad neighborhood?
Jüdischer Wohnbezirk
Rabbi Moishe explained to me that the word ghetto was for centuries used to describe an area where Jews were forced to live. During World War II, he himself was forced to live in a ghetto, where he lost most of his family.
The first ghetto, however, was in Venice, Italy, and dates back to the 16th century.
In the Venetian dialect, the word for foundry was geto; and the foundry was on the island where the Jews lived! A small and dirty island.
Back in the day when we founded the Ghetto Brothers, I had no idea about the roots of the word, and the connection to my own heritage.

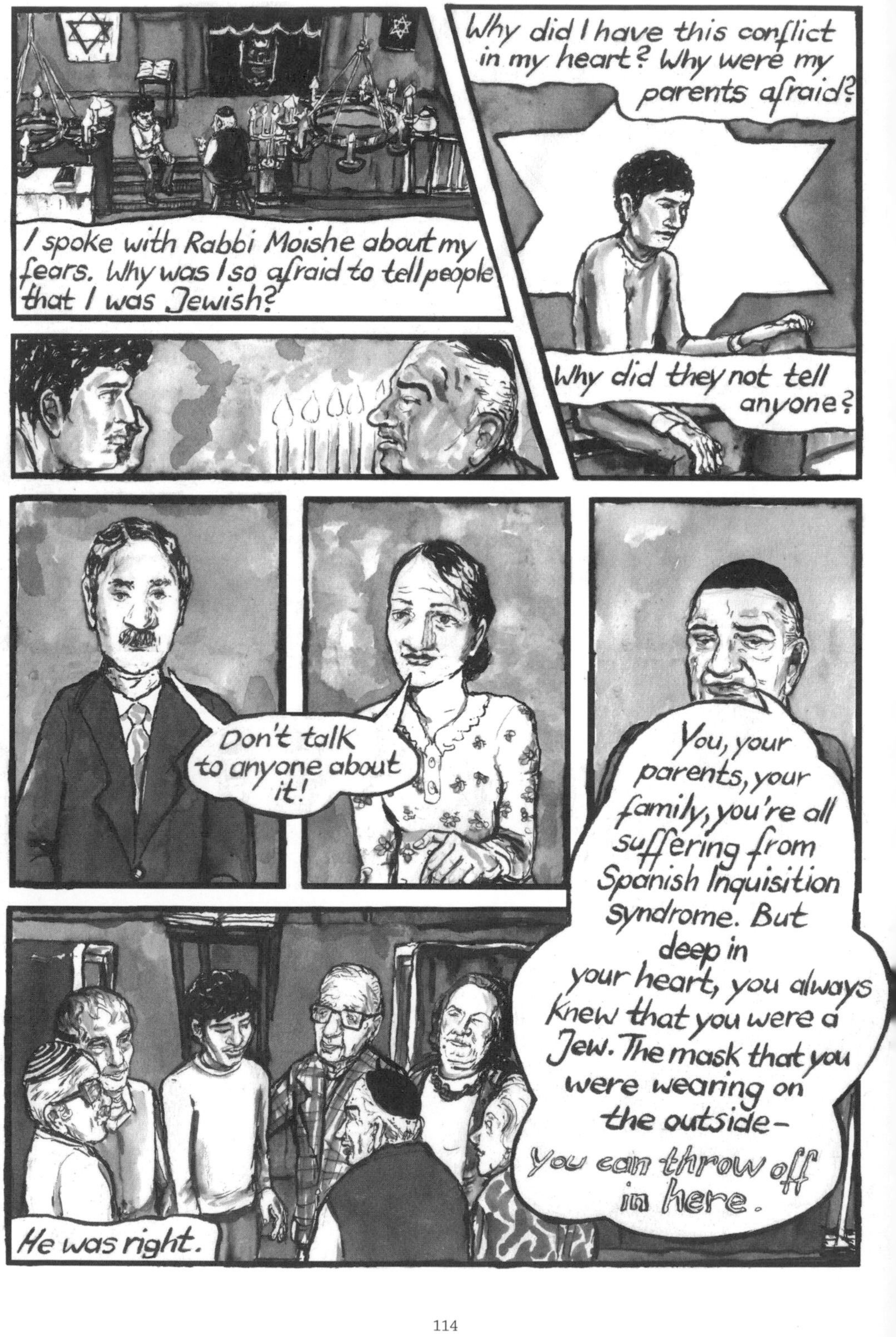
I spoke with Rabbi Moishe about my fears. Why was I so afraid to tell people that I was Jewish?
Why did I have this conflict in my heart? Why were my parents afraid?
Why did they not tell anyone?
Don't talk to anyone about it!
You, your parents, your family, you're all suffering from Spanish Inquisition syndrome. But deep in your heart, you always knew that you were a Jew. The mask that you were wearing on the outside-
you can throw off in here.
He was right.

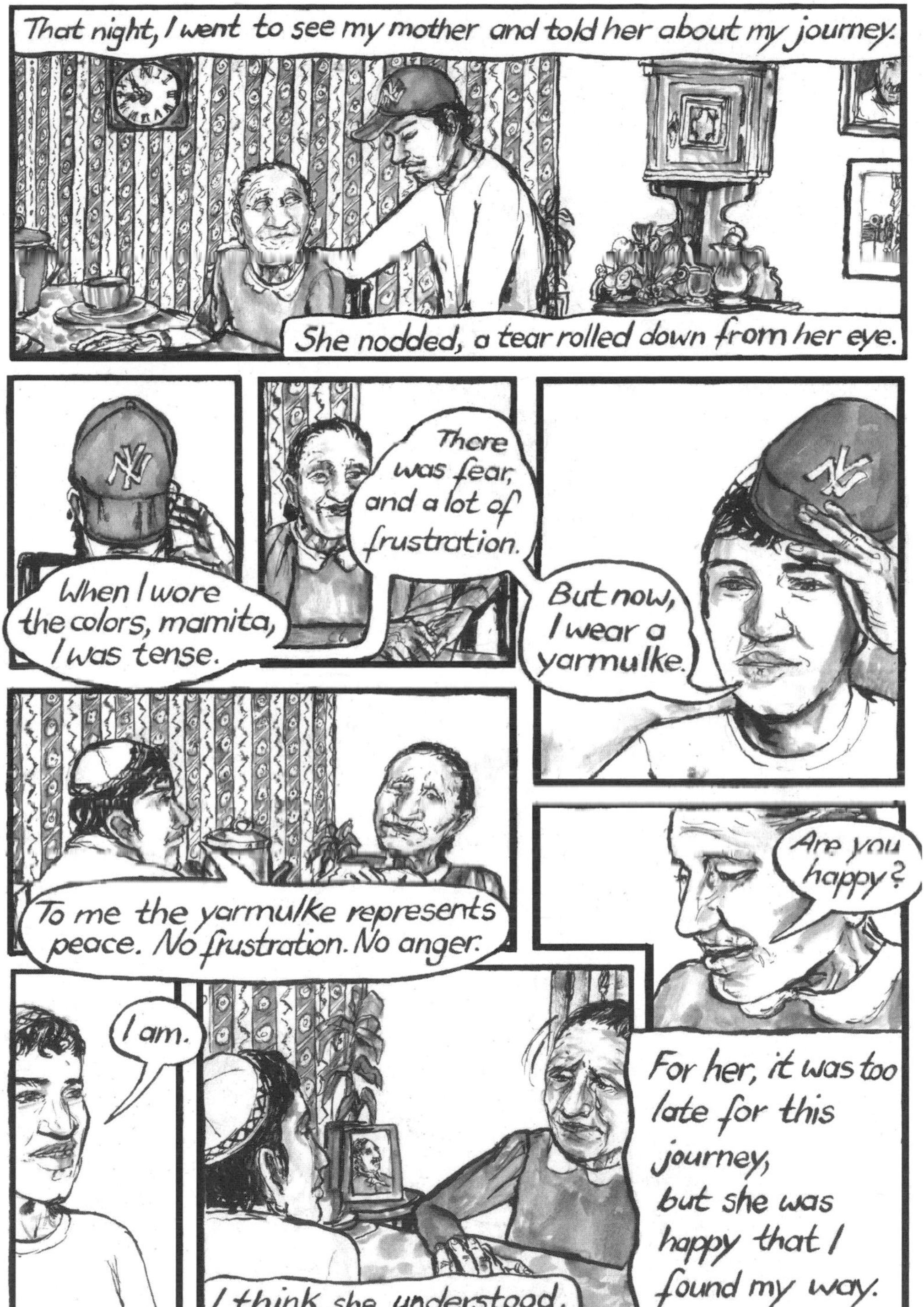

That night, I went to see my mother and told her about my journey.
She nodded, a tear rolled down from her eye.
When I wore the colors, mamita, I was tense.
There was fear, and a lot of frustration.
But now, I wear a yarmulke.
To me the yarmulke represents peace. No frustration. No anger.
Are you happy?
I am.
I think she understood.
For her, it was too late for this journey, but she was happy that I found my way.

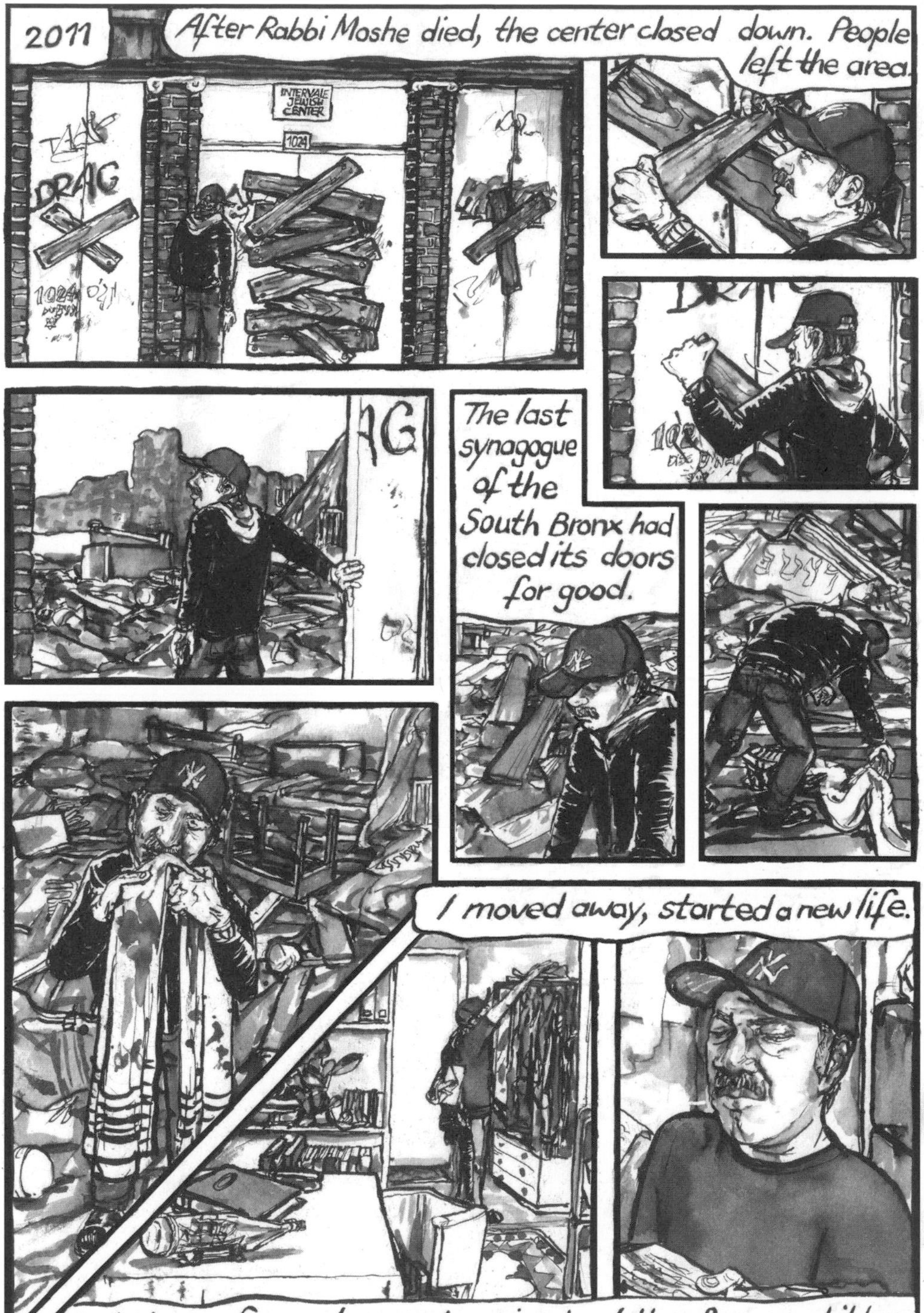
2011
After Rabbi Moshe died, the center closed down. People left the area.
INTERVALE JEWISH CENTER
1024
DRAG
The last synagogue of the South Bronx had closed its doors for good.
I moved away, started a new life.
And then, a few weeks ago, I received a letter from my children.

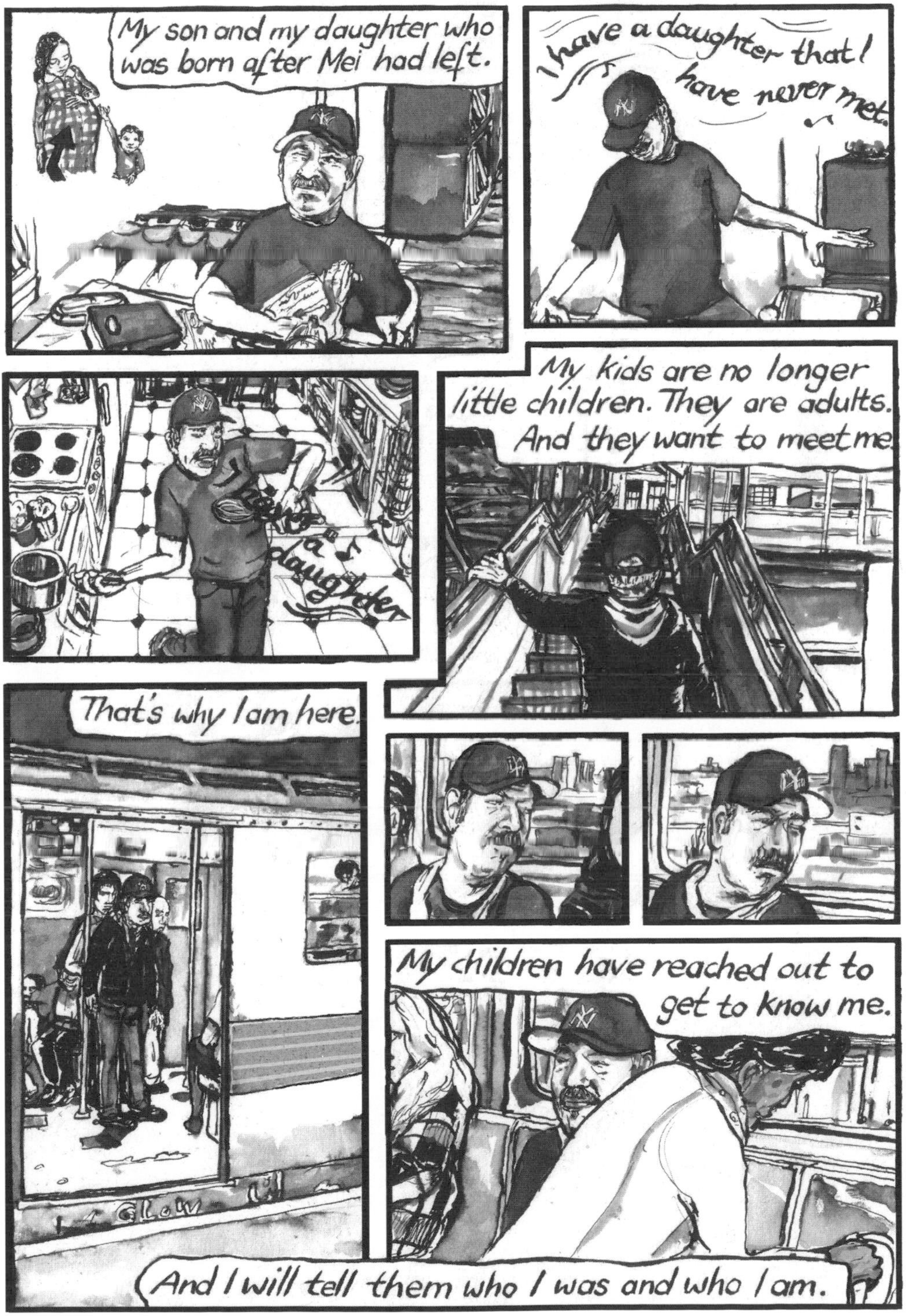
My son and my daughter who was born after Mei had left.
I have a daughter that I have never met.
My kids are no longer little children. They are adults. And they want to meet me.
That's why I am here.
My children have reached out to get to know me.
And I will tell them who I was and who I am.

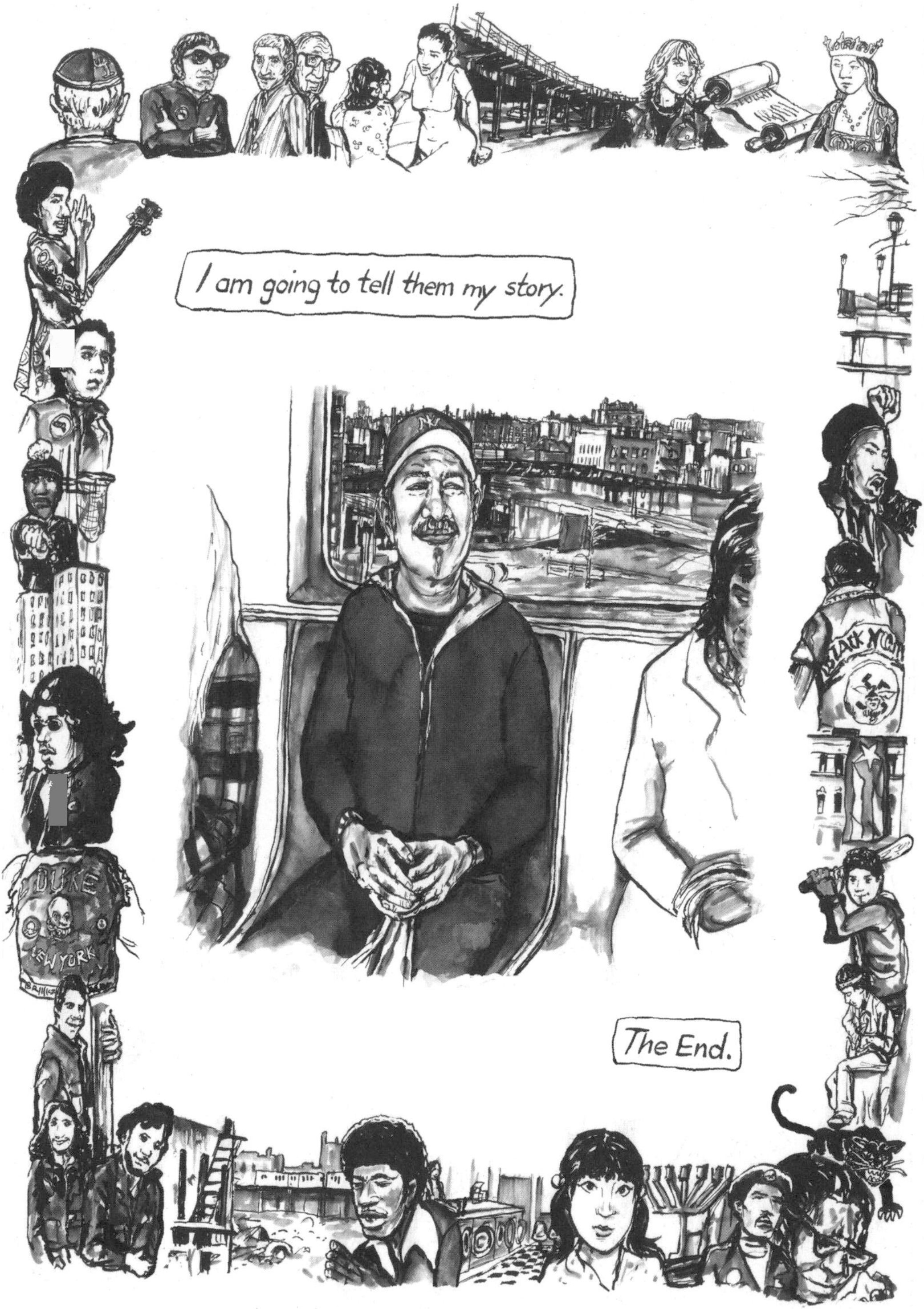
I am going to tell them my story.
The End.

THE STORY
BEHIND THE
STORY

place back then

"Can you dig it?" This is the iconic question in the opening scene of the 1979 cult movie "The Warriors." Cyrus, leader of the most powerful gang in New York City, has called a summit of all New York gangs, proposing a truce. But then Cyrus is killed. What would have happened if he hadn't been killed? What would have happened if this truce had come to life?

To many, "The Warriors" is – at least in part – inspired by the legendary Hoe Avenue Peace Meeting, a gathering organized by the Ghetto Brothers, then one of the most powerful gangs in the Bronx. In the aftermath of this summit, a culture today known as Hip Hop developed in the borough.

There are various creation myths about the roots of Hip Hop. Well known is the story of the 1973 back-to-school party in the recreation room of 1520 Sedgwick Avenue where Clive Campbell aka DJ Kool Herc experimented behind his turntables, isolating and elongating beats. The same year

HERNANDEZ

Photo by Alejandro Olivera

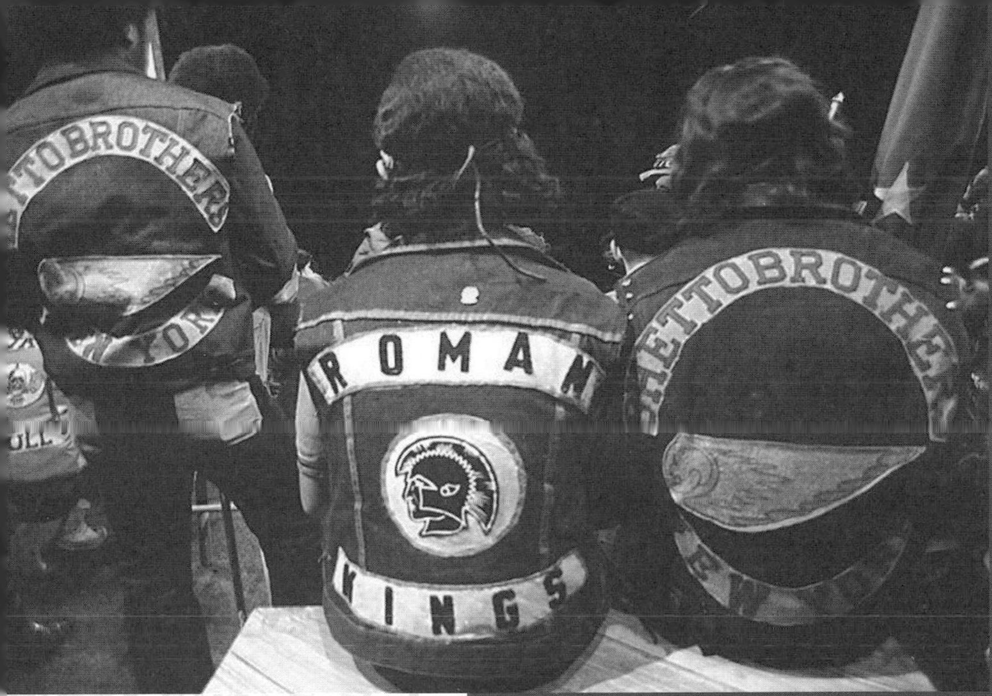
GHETTOBROTHERS
ROMAN
KINGS
GHETTOBROTHERS

Photo by Alejandro Olivera

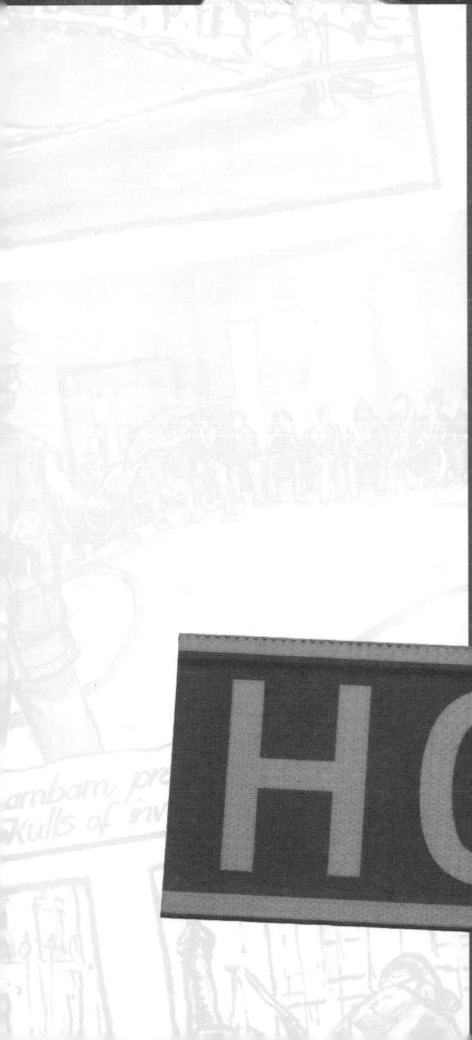

Afrika Bambaataa, the former warlord of the Black Spades, transformed the notorious gang into the Universal Zulu Nation and declared the elements of emceeing (oral), deejaying (aural), b-boying (physical), and graffiti (visual) as expressions of the same culture.

Lesser known is the story that created the environment in which these two milestones of Hip Hop occurred. Without the truce brokered during the Hoe Avenue Peace Meeting, Herc would not have been able to have his parties, and there is no doubt that the transformation of the Black Spades into the Universal Zulu Nation celebrating "Peace, Love, Unity, and Having Fun" was inspired by

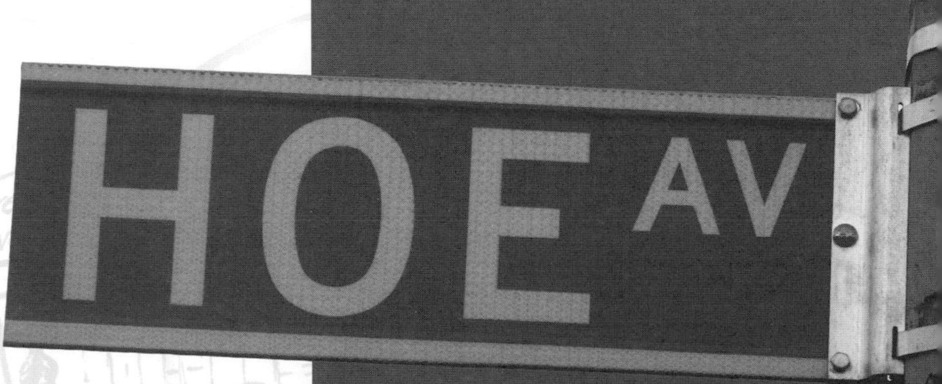
HOE AV

the similar transformation of the Ghetto Brothers initiated by Benjamin Melendez. "The gang truce with Brother Benjy was powerful," Bambaataa remembered 40 years later. "It was the time to put down the weapons against each other and try to organize."

BRONX

In 2010, I met Benjy doing a piece for the Swiss magazine "tachles." The founder of the Ghetto Brothers gave me a tour of his old neighborhood. The New York of his childhood was a very different place from today. The city was at the edge of bankruptcy, and neighborhoods such as the Lower East Side or South Bronx were in ruins. Violence ruled every street corner and without the backing of a gang, you were an easy target. So Benjy and his brothers joined the Cofon Cats, the same gang Kool Herc would later join, before founding the Ghetto Brothers. With the help of Carlos Suarez, a Vietnam vet better known under his street-name Karate Charlie, the Ghetto Brothers soon transformed into a powerful and influential gang.

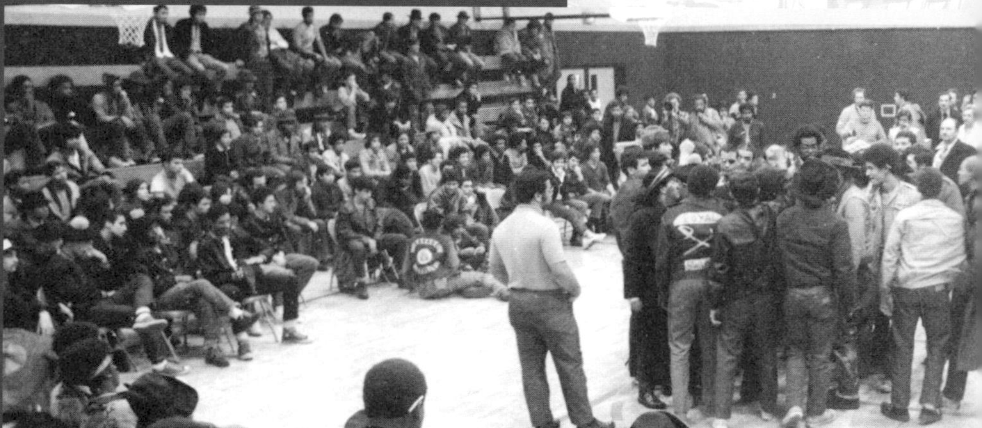

New York Daily News Archive / Getty Images

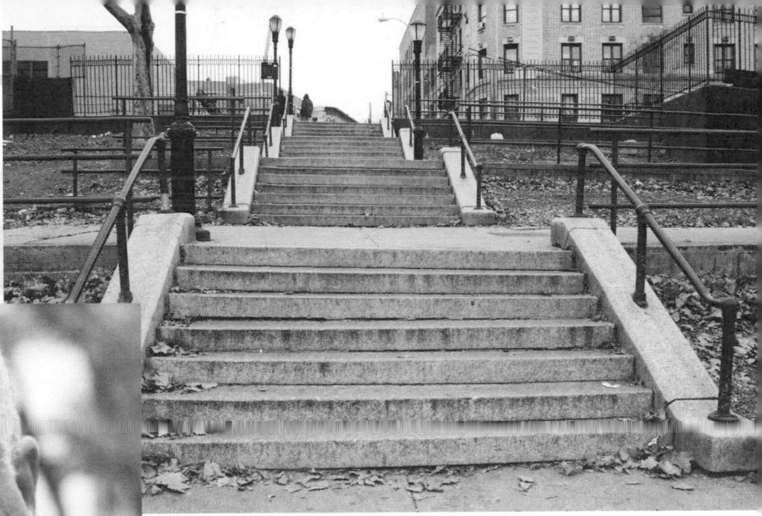

Photo by Julian Voloj

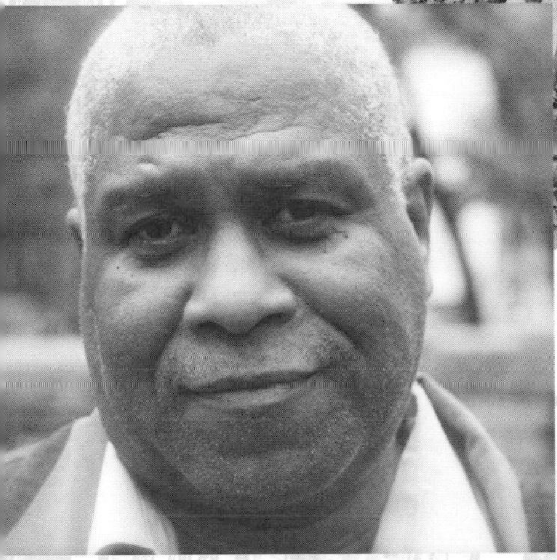

Left: Joseph Mpa, the former Black Panther who approached the Ghetto Brothers in 1971
Above: Stairs where Black Benjie was murdered

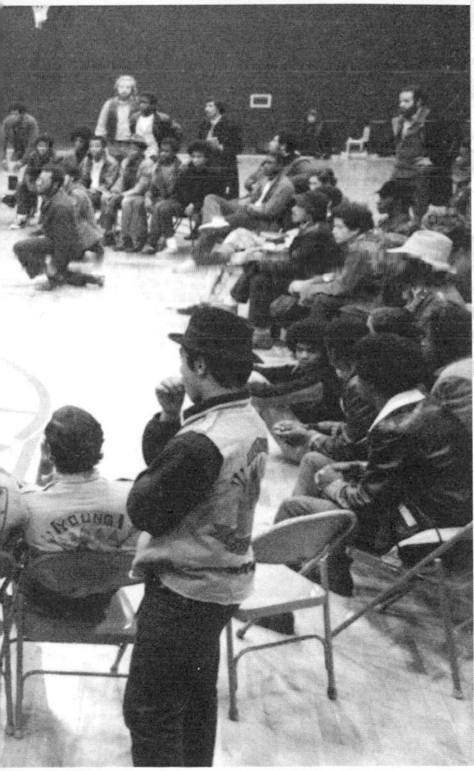

Hoe Avenue truce meeting

"The Ghetto Brothers were one of the largest gangs in the Bronx," remembers Joseph Mpa, a former Black Panther who visited the Ghetto Brothers during the violent summer of 1971. "The situation was getting off the hook. Gangs were killing other gang members. We felt we had to address the issue of the youth getting killed within our own community." The first gang they approached was the Ghetto Brothers. "The point that we made was that the other gangs were not the real enemy. The enemies were the people who were oppressing the community." After the meeting, the Ghetto Brothers got rid of the Warlord and introduced a new role into the gang structure: the Peace Counselor.

But on December 2nd, 1971, the GB Peace Counselor, 25-year old Cornell "Black Benjie" Benjamin was killed trying to mediate between rivaling gangs. Everyone expected the worst gang war in Bronx history, but instead of revenge, the Ghetto Brothers called for peace.

A key person behind the scenes was Rita Fecher, a public-school teacher who helped the Ghetto Brothers organize the gathering. In the 1960s, the daughter of a rabbi and ex-wife of another had left New Jersey for Greenwich Village, and from there made her way to the South Bronx. With her Super 8 camera she documented the borough's tough kids whom she saw as victims of a failed social policy. "Rita was the only person who believed in us," Benjy remembers of his old teacher.

Rita's tapes were unused for decades until Henry Chalfant, a photographer and filmmaker probably best known for his 1983 graffiti documentary "Style Wars," convinced her to revisit the project. Together, they found some of her former students and interviewed them about their post-gang lives. The documentary "Flyin' Cut Sleeves" was completed in 1993, and in it we see Benjy with Rabbi Moishe Sacks at the Intervale Jewish Center talking about his journey reclaiming his roots.

When Benjy and I visited the South Bronx in 2010, the Intervale Jewish Center, located only a stones' throw from the steps where Black Benjie was killed, was boarded up and abandoned. "Rabbi Sacks died in 1995, and this was the end of the congregation," Benjy told me with a melancholic tone in his voice.

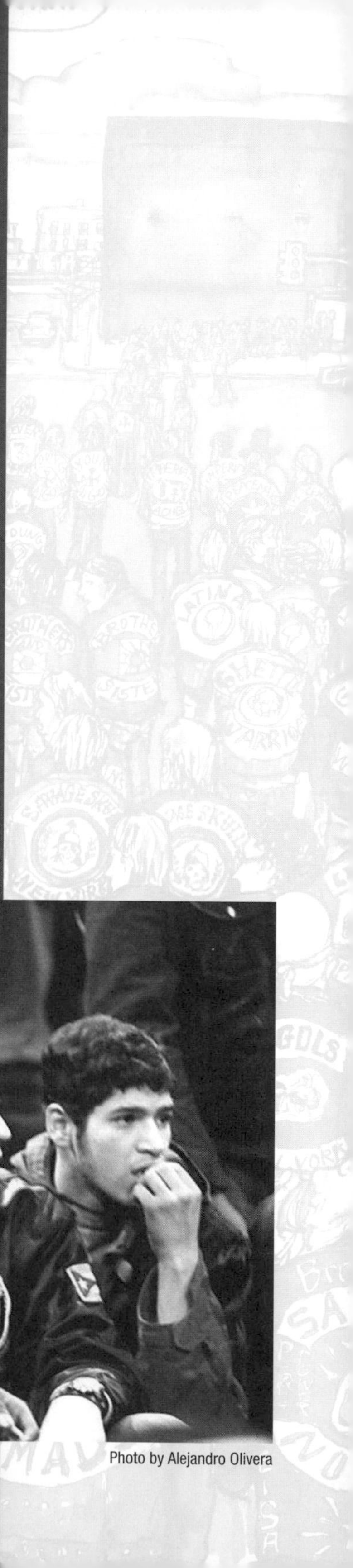

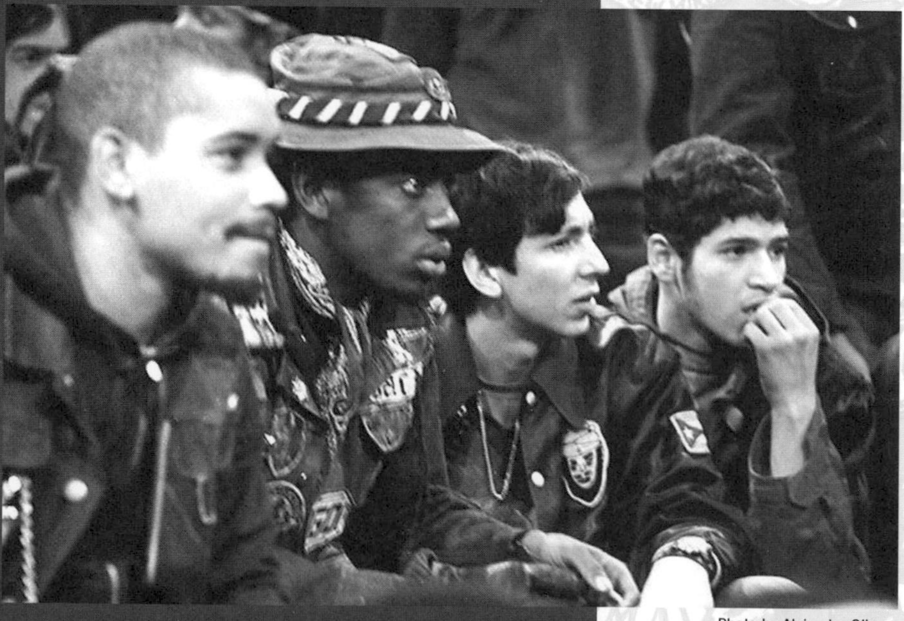

Photo by Alejandro Olivera

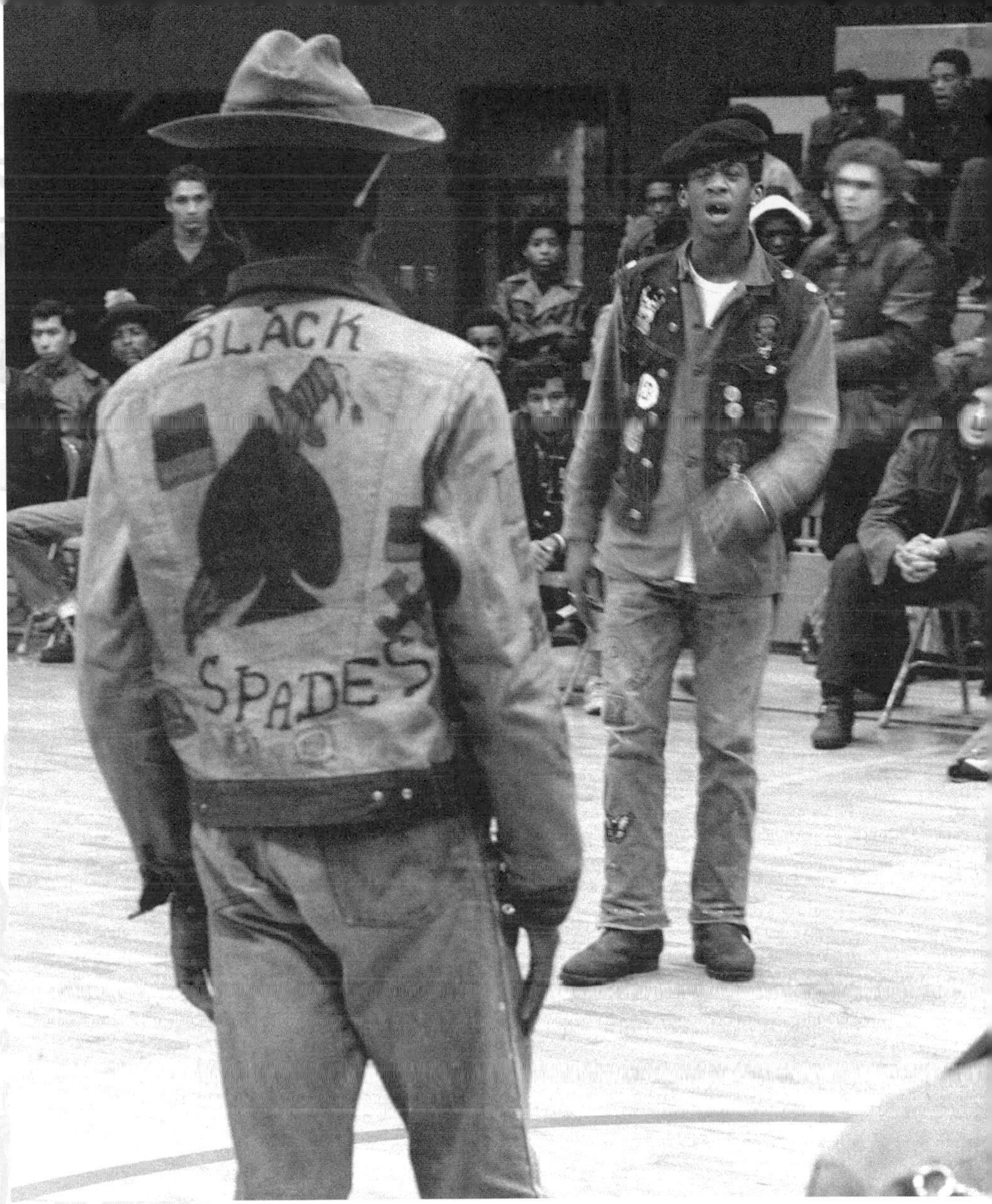
BLACK
SPADES

New York Daily News Archive / Getty Images

Hoe Avenue truce meeting

While Benjy's personal journey has no real happy ending, the Hoe Avenue Peace Meeting has a global legacy: the foundation of Hip Hop. In 2011, on the occasion of the meetings' 40th anniversary, I organized a reunion of former activists. There, it became clear that this nearly forgotten moment in Bronx history had even more connections to the pioneer days of Hip Hop.

The venue of the truce, the Boys & Girls Club on Hoe Avenue, would a decade later become one of the venues where the first Hip Hop crews would perform, as documented by photographer Joe Conzo. Many of Joe's images of the Bronx' urban decay were used for the illustrations of this book, but he also has another connection to the story: his grandmother was Evelina Antonetty, the founder of the United Bronx Parents, who gave Benjy his first job.

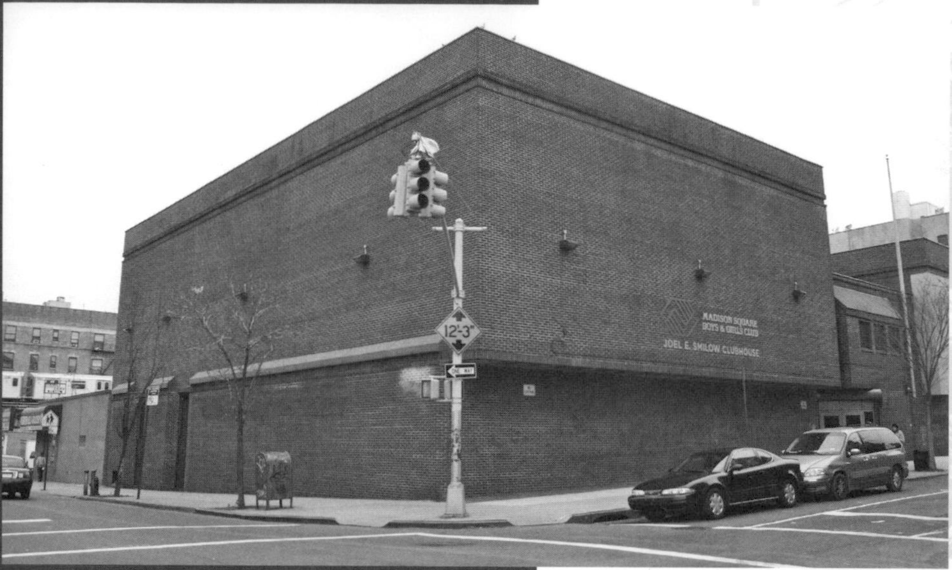
MADISON SQUARE
BOYS & GIRLS CLUB
JOEL E. SMILOW CLUBHOUSE

The Boys and Girls Club on Hoe Avenue. The truce meeting was held here.

Photo by Julian Voloj

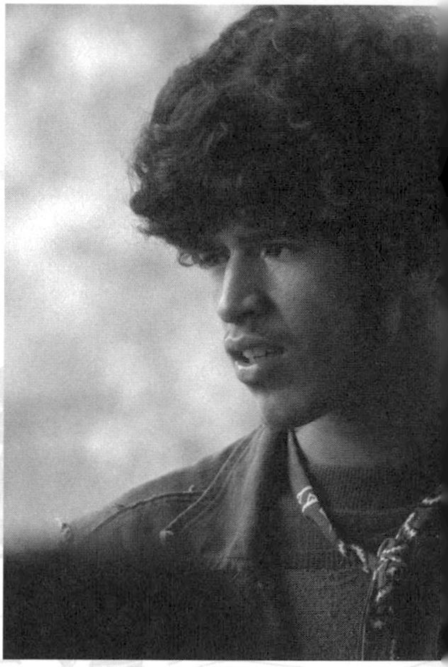

Benjamin Melendez

Conzo was introduced to the emerging Hip Hop scene by his friends, the legendary Cold Crush Brothers whose front man Grandmaster Caz wrote part of the lyrics of "Rappers Delight" (even if they were stolen from him, but that's another story…). The Cold Crush Brothers first manager was none other than Joseph Mpa, who is credited by Benjy for "planting the seed" for electing a Peace Counselor.

Over the course of three years, I had dozens, if not hundreds of conversations with Benjy Melendez and other people involved with the Hoe Avenue Peace Meeting. Even if some names were changed (e.g. Joseph Mpa became Joe Matumaini, the last name being the Swahili word for "hope") and some details were modified for a better narrative, this tale about the Puerto Rican migration to the US, this history of economic decline in the South Bronx, and this coming-of-age story about a young man struggling with his many identities is a true story. It is a piece of Bronx history that should not be forgotten.

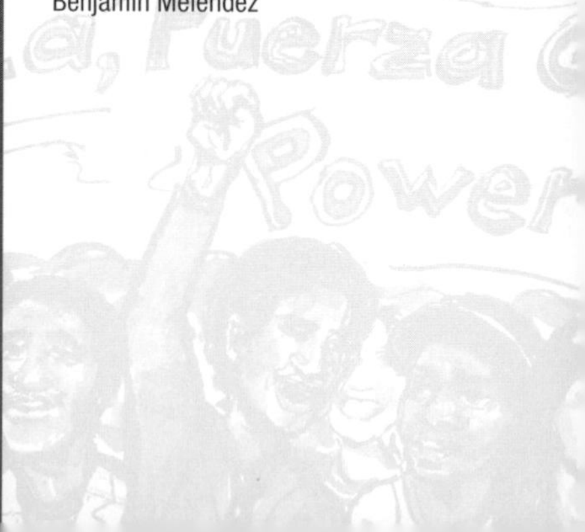